AF740468

financial econometrics

for researchers in finance and accounting

H. RUSSELL FOGLER
University of Florida, Gainesville

SUNDARAM GANAPATHY
Citibank, India

PRENTICE-HALL, INC., Englewood Cliffs, New Jersey 07632

Library of Congress Cataloging in Publication Data

FOGLER, H. RUSSELL.
Financial econometrics for researchers in finance and accounting.

Bibliography: p.
Includes index.
1. Econometrics. 2. Finance–Statistical methods. 3. Finance–Mathematical models.
4. Capital assets pricing model. I. Ganapathy, Sundaram. II. Title.
HE139. F63 330′.028 81-15387
ISBN 0-13-315887-X AACR2

Editorial/production supervision by *Linda Mason*
Cover design by *Frederick Charles Ltd*
Manufacturing buyer: *Ed O'Dougherty*

© 1982 by Prentice-Hall, Inc., Englewood Cliffs, N.J.07632

All rights reserved. No part of this book may be reproduced in any form or by any means without permission in writing from the publisher.

Printed in the United States of America

10 9 8 7 6 5 4 3 2 1

ISBN 0-13-315887-X

Prentice-Hall International, Inc., *London*
Prentice-Hall of Australia Pty. Limited, *Sydney*
Prentice-Hall of Canada, Ltd., *Toronto*
Prentice-Hall of India Private Limited, *New Delhi*
Prentice-Hall of Japan, Inc., *Tokyo*
Prentice-Hall of Southeast Asia Pte. Ltd., *Singapore*
Whitehall Books Limited, *Wellington, New Zealand*

WITHDRAWN
University of Bristol
UNIVERSITY OF BRISTOL

TELEPEN
10 0293610 7

contents

preface

Most business school curricula offer two Applied Statistics courses, and these are not specifically geared toward Finance and Accounting. This background is certainly not adequate for evaluating recent studies that use sophisticated statistical concepts. Economics departments have overcome this void by developing their own courses entitled Econometrics. The proper background for Econometrics is a one-year sequence in Probability (which requires one year of calculus) and one semester in Linear Algebra. Most Finance and Accounting students do not have these prerequisites, nor do these students relate to empirical studies about Economic topics. Yet, as future research outdates present theories, Finance and Accounting curricula will have to add "methodology" courses as the other disciplines have done. The goal of Financial Econometrics is to bridge this existing "gap."

Approximately 45% of this book is Appendices. This is because the Appendices provide general prerequisite background in Probability and Matrix Algebra. Yet, on first reading much of the text can be read with only minimal reference to Appendices. Thus, Finance and Accounting oriented readers can obtain an overview of the technical concepts. As they become more familiar with the technical concepts, they can increasingly use Appendices A through M on later readings. And finally for the more technically oriented, a number of proofs are provided in Appendix M. Thus, this book is envisioned as a primer and handbook to be used both in courses and later on as professional developments require one to update his (her) background.

Financial Econometrics will show the application of econometric techniques to capital market analysis. Throughout the book, the reader should remember that all statistical technqiues have two parts:

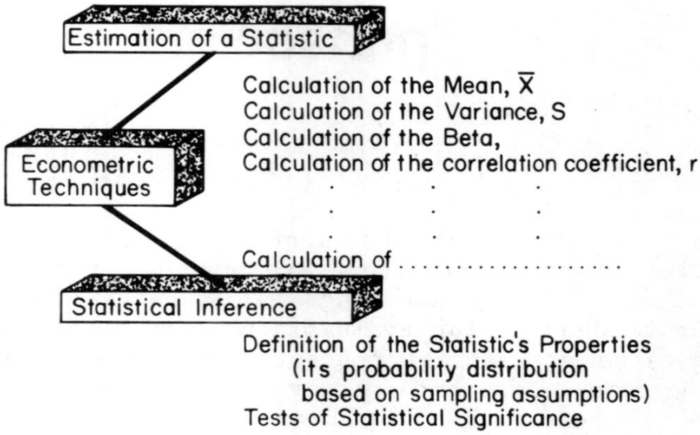

Estimating a statistic is merely computational. Understanding is required, however, to answer questions about the properties of the estimator. Each chapter begins by telling what questions are addressed, such as in Chapter 3, "Is the beta significantly different from a hypothesized value of 1.2, and how would it be affected if the risk-free rate and the stock market are correlated?" To answer questions such as this, the properties (e.g., unbiasedness, efficiency, etc.) of the sampling distribution of beta must be understood; to know the distribution, certain statements about normality and independence of errors are often required. 80%-90% of most Econometrics and Statistics texts are addressed to the properties of the estimators.

To provide the fundamental statistical knowledge, in an interesting way, each chapter addresses specific problems in capital market analysis. Chapter 2 is a review of simple linear regression applied to estimating beta. Then Chapter 3 addresses questions such as "What happens when the risk-free rate is correlated with the overall stock market return--how does this affect the estimate of beta?" The questions in Chapter 3 are all addressed to "exceptions" from the assumptions that are needed for simple calculation and testing of beta. Chapter 4 proceeds to answer, "What assumptions are necessary when several explanatory variables are used?" Chapter 5 then generalizes the estimation process by answering "What can you do about patterns in the error terms and simultaneous feedbacks?" For the reader who is willing to apply the contents of chapters to real data, by the end of this book, she or he will have a statistical background which will enable them to answer these questions. This knowledge, coupled with a knowledge of the major readings on capital market theory listed below, will provide the background to assess the trends which are currently underway in analysis of capital market risk and returns.

SUGGESTED REFERENCES

Derivation of the Capital Asset Pricing Model (CAPM)

Each of these readings requires knowledge of basic calculus. An introduction to the derivation of the Sharpe-Lintner-Mossin model is provided in the Copeland and Weston reference, as well as a review of calculus in the Appendices. The rigor and clarity of an article such as Mossin's is well worth the time to master each step in the derivations; this article is a must for an understanding of the aggregation procedures for establishing a partial equilibrium relationship. Finally, the Ross article provides a state-of-the-art survey of both past and present theoretical developments.

Thomas E. Copeland and J. Fred Weston, Financial Theory and Corporate Policy. Addison-Wesley, Inc. 1979, Chapters 6 and 7.

Jan Mossin, "Security Pricing and Investment Criteria in Competitive Markets," American Economic Review, Volume LIX (December 1969), pp. 749-756.

Stephen A. Ross, "The Current Status of the Capital Asset Pricing Model," Journal of Finance, Volume XXXIII (June 1978) pp. 885-901.

Time Horizon Bias

Although the purpose of this text is not to address capital market theory directly, the variables used in the regression must come from such theory, either explicitly or implicitly. The use of stock returns is from the standard one-period capital asset pricing model (CAPM) that is discussed in the above references. If such a model is assumed to hold, then either returns or excess returns (returns minus a risk-free rate of return) are appropriate variables, with the return variable model being more general. Because the references by Lee and Jensen show that nonlinearity will occur at any other horizon than the one assumed, the logarithm of returns is often used; this problem arises from the static equilibrium approach of the CAPM, and the logarithm is often felt to be an adequate adjustment. Thus, it quickly becomes clear that the reader must ultimately be educated in both theory and empirical measurement, and accordingly, mastery of these references is suggested.

Cheng F. Lee, "On the Relationship Between the Systematic Risk and Investment Horizon," Journal of Financial and Quantitative Analysis, Volume XI (December 1976), pp. 803-815.

Michael C. Jensen, "Risk, the Pricing of Capital Assets, and the Evaluation of Investment Portfolios," Journal of Business, Volume 42 (April 1969), pp. 167-247.

Non-Independence of Residuals

As indicated in the text, empirical research is finding increasing evidence of dependence in the residual-error terms. In addition to Farrell's paper, the Rosenberg and Marathe article indicates correlations of the residuals to various firm specific variables. Similar findings on dependence are shown by the Lee and Vinso research, which uses a standard simultaneous-equation analysis with generalized least-squares adjustment to allow pooling of both cross-section and time-series data. Finally, the Jensen piece makes it clear that problems with beta may explain the "superior" performance of some beat-the-market strategies, as well as elaborating on present research on this topic.

James L. Farrell, Jr., "Analyzing Covariation of Returns to Determine Homogeneous Stock Groupings," Journal of Business, April, 1974, pp. 186-207.

Barr Rosenberg and Vinay Marathe, "Common Factors in Security Returns: Microeconomic Determinants and Macroeconomic Correlates," Proceedings of the Seminar on the Analysis of

Security Prices, University of Chicago, May 1976, pp. 61-115.

Cheng Lee and Joseph Vinso, "The Single vs. Simultaneous Equation Model in Capital Asset Pricing: A Synthesis," Journal of Business Research, (forthcoming).

Michael C. Jensen, "Some Anomalous Evidence Regarding Market Efficiency," Journal of Financial Economics, Volume 6, (June-September, 1978), pp. 95-102.

Bias in Portfolio Measurement Techniques

Although beta may be a biased risk measure, the relative ranking is highly correlated between various performance measures (Tito and Smith). But, the impact of bias is present (Friend and Blume).

Keith V. Smith and Dennis A. Tito, "Risk-Return Measures of Ex-Post Portfolio Performance," Journal of Financial and Quantitative Analysis, December 1969, pp. 449-470.

Irwin Friend and Marshall Blume, "Measurement of Portfolio Performance Under Uncertainty," American Economic Review, September 1970, pp. 561-575.

Andrew Rudd and H. K. Clasing, Jr., Modern Portfolio Theory: The Principles of Investment Management, Dow-Jones Irwin, 1981, Chapter 7.

Econometric Tests and Procedures

There are at least four papers which are necessary for understanding procedures for detecting and eliminating bias and inefficiency from estimators. The papers by Miller-and-Scholes, Black-Jensen-and-Scholes, and Black-and-Scholes can be begun after Chapter III discusses probability limits. The paper by Litzenberger and Ramaswamy can be undertaken after the first half of Chapter V.

Merton Miller and Myron Scholes, "Rates of Return in Relation to Risk: A Re-examination of Some Recent Findings," in Michael Jensen, editor, Studies in the Theory of Capital Markets, Praeger Press (New York, 1972), pp. 47-78.

Fischer Black, Michael Jensen, and Myron Scholes, "The Capital Asset Pricing Model: Some Empirical Tests," in Michael Jensen, editor, Studies in the Theory of Capital Markets, Praeger Press (New York, 1972), pp. 79-121.

Fischer Black and Myron Scholes, "The Effects of Dividend Yield and Dividend Policy on Common Stock Prices and Returns," Journal of Financial Economics, Volume 1 (1974), pp. 1-22.

Robert H. Litzenberger and Krishna Ramaswamy, "The Effect of Personal Taxes and Dividends on Capital Asset Prices: Theory and Empirical Evidence," Journal of Financial Economics, Volume 7, June 1979, pp. 163-195.

I am grateful to the Literary Executor of the Late Sir Ronald A. Fisher, F.R.S. to Dr. Frank Yates, F.R.S. and to Longman Group Ltd. London, for permission to reprint Tables from their book Statistical Tables for Biological, Agricultural and Medical Research. (6th edition, 1974)

As with any book, numerous colleagues have contributed. Ira Horowitz, former department chairman, provided extensive improvements and numerous helpful comments on style. George Pinches, former consulting editor and friend, was the original supporter as well as a prompt reviewer. Joe Vinso was a major source of support, as he has taught material similar to this and therefore had significant classroom experience. The Frank Russell Company staff and clients have raised numerous practical questions indicating the need for more sophisticated econometric approaches, and as such have been a major intellectual impetus. Comments from Bill Lewellen, Chris Barry, Bill Carleton, Bill Beedles and Cheng Lee have also improved this manuscript. A number of students have made contributions: in particular, thanks are due especially to P. C. Padmanabhan for the extensive proof-reading which he did, Tony Rivers, and Pramood Kargonekar. Terrific typing support has been provided by Ms. Heidi Middleton and Ms. Vicki LaPlaca. Ms. Margie Summers has our sincere thanks for moving this from our typed copy to a camera-ready product. Finally, H. R. F. wants to thank his family for the many hours during which they have foregone his time and S. G. wishes to express his sincere thanks to his mentor Mr. S. Deenanathan and all his family members for their time, encouragement, support and guidance.

1

why financial econometrics?

"What should the corporation do about dividend policy? We don't know."
Fischer Black
Journal of Portfolio Management, Winter 1976
p. 8

Ignorance is both frustrating and embarrassing. And what could be more embarrassing than to admit that neither academicians nor financial consultants know how dividends affect a stock's return!

1. THE DIVIDEND PUZZLE AND ECONOMETRICS

Hypotheses about dividend policy can be arrayed in two camps. The "world without taxes" camp has shown mathematically that investors would be indifferent between receiving a dividend or selling an equal dollar amount of their stockholding (if the corporation retained the dividend, the stock's price would be higher by that amount, so it is equivalent to receiving the dividend). The "personal taxes" camp is equally effective in showing mathematically that for all investors with personal tax rates higher than the capital gains tax rate, earnings retention is preferred over dividend payout; thus, returns will have to be higher on higher dividend paying stocks, after adjusting for differences in risk (implying, therefore, that most companies shouldn't pay dividends because most shareholders are subject to higher tax rates).

In 1974, Professors Black and Scholes published an extensive study of stock returns and dividends. Their hypothesis was that a stock's return (R_j) would be a function of its risk (measured by a variable designated β_j) and the percentage difference of its dividend yield from the average yield of all stocks (D_j); i.e.,

$$\tilde{R}_j = \gamma_o + \beta_j(\tilde{R}_m - \gamma_o) + \gamma_1 D_j + \varepsilon_j,$$

where R_m represents the average return on a "market" portfolio of all stocks, γ_o and γ_1 are regression coefficients, ε_j is the residual error related to stock j in the cross-section regression, and tildes (~) indicate that the respective measure is specified as a random variable. A sample of their regression estimates of the coefficient for the dividend term are shown below

Period	γ_1	t-value
1936-66	0.0009	0.94
1947-66	0.0009	0.90
1936-46	0.0011	0.54
1947-56	0.0002	0.19
1957-66	0.0016	0.99
1940-45	0.0018	0.34

Because the t-values of these estimates were too low to reject a null hypothesis that the true population value of γ_1 was zero, they concluded that there was no significant evidence that dividend yield was a significant variable affecting stock returns.[1] Thus, the message to financial managers seemed to be that dividends didn't seem to matter.[2]

In performing the above study, Black and Scholes grouped their stocks into portfolios before estimating γ_1. This is a common procedure used to reduce measurement errors, thereby increasing accuracy. While such a procedure can be shown to improve accuracy, it also can reduce

[1]Also, although the above estimates of γ_1 are all positive, other time periods contained negative estimates.

[2]It is important to notice that "they don't matter" is not what was tested. Not finding a significant difference between an estimator and zero is based upon a Type 1 error test of a null hypothesis; when one concludes that "not finding a significant difference" means "there isn't a significant difference," then the Type 2 error must be considered. The implications of this are provided in Appendix F.

the efficiency of statistical tests to find significant differences. To account for this problem, Professors Litzenberger and Ramaswamy recently utilized econometric adjustments to account for estimation error from variations in risk between different time periods; such techniques allowed them to use both cross-section and time-series data on individual stocks, thereby enhancing statistical efficiency.

Litzenberger and Ramaswamy found the following coefficient (γ_2) on their dividend term:

Period	γ_2	t-value
1936-40	0.335	2.64
1941-47	0.408	7.35
1948-54	0.158	4.37
1955-61	0.018	0.32
1962-68	0.171	2.33
1969-77	0.329	6.00

Thus, their results indicate that, except for the period 1955-61, the dividend coefficient was significantly positive.

What are the implications of the foregoing? First, econometric adjustment procedures will be increasingly used in financial studies because greater accuracy is needed. Second, financial executives must know the limitations of such techniques if they are to make reasoned financial decisions.[3] And third, the most crucial limitations are often the statistical assumptions about independence between error terms both between stocks and between time periods. This third implication is well illustrated below by attempts to explain a stock's return and risk using simple linear regression.

2. BETA ESTIMATES--TWO PROBLEMS

In the above studies, the risk measure (β_i) referred to was "beta." A simplified way of describing beta is that it measures the relative volatility of a stock's return

[3]The real world importance attached to this can be shown by the fact that a corporate client of a major consulting firm called for an opinion on the Litzenberger and Ramaswamy article prior to its publication. The client is the sponsor of a pension fund, and since pension fund earnings are tax exempt, the client wanted to know if they should be shifting their portfolio toward stocks with higher dividends.

compared to the market. For example, if market indexes rise 10% and a stock's value rises 15%, and if such a one-and-a-half times volatility persists over both rises and falls in market indexes, then the stock's beta is said to be 1.5. Beta's name is derived from the beta coefficient $\hat{\beta}$ in the linear regression of a stock's returns in period t, ($R_{s,t}$), against the market return ($R_{m,t}$), where the estimated relationship is $R_{s,t} = \hat{\alpha} + \hat{\beta}_s R_{m,t}$.[4]

As might be expected, beta is not always accurate. For example, Jim Farrell of Citibank examined the returns of two mutual funds, one with a beta of 1.09 versus another with 1.11. Such similar betas would suggest nearly similar performance--but such was not the case! During the 1973-74 bear market, one fund lost only 16%, while the market lost 29% and the other fund lost 42% (Table 1.1).

Table 1.1
FARRELL'S RESULTS WITH BETA

Stock Group	S&P 500	Affiliated Fund	T. Rowe Price
Growth	39.8%	10.5%	80.2%
Cyclical	24.0	57.5	8.7
Stable	20.0	18.0	4.1
Oil	16.2	14.0	7.0
Total	100.0%	100.0%	100.0%
Portfolio Beta	1.00	1.09	1.11
Fund Performance	-29%	-16%	-42%

Source: James L. Farrell, Jr., "Homogenous Stock Grouping," Financial Analysts Journal, May-June 1975, p. 58.

[4]A better procedure for estimating beta is to use excess returns (i.e., returns minus a riskfree rate) rather than returns themselves. This will eliminate estimation bias if the riskfree rate and the market return are correlated. For a discussion of this, see the reference to Miller and Scholes in the Introduction, as well as the analysis of Chapter 3.

Rather than being explained by beta, Farrell's results for the two funds appear attributable to two other facts: cyclical stocks performed especially well during this period, and growth stocks performed much worse. You might wonder if, "Affiliated was able to select the better performing stocks!" Such a doubt, however, was not warranted by historical facts. From 1966-1975, Affiliated Fund's returns from price appreciation and dividends respectively were 1.2 percent and 3.9 percent versus T. Rowe Price's 2.4 percent and 2.0 percent. Affiliated Fund had consistently concentrated in the cyclical stocks that pay relatively higher dividends, while T. Rowe Price had consistently played the growth stocks. Thus, rather than good or bad selection, the results were related to diversification strategies, which certainly were not adequately captured by beta.

Another problem with beta was shown in a study by Professors Friend and Blume at the Wharton School. Their study found consistent bias in evaluating portfolio performance over longer periods. The monthly performance was analyzed for 200 randomly selected portfolios, constructed from 788 common stocks listed on the New York Stock Exchange for the period January 1960 through June 1968. For each portfolio, three risk adjusted statistics of performance were calculated--the Sharpe measure (S), the Treynor measure (T), and the Jensen measure (J) (if you are not familiar with these, the bias can still be understood at an intuitive level!). Each of these statistics implicitly or explicitly account for the portfolio beta, and thus each of the statistics should be statistically independent of the portfolio beta. Such independence is equivalent to the statement, that, "if a regression analysis were performed between the performance statistic and beta (i.e., statistic $= \alpha + b\beta_p$, where β_p is the portfolio beta), there should be no relationship." Friend and Blume performed three tests for such a linear relationship: (1) a regression test with the portfolio beta on the right hand side; (2) the same test with the portfolio standard error as the right-hand-side variable; and (3) test #1, but with the beta calculation based upon the logarithms of returns (a popular adjustment procedure discussed in the section on "Time Horizon Bias" in the references suggested in the Introduction).

As Table 1.2 indicates, all of the measures were highly correlated to both portfolio betas and standard errors (a quick way to assess whether the coefficients are significant is from the t-ratios, with a ratio above 3 being regarded as statistically significant--more on this in Chapter 2). Thus, some of the assumptions in the use of beta for risk adjusting must be inadequate. Because all of

Table 1.2

REGRESSIONS OF ONE-PARAMETER PERFORMANCE MEASURES ON RISK RANDOM PORTFOLIOS, JANUARY 1960-JUNE 1968

Performance Measure	=	α	+	β Risk Measure	R^2	Standard Error
1) S	=	0.2677 (45.50)	-	0.0557 X_1 (-9.17)	0.2944	0.0215
2) S	=	0.2724 (42.00)	-	1.3614 X_2 (-9.01)	0.2871	0.0216
3) T	=	0.0134 (45.10)	-	0.0039 X_1 (-12.82)	0.4510	0.0011
4) T	=	0.0136 (39.82)	-	0.0921 X_2 (-11.59)	0.4012	0.0011
5) J	=	0.0028 (11.34)	-	0.0018 X_1 (-7.13)	0.2004	0.0009
6) J	=	0.0029 (10.42)	-	0.0429 X_2 (-6.61)	0.1768	0.0009
7) S'	=	0.2648 (44.57)	-	0.0741 X_1' (-12.04)	0.4199	0.0214
8) S'	=	0.2714 (41.49)	-	1.8356 X_2' (-11.92)	0.4146	0.0215
9) T'	=	0.0130 (44.98)	-	0.0046 X_1' (-15.29)	0.5391	0.0010
10) T'	=	0.0133 (39.92)	-	0.1097 X_2' (-13.99)	0.4946	0.0011
11) J'	=	0.0345 (31.04)	-	0.0311 X_1' (-27.03)	0.7857	0.0040
12) J'	=	0.0372 (29.80)	-	0.7698 X_2' (-26.16)	0.7745	0.0041

Note: S represents the Sharpe measure of performance; T represents the Treynor measure of performance; J represents the Jensen measure of performance; X_1 represents the Beta coefficient of a random portfolio; X_2 represents the standard deviation of portfolio return; $\bar{R}^2$ represents the coefficient of determination adjusted for degrees of freedom. The figures in parentheses are t-values. The unprimed variables are calculated using monthly relatives; the primed variables using the logarithm of the monthly relatives.

Source: Irwin Friend and Marshall Blume, "Measurement of Portfolio Performance Under Uncertainty," American Economic Review, September 1970, pp. 561-575.

the slope coefficients are negative, the performance measures were proportionately lower for (biased against) higher beta portfolios during this time period. Thus, if managers of high beta portfolios are compared against managers of lower beta portfolios, the lower beta managers have an unfair advantage. Could it be that the lower beta portfolios were high dividend portfolios, and therefore received higher returns? Could the rate used for the riskless rate be too low, thereby causing this type of bias? Presently, the reasons for this bias are not fully understood, although, as more sophisticated methods are employed by researchers, such discrepancies will become understood.

3. OUR STATE-OF-THE-ART

The above two examples raise two questions:

(a) Is the single beta model useful?

(b) Can the single beta model be improved?

To answer the first question, it is important to have some historical perspective. Before 1966, no consistent risk adjustment procedure was available. Thus, if a broker earned 15% when the market went up 10%, there was no way to know whether he was a stock market genius or merely a gambler in volatile stocks (of course, you would know when the market went down!). Thus, the answer to the first question is "Sure, if you do not have something better, and until better measures are developed!"

The answer to the second question is "yes, and research is underway." The most basic form of this research has been to examine the residual error term ($e_{s,t}$). For example, Farrell in a doctoral dissertation at New York University used a heuristic procedure to group stocks together based upon their tendency to have similar residual errors and patterns over time. He found that the monthly residuals from 100 large companies during the period 1961-1969 tended to fall into four groups of stocks--growth, stable, cyclical, and oil. Then he constructed an index for each of the four groups, as well as analyzing the <u>correlation</u> of the residual errors of each type of stock with each type of index. <u>If residuals were not independent</u>, he hypothesized that they would correlate with that group index which was similar to the type of the stock. Such a result would be indicated by positive and high correlation coefficients (such coefficients range from -1 to +1 depending on the degree of correlation). As Table 1.3 indicates, the results confirmed this hypothesis (e.g., growth stocks had an average correlation of .43 with the growth index versus low negative correlations with the other indexes, as well as a high average t-statistic of

5.04 versus insignificant t-statistics for correlation with the other three indexes). Also, in another part of his study, Farrell found that, for the period studied, beta only explained 31% of a stock's return, while the group indexes explained another 15%.

Table 1.3
MATRIX OF RESIDUAL CORRELATION COEFFICIENTS, AVERAGES OF STOCKS AND FOUR STOCK INDEXES (1961-69)

	Index			
Average	Growth	Stable	Cyclical	Oil
Of 31 growth stocks	.43	-.05	-.05	-.17
	(5.04)	(-0.56)	(-0.61)	(-1.79)
Of 25 stable stocks	-.06	.38	-.04	-.02
	(-0.61)	(4.32)	(-0.29)	(-0.18)
Of 36 cyclical stocks	-.05	-.03	.37	-.07
	(-0.49)	(-0.34)	(4.22)	(-0.77)
Of 8 oil stocks	-.26	-.03	-.12	.64
	(-2.88)	(-0.32)	(-1.34)	(8.92)

<u>Source</u>: Reprinted from "Analyzing Covariation of Returns to Determine Homogeneous Stock Groupings," by James L. Farrell by permission of the University of Chicago Press. Journal of Business, April 1974, Table 4, p. 205.

Farrell's results indicate that <u>residuals are not independent</u>, and thus simple beta estimates may capture only one source of variation in stock returns. Other causes of variation could be:

> <u>Returns on Every Other Stock</u>: If one group of stocks declines relative to others, then investors may sell some of the higher stocks to buy more of the lower ("taking profits" and "rebalancing the portfolio"). Or, because some of the stocks have declined, investors may become fearful and sell-off a portion or all of their portfolio. Or they may rebalance to improve diversification. Other reactions are also possible, although little conclusive research is available on such adjustments.

Macro-Economic Events: If a war breaks out, almost all stocks will be affected. Similarly, all stocks might be affected by interest rate moves, economic depression, and so on. Beta probably reflects the influence of these factors.

Company Specific Financial Data: If a company's earnings rise unexpectedly, its stock price will probably jump also. Similar price changes would be likely for favorable changes in its debt/equity ratio, dividend payout, and so on. These company statistics, specific to the individual company, are probably not captured in beta.

Residual or Unexpected Variables: Even after all of the foregoing variables are considered, stock returns behave in too complex a manner to obtain a perfect explanation; however, the unexplained variables can often be found if they have a systematic effect on the stock's return; these variables will be reflected in the residual error term in the regression.

Figure 1.1 shows the simultaneous feedbacks that could occur between types of variables, as well as clarifying the assumptions of the beta model. Estimating beta assumes that feedbacks both within stocks returns, between company data and stock returns, and related to omitted variables are random and unexpected, i.e., can be assigned to a random error term that is unrelated to the macroeconomic events. Then, beta captures the macro-economic events that affect all stocks.[5]

The next four chapters explain how econometric techniques are used to isolate the causes of stock returns. Chapter 2 is a quick review of simple linear regression, while Chapters 3 and 4 present the important assumptions of regression analysis and extend it to the use of several independent variables. Finally, Chapter 5 presents more sophisticated single-equation methods, such as used in the study by Litzenberger and Ramaswamy, as well as introducing the role of simultaneous equation systems for analysis.

[5]The statements in this paragraph, although accurate, are overly general. This generality will be eliminated in Chapter 5, when econometric methods are evaluated for their role in estimating beta more accurately.

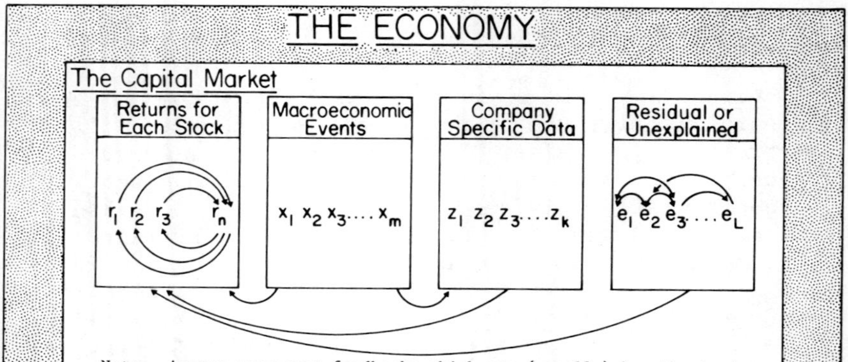

Note: Arrows represent feedbacks which are (usually) hypothesized. Other feedbacks are more tenuous, such as the belief (hypothesis) that falling stock prices cause people to spend less, thus affecting the macroeconomic variables. Further, the macroeconomic variables (x_i) are <u>assumed</u> independent of each other, as is also <u>assumed</u> of company specific variables (z_i).

2

the basics of simple linear regression

Econometric techniques can be viewed in two parts: (1) estimation, and (2) statistical inferences from the estimators. These two parts will be presented as they relate to simple linear regression; specifically, we will discuss

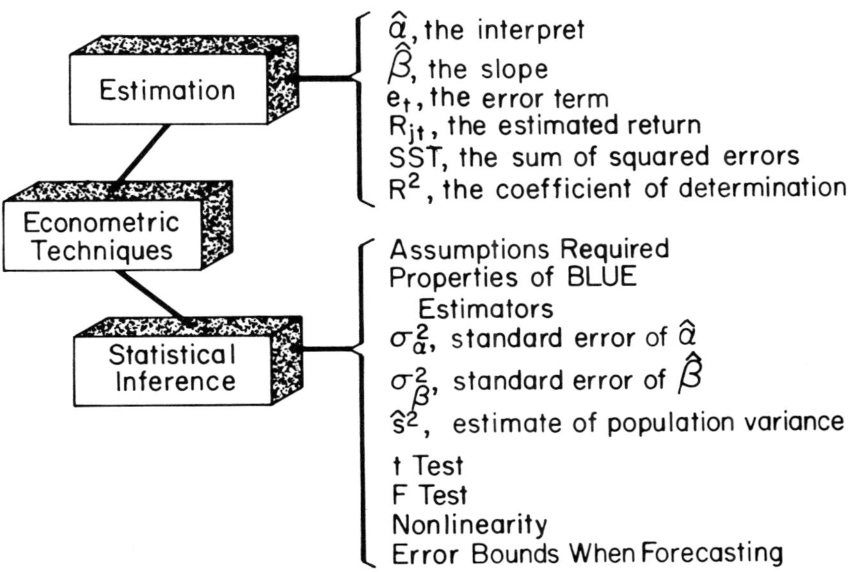

1. FITTING A REGRESSION LINE OF IBM'S RETURNS

Figure 2.1 is a graph of 240 monthly returns on IBM's stock compared to the returns on the University of Chicago Index (CRSP).[1] Table 2.1 (under Figure 2.1) contains the computer output from the regression of IBM's returns versus the CRSP. Superimposed on this graph is a line that gives the "best fit" assuming that there is a linear relationship between these two sets of returns. If you accept the line as a reasonable representation of the relationship, you are implicitly hypothesizing that the underlying "true" probabilistic mathematical model is of the form:

$$R_{jt} = \alpha_j + \beta_j R_{mt} + u_{jt} \tag{2.1}$$

where R_{jt} represents the return on stock j (IBM, in this case) in period t, R_{mt} is the return on the market index in period t, α_j and β_j are the intercept and slope of the true linear relationship between the market return and stock j, while u_{jt} is a stochastic disturbance term.[2]

It is important to understand two assumptions at this point. First, while α and β are assumed to be the true population parameters, the statistics of .73 and 1.06 are only estimates. This is because you only have a specific sample from which to estimate the true model. That is, although 240 observations is a relatively large sample size, still there will be some error in trying to estimate the true intercept and slope--we will return to this sampling problem later. Second, a stochastic disturbance term has been included, thereby indicating less than perfect explanatory power. The inclusion of such a term is often justified by several conditions (see Johnston, 1972):

(i) u_t is inserted to capture imperfect specification such as unwittingly ignoring variables that relate to the dependent variable.

---

[1]These data points are included at the end of the chapter for readers who want to try their own calculations.

[2]Readers must continually be aware of the difference between population parameters (α, β) and error terms (u_t) versus sample estimates of these $(\hat{\alpha}, \hat{\beta}, e_t)$ that are discussed shortly. Remember you never see α, β, and/or u_t; you only see the sample estimates. The population stochastic disturbance term is variously called "the error term," or the "random error"; "residual" or "residual-error" is reserved for the sample term.

Figure 2.1
IBM VS. MARKET INDEX (1956-1976)

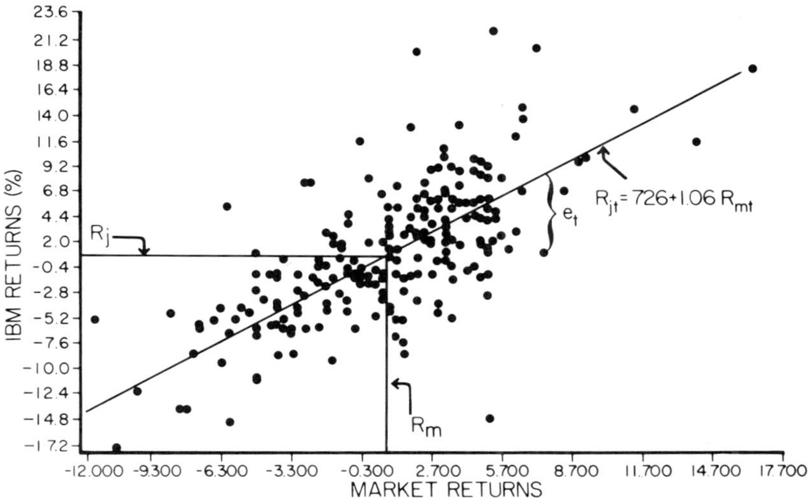

Table 2.1
IBM RETURNS REGRESSED ON CRSP MARKET INDEX: MONTHLY 1956-1975

ORDINARY LEAST SQUARES
VARIABLES...

STKRET (R_{jt})
C(1)
MKTRET (R_{mt})

INDEPENDENT VARIABLE	ESTIMATED COEFFICIENT	STANDARD ERROR	T-STATISTIC
C	0.726428	0.300108	2.42056
MKTRET	1.05976	0.728027E-01	14.5567

R-SQUARED = 0.4710

F-STATISTIC(1,238) = 211.896

DURBIN-WATSON STATISTIC (ADJ. FOR 0 GAPS) = 1.8457

NUMBER OF OBSERVATIONS = 240

SUM OF SQUARED RESIDUALS = (SSE) 4997.71

STANDARD ERROR OF THE REGRESSION = $(\sigma_u^2/n\text{-}2)$ = 4.58244

ESTIMATE OF VARIANCE-COVARIANCE MATRIX OF ESTIMATED COEFFICIENTS

0.901E-01 -0.369E-02
-0.369E-02 0.530E-02

VARIABLE ********	MEAN ****	VARIANCE ********	STANDARD DEVIATION ******************
STKRET	1.46434	39.5284	6.28716
MKTRET	0.696296	16.5768	4.07146

COVARIANCE MATRIX
****

	STKRET	MKTRET
STKRET	39.528	17.568
MKTRET	17.568	16.577

CORRELATION MATRIX
****

	STKRET	MKTRET
STKRET	1.0000	0.68629
MKTRET	0.68629	1.0000

(ii) It is not always possible to quantify all the variables contributing to the model. Such variables will be reflected in the error term u_t.

(iii) Even when the variables are quantifiable, it is not always possible to measure them with precision. Thus, u_t also accounts for these measurement errors.

In other words, there is an element of randomness in the behavior of any system and as such, insertion of u_t is called for. Up until the last section of this chapter, it will be assumed that this error term accounts for randomness associated with the dependent variable (R_{jt}), while the independent variable (R_{mt}) is assumed to be exogenously supplied, i.e., R_{mt} is assumed non-random or fixed.

In contrast to the hypothesized true model of equation (2.1), the estimated ("fitted") simple regression line has "hats," or (^), covering its parameters to indicate that they are sample estimates; i.e.,

$$\hat{R}_{jt} = \hat{\alpha} + \hat{\beta}R_{mt} \tag{2.2}$$

The $\hat{\alpha}$ and $\hat{\beta}$ are <u>point estimators</u> (Appendix D) of the unknown population parameters α and β respectively. R_{jt} is the 'fitted' value corresponding to a given value of R_{mt}, i.e., the exact line.

The term e_t, shown in Figure (2.1) is the <u>sample residual</u> or the deviation of the fitted value from the actual value; i.e.,

$$e_t = R_{jt} - \hat{R}_{jt} \tag{2.3}$$

The term e_t can be positive or negative depending upon whether R_{jt} lies above or below the fitted line.

Now, the logical question is, "How did we derive the estimated line?" The answer is "by the method of ordinary least squares (OLS)." By this method, the line of best fit is chosen such that the sum of squares of deviations[3] of the observed values, R_{jt}, from those predicted, $\hat{R}_{jt}$, is a minimum; i.e.,

$$\min \Sigma e_t^2 = \Sigma(R_{jt} - \hat{R}_{jt})^2$$
$$= \text{Sum of Squares for Error (SSE)} \tag{2.4}$$

[3]Note that the sum of the deviations squared will be zero.

While the mathematical mechanics of this method are presented in Appendix M, it is sufficient for the reader to understand only that the estimated coefficient $\hat{\beta}$ is a function of the "deviations" from each mean. In Figure 2.1, $\bar{R}_j$ and $\bar{R}_m$ correspond to the means of stock returns and market returns. The objective of minimization is accomplished by setting (see App. M-1 and M-2 for proofs)

$$\beta = \frac{\Sigma(R_{mt} - \bar{R}_m)\ (R_{jt} - \bar{R}_j)}{\Sigma\ (R_{mt} - R_m)^2} = \frac{\sigma_{jm}}{\sigma^2_m} \qquad (2.5a)$$

and for the example,

$$= \frac{17.568}{16.577} = 1.06$$

where σ_{ij} is defined as the covariance of variable i with variable j. Consequently,

$$\hat{\alpha} = \bar{R}_j - \hat{\beta}\ \bar{R}_m \quad ^4 \qquad (2.5b)$$

and for the example,

$$= 1.464 - 1.060(.696) = .726$$

2. R^2 - HOW MUCH OF THE DOTS IS EXPLAINED?

Having fitted the line, how does one go about evaluating the 'goodness of fit' or the strength of the relationship? One method is to calculate R^2, the coefficient of determination. R^2 can be interpreted as 'a measure of indicating how close the scatter of points resembles a straight line' (Yamane, 1967). In simple two-variable models, R^2 is computed as the square of the correlation coefficient between the dependent and independent variables. $R^2 = 1$ signifies a 'perfect fit'; $R^2 = 0$, indicates a 'no meaningful relationship'. For the IBM regression in Figure 2.1, $R^2 = .471$; the significance of .471 can be subjected to standard statistical tests. Before discussing the available tests, however, more detailed discussion of R^2 and its calculation is appropriate.

Because econometric calculations often use "deviations from the mean" for computational convenience in

[4]Using $R = \hat{\alpha} + \hat{\beta}R_{mt} + e_t$, and taking the expected values (Appendix A) gives $\bar{R}_j = \hat{\alpha} + \hat{\beta}\ \bar{R}_m$; hence $\hat{\alpha} = \bar{R}_j - \hat{\alpha}\bar{R}_m$.

multivariate models, it is necessary to view R^2 as related to such deviations (although the concept of a close fit is still the same). Figure 2.2 illustrates how this would be done for just one observation, R_{jt} = 13%. The total variation of the observed R_{jt} value about <u>its</u> sample mean, (BD=5%) can be broken up into two components: (1) variation of the <u>fitted</u> value from its sample mean (BC=2%) and (2) variation of the <u>observed</u> value from the corresponding fitted value, which the reader would recall as the residual-error term (CD=e_t=3%).

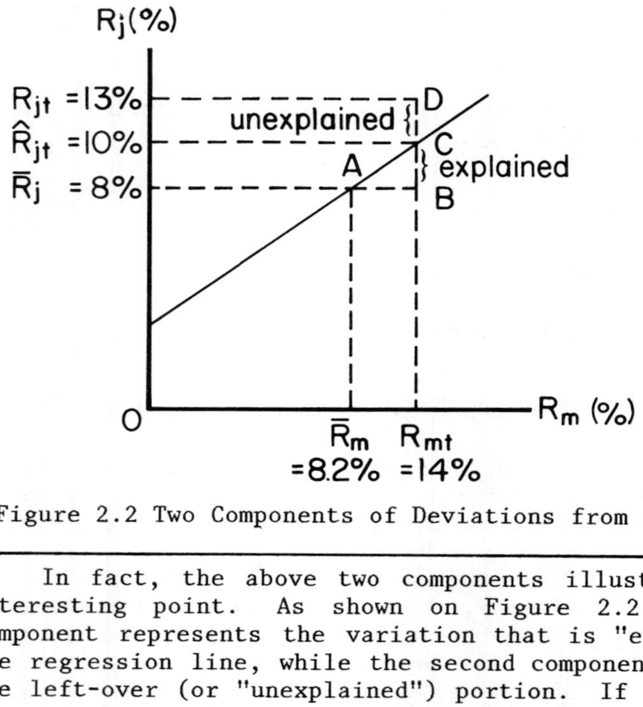

Figure 2.2 Two Components of Deviations from the Mean $\bar{R}_m$

In fact, the above two components illustrate a very interesting point. As shown on Figure 2.2, the first component represents the variation that is "explained" by the regression line, while the second component represents the left-over (or "unexplained") portion. If the observed return were on the fitted line, a <u>perfect</u> fit would occur; the unexplained portion would be zero. Thus, we can easily see that the magnitude of the explained versus the unexplained portions indicates the closeness of the observed values to the estimated values. As will be shown below, R^2 actually is a measure based upon the ratio of the explained divided by the total variation for <u>all</u> observations.

Because Figure 2.2 shows only one return observation (R_{jt}), it is necessary to generalize for a series of returns. Accordingly, each segment of BD, as well as the horizontal distance AB, must be subscripted for successively timed returns of security j. (This subscripting also follows conventional econometric notation, thereby furthering readability with the standard reference sources).

Expressed mathematically, the actual returns (R_{jt}) are

$$R_{jt} = \hat{R}_{jt} + e_t \tag{2.6a}$$

Subtracting $\overline{R}_j$ from both sides provides the deviations,

$$R_{jt} - \overline{R}_j = \hat{R}_{jt} - \overline{R}_j + e_t \tag{2.6b}$$

Squaring both sides and taking the sum over the entire sample (see Appendix M-3), we get

$$\Sigma(R_{jt} - \overline{R}_j)^2 = \Sigma(\hat{R}_{jt} - \overline{R}_j)^2 + \Sigma e_t^2 \tag{2.6c}$$

The first term on the right hand side of equation (2.6c) is called the "explained" variation due to the linear relationship and the second term is the "unexplained" variation. An equivalent statement is that the total sum of squares (SST) is composed of the sum of squares explained by the regression (SSR) plus the sum of squares due to the error term (SEE): i.e.,

$$SST = SSR + SSE$$

Thus, R^2 is the ratio of the explained sum of squares (SSR) to the total sum of squares (SST); i.e.,

$$R^2 = \frac{SSR}{SST} = \frac{\text{Explained variation}}{\text{Total variation}}$$

$$= \frac{\Sigma(\hat{R}_{jt} - \overline{R}_j)^2}{\Sigma(R_{jt} - \overline{R}_j)^2} = 1 - \frac{\Sigma e_t^2}{\Sigma(R_{jt} - \overline{R}_j)^2} \tag{2.7}$$

and, for the IBM example,

$$= 1 - \frac{4997.71}{39.528 \times 240} = .47$$

We hasten to add a word of caution regarding the use of R^2. There are several problems associated with blindly using R-squared values. To elucidate, before comparing two models, one has to make sure that the left-hand-side variables of the two models are the same. For instance, one will be making gross mistake if one tries to compare the following equations on the basis of R-squared:

$$y = a + bx \qquad R^2 = 0.9$$

$$\ln y = p + qx \qquad R^2 = 0.79$$

because the left hand side variables are different (and their total variation will be different after the logarithmic transformation). We will enumerate other pitfalls associated with R-squared as we go along. In passing, we do want to mention that one should not rush to conclusions about the assumed model based on R-squared before ascertaining whether certain other results (e.g., the signs and significance of the coefficients) conform to the parameters of the model being hypothesized. We will delve into this topic at length later. For now, our suggestion is that the reader should neither be bogged down nor carried away by R-squared.

3. ASSUMPTIONS PROVIDING BEST LINEAR UNBIASED ESTIMATORS (BLUE)

Standard tests of the simple linear model

$$R_t = \alpha + \beta R_{mt} + u_t \tag{2.8}$$

require several underlying assumptions (called the "spherical" assumptions) about the random disturbance term, u_t:

(i) u_t has a mean (or expectation) of zero; $E(u_t) = 0$.

(ii) All u_t have a <u>common constant and finite variance</u> for all t; $V(u_t) = \sigma_u^2$. This property is known as 'homoscedasticity'.

(iii) Error terms are <u>not correlated</u>; $E(u_t, u_{t-k}) = 0$ for all t, k, $k \neq 0$. This property is referred to as 'non-autoregression'.

(iv) Error terms are <u>independent of the explanatory variables</u>; i.e., $E(R_{mt}, u_t) = 0$ for all t.[5] This assumption is upheld if all R_{mt} are treated as nonrandom.

(v) We will mention, for the sake of completeness, one other tacit assumption; viz, $E(u_{it}, u_{jt}) = 0$, where i , j are two different securities. Stated verbally, this means

[5] $\text{Cov}(R_{mt}, u_t) = E(R_{mt})E(u_t) - E(R_{mt}, u_t)$. By assumption (i), $E(u_t) = 0$ and, by (iv), $E(R_{mt}, u_t) = 0$, implying Cov $(R_{mt}, u_t) = 0$.

that the error term of "our" simple linear model (think of it as R_{jt} vs. R_{mt}) is not correlated with that of another regression model (say R_{jt} vs. R_{mt}). The implications of this assumption will be clear when we discuss the 'seemingly unrelated regressions' (Chapter 5).

4. PROPERTIES OF BLUES

Under the set of assumptions (i)-(v), it can be proved that $\hat{\alpha}$ and $\hat{\beta}$ are the best linear unbiased estimators (BLUE) of the parameters α and β respectively [App. E]. What does BLUE mean, per se? Simply put, it indicates the presence of three properties--linearity, unbiasedness, and efficiency. In Appendix M, it is shown that both $\hat{\alpha}$ and $\hat{\beta}$ are linearly dependent on R_{jt} [M-4], as well as that $E(\hat{\alpha}) = \alpha$ and $E(\hat{\beta}) = \beta$ [unbiasedness M-5], and that the estimators obtained by the method of least squares have the smallest variance (efficiency). Since the proofs are available for your interest, we will assume these results and go on.

Yet, even with the above properties, it is very reasonable to ask a question which is slightly different: "How much confidence do you have in the results?" Intuitively, less confidence might be expected of $\hat{\alpha}$ and $\hat{\beta}$ fitted from a sample size of say 10 observations versus a sample size of, say, 10,000 observations. Correspondingly, if the scattered dots were very far from the line, the fitted $\hat{\alpha}$ and $\hat{\beta}$ might intuitively be expected to be less precise than if all of the dots were nearly on the line. This type of appeal to intuition makes it easy to comprehend the basic calculations for the variance (or degree of confidence) of the fitted estimators $\hat{\alpha}$ and $\hat{\beta}$.[6]

Basically, each calculation adjusts the square of the assumed population standard error (i.e., dots around the true linear relation) for the variance in the explanatory variable, R_m. Because the summation is over the number of observations in the sample, the denominator will correspondingly be larger (and the resultant estimate of σ^2 smaller) for larger sample sizes, as well as for more variation of R_{mt} from its mean.

$$\sigma^2_{\hat{\alpha}} = \sigma^2_u \left[\frac{\Sigma R^2_{mt}}{n\Sigma(R_{mt}-\bar{R}_m)^2} \right] \tag{2.9a}$$

[6]For either "doubting Thomases'" or our "Appendix-lovers," the derivations are provided in Appendix M-6.

$$\sigma^2_{\hat{\beta}} = \sigma^2_u / \Sigma(R_{mt} - \bar{R}_m)^2 \qquad (2.9b)$$

Since we do not know the actual value of σ^2_u, the population variance, we need to derive an unbiased estimator ($\hat{s}^2$) for this parameter. Such as estimator is [see App. M-7],

$$\hat{s}^2 = \frac{\Sigma e^2_t}{n-2} \qquad (2.10)$$

which enables us to estimate the variances of the regression coefficients, $\hat{\alpha}$ and $\hat{\beta}$. Substituting (2.10) into both equation (2.9a) and equation (2.9b) yields:

$$\hat{s}^2_{\hat{\alpha}} = \hat{s}^2 \left[\frac{\Sigma R^2_{mt}}{n\Sigma(R_{mt} - \bar{R}_m)^2} \right] = \frac{\Sigma e^2_t}{n-2} \left[\frac{\Sigma R^2_{mt}}{n\Sigma(R_{mt} - R_m)^2} \right] \qquad (2.11a)$$

$$\hat{s}^2_{\hat{\beta}} = \hat{s}^2 \left[\frac{1}{\Sigma(R_{mt} - \bar{R}_m)^2} \right] = \frac{\Sigma e^2_t}{n-2} \left[\frac{1}{\Sigma(R_{mt} - \bar{R}^2_m)} \right] \qquad (2.11b)$$

The square roots of the estimated variances are known as the <u>standard errors</u>. Why estimate the standard errors at all? Besides estimating the $\hat{\alpha}$ and $\hat{\beta}$ coefficients, we want to compute the confidence intervals [App. E] for these coefficients and make certain statements about their statistical significance.

Before using standard errors for testing statistical significance, we have to make certain assumptions about the distribution of the errors. A common assumption, is that the errors can be assumed to follow a normal distribution [App. C]; that is,

$$u_t \sim N(0, \sigma_u^2) \tag{2.12a}$$

Since R_1, R_2, ..., R_n are linearly dependent on u_1, u_2, ..., u_n respectively (equation 2.8), and u_1, u_2, ..., u_n are distributed independently, it follows that R_1, R_2, ..., R_n are also normally distributed and independent of each other. This leads us to the conclusion that the sample estimators, $\hat{\alpha}$ and $\hat{\beta}$, will also be distributed normally since both are linear combinations of the R_{jt}'s (App. M-4). So we write

$$\hat{\alpha} \sim N(\alpha, \sigma_\alpha^2) \tag{2.12b}$$

$$\hat{\beta} \sim N(\beta, \sigma_\beta^2) \tag{2.12c}$$

And lastly, the implications of assuming nonnormal errors will be discussed in the next chapter.

5. DO THE RESULTS SUPPORT THE HYPOTHESIZED MODEL?

Several significance tests can be carried out to check whether it is reasonable to conclude that any relationship exists between the two variables in question. For a fuller discussion, the reader can refer to Appendix E, but the following discussion will provide a general level of review and understanding.

t-Test

As shown in Appendix M-8, both $\hat{\beta}$ and $\hat{\alpha}$ can be subjected to standard t-tests; i.e.,

$$\frac{\hat{\beta}-\beta_H}{\hat{s}_{\hat{\beta}}} \sim t_{n-2} \tag{2.13}$$

$$\frac{\hat{\alpha}-\alpha_H}{\hat{s}_{\hat{\alpha}}} \sim t_{n-2} \tag{2.14}$$

where β_H and α_H are the hypothesized population parameters (note: often a null hypothesis that there is no relationship--that is, either $\beta_H = 0$ or $\alpha_H = 0$ -- is used to test for "significant difference from zero").

Establishing the linear relation between R_{jt} and R_{mt} is tantamount to rejecting the null hypothesis that $\beta=0$. The null hypothesis can be rejected using a two tail test at a 0.05 level of signifiance if $|\beta| > 1.96\ \hat{s}_{\hat{\beta}}$ or $|\beta|/\hat{s}_{\hat{\beta}} > 1.96$.[7] For the IBM example, $\hat{\beta} = 1.06$ and $\hat{s}_{\beta} = .07$, and therefore, $t = \beta - 0/\hat{s}_{\hat{\beta}} = 1.06/.07 = 14.56$.[8] Since the resultant t value is larger than 1.96, we are led to conclude that β is significantly different from zero and that there exists a linear relation between R_{jt} and R_{mt}.[9]

It is customary to provide the t-statistics for the coefficients below the coefficients themselves (although some authors include the standard errors instead). For the IBM regression model, the results would be written as

$$R_{jt} = \underset{(2.42)}{0.73} + \underset{(14.56)}{1.06}\, R_{mt} + e_t$$

If an 0.05 level of significance is assumed, we would conclude that the coefficients are significantly different from zero because the t-values are greater than 1.96. Of course, if it were hypothesized that either $\hat{\alpha}$ or $\hat{\beta}$ were to be positive (negative), then a one tail test would be appropriate because you are only testing whether $\hat{\alpha}$ or $\hat{\beta}$ is significantly greater (less) than zero.

There are numerous situations where t-tests are useful. An interesting example of such a situation is provided by our IBM data, when combined with the question "Does the fitted function appear to confirm that the capital-asset-pricing-model (CAPM) is a good explanation of IBM's stock return movements?" One way to test this is based upon the fact that, since the CAPM postulates the expected return of a security i, $E(R_i)$, would be equal to the riskless rate, r_f, plus the security's beta times the excess return of the market return, R_m, minus the risk-free rate -- i.e.,

---

[7]A t-value of 1.96 is suggested here only as a benchmark. Another common benchmark for large samples is 3.00, as this greater than the .01 significance level. For lower levels of significance the t-value will be greater and vice versa. There is no set rule for imposing significance levels, although the decision should depend upon the seriousness of not rejecting a false null hypothesis.

[8]Since $n \geq 30$, the t distribution can be approximated with a normal distribution.

[9]A similar test can be performed to check the significance of $\hat{\alpha}$.

$$E(R_i) = r_f + \beta_i(E(R_m)-r_f)$$

By some simple multiplication and subtraction, it is evident that an equivalent statement is that

$$E(R_i) = (1-\beta_i)r_f + \beta_i\ E(R_m)$$

which would suggest that the intercept of our IBM regression should be equal to $(1-\beta_i)r_f$, or equivalently, that

$$\hat{r}_f = \frac{\hat{\alpha}}{1-\hat{\beta}_i}$$

$$= \frac{.73}{-.06}$$

$$< 0$$

Thus, by calculating the actual compounded risk-free rate over this period, and then by using this actual rate as the hypothesized population value, one could test

$$t_{n-2} \simeq \frac{\hat{r}_f - \text{actual } r_f}{\hat{s}_{\hat{r}_f}}$$

where the standard error of $\hat{r}_f$ would be calculated as the standard deviation of the actual rates divided by $n/n-1$ (see Appendix B).

In contrast to the above test about a hypothesized intercept, t-tests can be used for null hypotheses about hypothesized slope coefficients. For example, in an interesting article by Gibson (1972), a linear relation was hypothesized between the nominal rate of interest (NI) and the expected inflation, where EI was the expected rate of price change; i.e.,

$$NI_t = \gamma + \delta(EI_t) + u_t$$

where his gamma (γ) is equivalent to our previously discussed α, and his delta (δ) is equivalent to our β. U.S. Treasury Securities were used as a surrogate for the market rates. He was interested in testing the hypothesis that $\delta=1$. Such a hypothesis is equivalent to a statement that nominal interest rates fully reflect expected inflation plus a real rate of interest. His results indicated that, for 3-month Treasury Bills (he also tested numerous other regressions),

$$NI = 2.21 + .93\ EI \quad R^2 = .76 \quad \hat{s}^2_{\delta} = .085 \qquad (2.15)$$

Given $\hat{\delta} = 0.93$ and $\hat{s}_{\delta} = 0.085$,

$$t = \frac{\hat{\delta}-1}{\hat{s}_{\hat{\delta}}} = \frac{-.07}{.085} = 0.82 < 1.96$$

Hence, the null hypothesis that $\hat{\delta} = 1$ would not be rejected with 95% confidence. So, it is possible to present equation (2.15) as NI = 2.21 + EI. In such a case, γ=2.21 would be taken as the real rate of interest. (Note: because he ran many regressions, the example here is taken out of the full context and is solely for illustrative purposes.)

F Test

Earlier on we decomposed the total sum of squares (SST) into sum of squares due to the regression (SSR) and the sum of squared errors, SSE. That is,

$$\Sigma(R_{jt}-\bar{R}_j)^2 = \Sigma(\hat{R}_{jt}-\bar{R}_j)^2 + \Sigma e_t^2 \qquad (2.6c)$$

$$SST = SSR + SSE \qquad (2.6d)$$

Where SSR is the variation explained by changes in R_{mt}. If changes in R_{mt} did not really affect R_{jt}, we would expect the SSR to be zero; i.e., R_{jt} would be independent of R_{mt}, and $R^2 = 0$. [See Appendix M-9]. Due to sampling errors, however, SSR would still usually be different from zero, even when R_{jt} was not related to R_{mt}.

To test the null hypothesis that there exists no relationship between R_{jt} and R_{mt}, we will use a probability distribution called the F-distribution (Appendix I). The important feature of this distribution is that it can be proved that, under the null hypothesis, the ratio (test statistic)

$$\frac{SSR/1}{SSE/n-2} \sim F_{1,\, n-2} \qquad (2.16)$$

where the subscripts 1, n-2 represent the degrees of freedom associated with the numerator and denominator respectively.[10] Alternatively, the test statistic can also be written equivalently in terms of R^2 as

[10]"Degrees of freedom" is a concept that is troublesome to most users, even sophisticated ones. Degrees of freedom are the total number of sample observations minus the number of sample statistics used for a subsequent calculation. The idea of freedom can be seen by thinking of three observations {2,4,6}, or n=3. If the sample mean is calculated ($\bar{X}$=4), then there are only two degrees of freedom

$$\frac{SSR/1}{SSE/n-2} = \frac{(SSR/SST)/1}{(SSE/SST)/n-2}$$

$$= \frac{(SSR/SST)/1}{[(SST-SSR)/SST]/(n-2)}$$

$$= \frac{R^2/1}{(1-R^2)/(n-2)} \sim F_{1,n-2}$$

Thus, the F test can also be thought of as a test for the significance of R^2, and we will reject a null hypothesis of no relationship if the F ratio so computed exceeds a critical theoretical F value.

For example, in our IBM regression, SSR = 4449.0, SSE = 4997.1, n = 240, and therefore

$$\frac{SSR/1}{SSE/n-2} = \frac{4449.0}{20.996} = 211.9$$

Referring to Table 4A (at back of book) for 1 and 238 degrees of freedom for $\alpha = .05$, we find the F statistic is between 3.84 and 3.92. Thus, we would reject the null hypothesis of no relationship.

---

[10]continued.
left in the sample because the third number can be determined by the mean and any two of the others (e.g., if $\overline{X}=4$ and $X_1=2$, $X_2=4$, then X_3 must be 6). Another example would be to think of just two observations (dots) in a two dimensional space; drawing a line through the dots would leave no degrees of freedom. Since all statistical tests use sample information, the test must be adjusted for the degrees of freedom left over after calculating sample statistics. Because calculating the degrees of freedom can often be confusing, the exact calculations are provided with each test. For those who want to examine this further, however, the paragraph below discusses the degrees of freedom for the three terms discussed in the text above.

In the above sample, once regression estimators $\hat{\alpha}$ and $\hat{\beta}$ have been calculated, the n error terms $(R_{jt}-\hat{\alpha}-\hat{\beta}R_{mt})$ lose two degrees of freedom. That is, if any n-2 sample observations are given, plus the values of $\hat{\alpha}$ and $\hat{\beta}$, all n of the errors can be determined; thus, two of the error terms are not independent. For the total sum of squares, the only statistic calculated is the sample mean, which leaves n-1 independent observations. Finally to obtain the SSR, it would be necessary to use n-1 of the sample statistics plus <u>any</u> (independent) other observation to estimate $\hat{\alpha}$, $\hat{\beta}$, and therefore $\hat{R}_{jt}$, thus indicating only one independent observation.

The main difference between the t-test and the F test outlined here is that the t test is applicable to test the significance of each one of the coefficients whereas the F test concerns itself with the linear hypothesis as a whole. This distinction will be brought out more clearly when we deal with multivariate regressions (Chapter 4). Further insight can be obtained from Appendix I where, for example, the F value is shown as obtainable from squaring the t value.

6. FORECASTING

One of the main purposes of the regression analysis is to predict the future values of the dependent variables for a known (or hypothesized) value of the independent variable. For instance, if we hypothesize that the market return R_{mt} is going to be 10% in the next period, the estimated model,

$$\hat{R}_{jt} = \hat{\alpha} + \hat{\beta} R_{mt} \quad (2.17)$$

would predict the value of IBM's stock return as

$$\hat{R}_{jt} = 0.73 + 1.06 R_{mt}$$

$$= 11.33\%$$

As shown below, however, there are three sources of "imprecision" in our forecast, and thus we have to construct a confidence interval around $\hat{R}_{jt}$. To do so, let us determine the standard error of the estimate. For $t = n+1$, the prediction equation is

$$\hat{R}_{j(n+1)} = \hat{\alpha} + \hat{\beta} R_{m(n+1)}$$

while the true model is assumed to be

$$R_{j(n+1)} = \alpha + \beta R_{m(n+1)} + u_{n+1}.$$

Therefore the prediction error is

$$\hat{R}_{j(n+1)} - R_{j(n+1)} = (\hat{\alpha} - \alpha) + (\hat{\beta} - \beta) R_{mt} - u_{n+1}$$

with an expected value of zero, i.e.,

$$E(R_{j(n+1)} - R_{j(n+1)}) = 0 \quad (2.18)$$

because $E(\hat{\alpha}) = \alpha$; $E(\hat{\beta}) = \beta$ and $E(u_{n+1}) = 0$. Thus $\hat{R}_{j(n+1)}$ is an unbiased estimator of $R_{j(n+1)}$. Yet, although our estimates are unbiased, the precision of our estimation depends on three factors: (i) dispersion of the explanatory variable forming the sample, i.e. $(R_{mt} - \bar{R}_m)$; (ii) the size of the sample, n; and(iii) the distance between the future value of R_{mt} and the sample mean $\bar{R}_m$ (the further away from the mean of explanatory variable, the less the expected precision, i.e., extrapolation is less reliable than interpolation). Figure 2.3 shows graphically the cumulative effects of all these factors as they bear upon our 'successful' estimation. Mathematically, the variance of the estimator R_{jn+1} can be shown to be equal to

$$V\left[\hat{R}_{jn+1}\right] = \sigma_u^2\left[1 + \frac{1}{n} + \frac{(R_{m(n+1)} - \bar{R}_m)^2}{\Sigma(R_{mt} - \bar{R}_m)^2}\right] \quad (2.19a)$$

Hence, the standard error of the estimate is

$$SE(R_{j(n+1)}) = \sqrt{\frac{\Sigma e_t^2}{n-2}\left[1 + \frac{1}{n} + \frac{(R_{m(n+1)} - \bar{R}_m)^2}{\Sigma(R_{mt} - \bar{R}_m)^2}\right]} \quad (2.19b)$$

where we substituted (2.10) for σ_u^2. From equations (2.19) we gather that the standard error increases as we go farther away from the mean of the independent variable. Also, the greater the sample size and greater the dispersion of R_{mt} in the sample, the smaller the variance of our estimation.

To continue with our IBM example, the 95% confidence interval for $R_{j,(n+1)}$ is

$$R_{j,n+1} \pm 1.96 \times [SE(R_{j,n+1})]$$

which equals to

$$R_{j,n+1} \pm 1.96\sqrt{4.58\left[1 + \frac{1}{240} + \frac{(R_{m(n+1)} - .696)^2}{16.577}\right]}$$

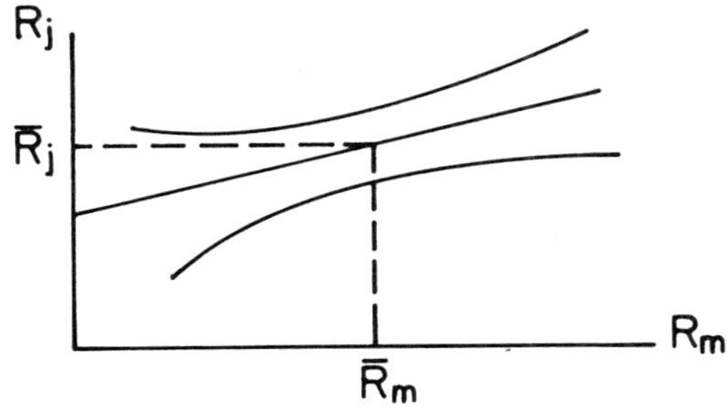

Figure 2.3 'Precision' of Forecasts

On the computer output for the regression analysis (Table 2.1), the phrase 'standard error of the regression' refers to equation (2.10) i.e., $\sqrt{s^2} = \sqrt{\Sigma e_i^2/n-2}$. Often this standard error is used, instead of that in equation (2.19b) for the sake of convenience, without causing too much error. Such a practice will be reasonably accurate if a large sample was used and if $R_{m,n+1}$ is very close to $\bar{R}_m$. Strictly speaking, however, we can use the regression model only for future values of R_{jt} that fall within the range of R_{mt} (t=1,2,...,n) from which the regression model was built, and with the SE expressed in (2.19).

Data Points for Figure 2.1 and Regression

PERIOD	STOCK RETURN	MARKET RETURN	PERIOD	STOCK RETURN	MARKET RETURN	PERIOD	STOCK RETURN	MARKET RETURN
1	-3.226	2.771	81	-10.789	-4.890	161	-2.500	0.304
2	5.128	3.948	82	-2.122	0.413	162	5.878	-6.286
3	21.027	6.914	83	15.390	11.103	163	-3.923	-6.406
4	7.071	0.558	84	-2.133	1.401	164	6.626	5.006
5	1.533	-4.889	85	8.654	5.061	165	0.072	-2.227
6	13.970	3.630	86	-5.428	-2.280	166	4.417	5.370
7	5.209	5.104	87	5.316	3.443	167	-0.694	-3.059
8	-5.728	-2.956	88	10.154	4.771	168	2.101	-1.761
9	-6.502	-4.980	89	3.127	2.040	169	-8.025	-7.580
10	3.090	0.746	90	-8.591	-1.773	170	1.849	5.883
11	4.711	0.660	91	-0.401	-0.191	171	-0.514	-0.149
12	10.656	3.276	92	2.589	5.367	172	-11.964	-9.959
13	-4.074	-3.217	93	1.630	-1.256	173	-6.309	-6.081
14	-1.641	-1.815	94	9.292	2.831	174	-10.072	-4.851
15	2.163	2.431	95	-1.518	-0.317	175	1.380	7.457
16	10.106	4.326	96	4.482	2.176	176	5.550	5.024
17	6.162	3.913	97	6.903	2.289	177	9.578	4.262
18	12.394	-0.412	98	5.212	1.821	178	1.182	-1.447
19	1.662	0.976	99	4.438	1.707	179	4.507	4.950
20	-5.914	-5.036	100	-4.039	0.757	180	3.417	6.087
21	-4.905	-5.877	101	5.491	1.934	181	2.439	4.737
22	-0.666	-4.289	102	-0.625	1.539	182	3.779	1.520
23	4.054	2.513	103	-3.145	1.809	183	6.241	4.354
24	0.847	-3.880	104	-4.383	-1.168	184	0.070	3.537
25	5.410	5.026	105	-0.908	3.423	185	-8.232	-3.427
26	2.379	-1.456	106	-3.780	0.726	186	-3.058	0.410
27	5.327	3.427	107	-1.488	-0.173	187	-8.123	-3.944
28	1.445	3.162	108	-0.727	0.443	188	4.824	4.002
29	-0.456	2.417	109	9.524	3.869	189	-0.082	-0.582
30	5.806	2.912	110	1.951	0.726	190	-1.070	-3.919
31	0.135	4.438	111	-0.329	-1.172	191	2.096	-0.147
32	0.852	1.823	112	6.769	3.450	192	10.147	8.895
33	9.677	4.905	113	-1.134	-0.479	193	9.361	2.459
34	6.618	2.761	114	-4.184	-5.145	194	0.503	3.112
35	2.908	3.021	115	4.585	1.796	195	3.731	0.799
36	22.679	5.129	116	4.488	3.096	196	0.981	0.630
37	-6.495	0.950	117	2.705	3.326	197	3.394	1.865
38	5.877	0.908	118	4.000	3.088	198	-1.446	-2.298
39	2.646	0.520	119	-1.219	0.239	199	2.232	-0.006
40	7.919	3.807	120	-4.952	1.233	200	2.271	3.731
41	20.435	1.993	121	-0.601	1.089	201	-0.490	-0.706
42	-4.681	0.109	122	4.133	-1.029	202	-5.166	1.002
43	-4.464	3.482	123	0.194	-2.170	203	1.777	4.997
44	-0.701	-1.068	124	8.043	2.371	204	2.813	1.319
45	-3.062	-4.555	125	-2.103	-5.009	205	8.333	-2.599
46	-0.607	1.690	126	-2.964	-1.116	206	-0.597	-3.904
47	6.748	1.805	127	-2.782	-1.283	207	0.000	-0.425
48	0.516	2.876	128	-5.620	-7.481	208	-5.446	-4.363
49	-5.077	-6.691	129	-0.936	-0.567	209	-3.226	-1.884
50	0.661	1.123	130	4.567	4.623	210	0.715	-0.877
51	5.024	-1.169	131	13.584	1.515	211	-0.789	5.062
52	3.075	-1.654	132	-1.197	0.394	212	-3.936	-3.088
53	11.547	3.271	133	7.537	8.397	213	-14.286	5.092
54	3.571	2.329	134	7.910	0.951	214	8.624	-0.141
55	0.479	-2.186	135	4.884	4.361	215	-5.042	-11.702
56	2.336	3.020	136	10.089	4.210	216	-6.887	1.405
57	-3.731	-5.636	137	-3.523	-4.098	217	-0.608	-0.064
58	-0.969	-0.498	138	6.702	2.410	218	-2.485	0.394
59	9.149	4.731	139	2.060	4.794	219	-0.893	-2.436
60	6.463	4.720	140	-1.359	-0.560	220	-3.605	-4.174
61	7.251	6.532	141	9.705	3.430	221	-5.927	-3.672
62	6.250	3.657	142	8.254	-2.702	222	0.118	-2.071
63	2.963	3.204	143	3.302	0.785	223	-5.229	-7.218
64	2.734	0.579	144	2.451	3.035	224	-4.030	-8.628
65	2.752	2.419	145	-5.183	-3.792	225	-17.188	-10.881
66	-2.661	-2.924	146	-2.220	-3.024	226	18.946	16.416
67	2.418	3.036	147	5.603	0.870	227	-5.486	-4.058
68	6.797	2.640	148	10.612	9.031	228	-5.219	-2.248
69	3.561	-1.903	149	5.579	2.366	229	12.054	14.060
70	9.201	2.703	150	-0.910	1.219	230	15.272	6.403
71	-1.174	4.626	151	-4.240	-2.011	231	-4.118	2.705
72	-0.172	0.056	152	-0.915	1.618	232	1.573	4.833
73	-6.390	-3.595	153	0.000	4.159	233	3.157	5.548
74	-0.784	2.035	154	-8.164	1.215	234	-2.791	4.984
75	-0.791	-0.575	155	8.713	5.552	235	-8.971	-6.343
76	-14.782	-6.117	156	-5.618	-3.568	236	-1.183	-1.750
77	-13.381	-8.341	157	-5.952	-0.665	237	1.074	-3.615
78	-13.567	-8.083	158	-0.700	-5.066	238	12.749	6.003
79	14.075	6.566	159	7.030	3.199	239	7.479	3.101
80	2.584	2.256	160	4.459	2.146	240	-0.939	-0.841

3

what happens when the real world doesn't fit the assumptions?

In Chapter 2, we built the simple linear regression model based upon the five assumptions below:

(i) The error term u_t has a mean (or expectation) of zero; $E(u_t) = 0$.

(ii) All u_t have a common constant and finite variance for all t; $V(u_t) = \sigma_u^2$.

(iii) Error terms are not correlated; $E(u_t, u_{t-k}) = 0$ for all t,k, $k \neq 0$.

(iv) Error terms are independent of the explanatory variable; i.e., $E(R_{mt}, u_t) = 0$ for all t. This assumption is upheld if all R_{mt} are treated as nonrandom.

(v) The error term of one model is uncorrelated with that of another; $E(u_{jt}, u_{it}) = 0$, where j, i are two different securities.

What happens if these assumptions are violated? Two results can occur: (1) biased sample estimators may be expected under violation of certain of the assumptions and (2) standard formulas and tests for statistical inference are invalid.

UNIVERSITY
OF BRISTOL
LIBRARY

In this chapter, we will be seeing the kinds of problems that arise if one or more of the above assumptions are violated, as well as discovering how to rectify such problems. Because this chapter focuses on how the properties of $\hat{\alpha}$ and $\hat{\beta}$ are affected by violated assumptions, the chapter contents present an unusual balance in our previously presented diagram of econometric boxes:

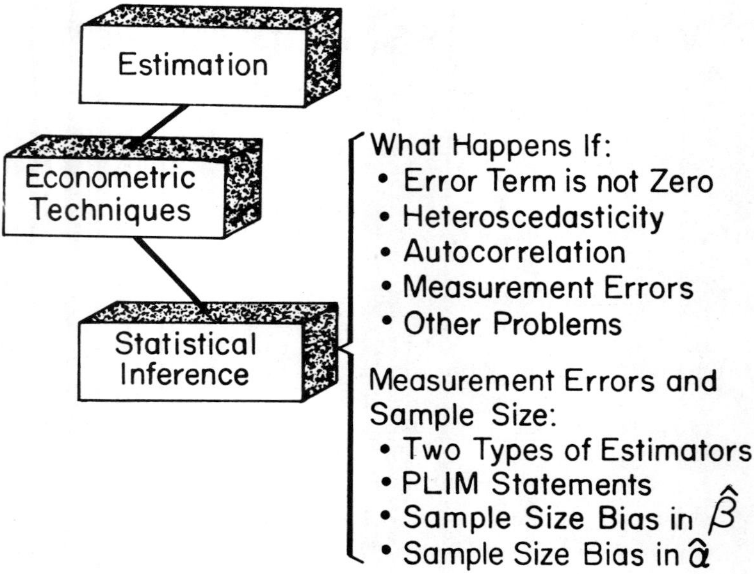

As can be seen, the whole focus will be on the bottom half of the diagram. This focus is appropriate because each violation will cause "odd" results when the estimators are assumed to be unbiased (remember the poor results that occurred in Chapter 1 when beta was assumed to an adequate representation of all risk--i.e., that the residual-error terms were independently distributed!)

Finally, since the five assumptions above are about the error term (u_t), you should not be surprised to find that the residual error term (e_t) often plays a vital role in giving us clues about the existence and cause of violated assumptions. Thus, in what follows, the analysis of the residuals performs a crucial role in dealing with the problematic situations.

1. TYPES OF VIOLATIONS AND THEIR TREATMENT

Below are eleven cases that violate the five required assumptions. Each will be discussed in a way that assists in detecting its presence, as well as indicating how to compensate for its effect.

EXPECTATION OF THE ERROR TERM IS NOT ZERO

The first assumption of the linear model was that the mean of the error term is zero, i.e., $E(u_t) = 0$. What if $E(u_t)$ is equal to a constant, say γ? Then we have,

$$\tilde{u}_t = \gamma + \tilde{\Theta}_t$$

where $\tilde{\Theta}_t$ is a random variable with a mean of zero. Now, the simple regression model in equation (2.1) becomes,

$$\begin{aligned} R_{jt} &= \alpha + \beta R_{mt} + \tilde{u}_t \\ &= \alpha + \beta R_{mt} + \gamma + \tilde{\Theta}_i \\ &= (\alpha + \gamma) + \beta R_{mt} + \tilde{\Theta}_t \end{aligned}$$

which resembles equation (2.1) in form but with a different intercept term $(\alpha + \gamma)$, although the slope coefficient β remains unaffected. But, unfortunately, α and γ cannot be separated and identified, and thus the estimated intercept will be a biased estimate of the true α (however, the estimate will be efficient, linear, and best).

HETEROSCEDASTICITY

The second assumption of the simple linear model was that the residual terms have a constant variance around the regression line (see Figure 3.1). But if the disturbances do exhibit non-constant variance (see Figure 3.2, for example) the least-squares estimators for the simple two-variable model are unbiased, but not BLUE.

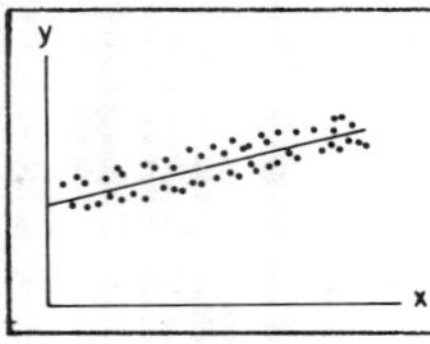

← Figure 3.1
Homoscedasticity

Figure 3.2 →
Heteroscedasticity

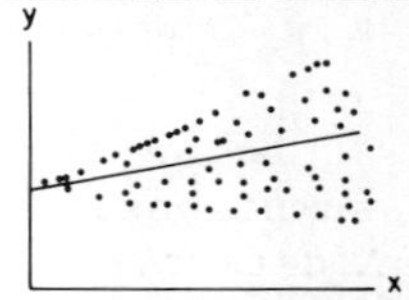

Miller and Scholes (1972) observed that "the variance of the disturbance term ... is not constant but is higher at higher values of R_i (and b_i)" where R_i are the mean annual rates of return for various common stocks in a portfolio, and b_i represent the covariance between a particular stock and the portfolio.[1] Their statement can be graphically portrayed much like Figure 3.2 with R_i = y and β_i = x, and this a problem when estimating the Security Market Line.

By taking recourse to a method known as weighted least squares we can eliminate the problem of heteroscedasticity. This requires certain assumptions about the variation of the disturbance term. For example, suppose we can hypothesize that the variance of disturbance u_i is proportional to the square of the explanatory variable x, i.e., $V(u_i) = \sigma^2 x^2$. Then we can transform the regression model $y = \alpha + \beta x + u_i$ into equivalent model that would be free of heteroscedastic disturbances. To illustrate,

$$y = \alpha + \beta x + u_i$$

dividing both sides by x, we get

$$\frac{y}{x} = \frac{\alpha}{x} + \beta + \phi_i$$

where $\phi = u_i/x$, and thus $V(\phi_i) = V(u_i/x) = 1/x^2\, V(u_i) = \sigma^2 x^2/x^2 = \sigma^2$. Thus the variance of the disturbance term is forced to become constant to facilitate the application of LS regression. We then have a new model which has an interesting relationship to the old model. Now, y/x is the dependent variable and 1/x can be the independent variable; thus the slope of the new model is the intercept of the original model, and the intercept of the new model is the slope of the original model.

Is heteroscedasticity a problem for estimating risk/return relationships? Rogalski and Vinso (1978) examined this problem when estimating the market model for security i's return. They ran a regression of the type $|e_{it}| = c_i + d_i R_{mt} + N_{it}$ (where || stands for absolute value) to investigate any relationship between the error term on security i's return and the market returns (explanatory variable).

[1]Heteroscedasticity is more common in models dealing with cross-section data than time-series data, although it can be a problem in both as discussed in the first part of Chapter V.

They found that c_i and d_i were jointly significant[2] at the 10% level for 13%-16% of the stocks on various exchanges, leading to the conclusion that heteroscedasticity should not be disregarded when using the market model.

AUTOCORRELATION

If the residuals of the regression equation are correlated, contrary to the assumption that $[E(u_t, u_{t-j}) = 0, j \neq 0]$, the estimates of α and β obtained using the least-squares procedure are no longer BLUE, although they are still unbiased. Also, the values of R^2 as well as t and F statistics tend to be exaggerated (Maddala, 1977). Thus, you must insure that the residuals are not correlated to make inferences from the regression equation.

To understand how autocorrelation might be detected, let us assume that our stock return model

$$R_{jt} = \alpha + \beta R_{mt} + u_t$$

has a first order autoregressive scheme[3] in its residual errors, shown in Figure 3.3, i.e.,

$$u_t = \rho u_{t-1} + \varepsilon_t$$

where ρ is called the autocorrelation coefficient.[4]

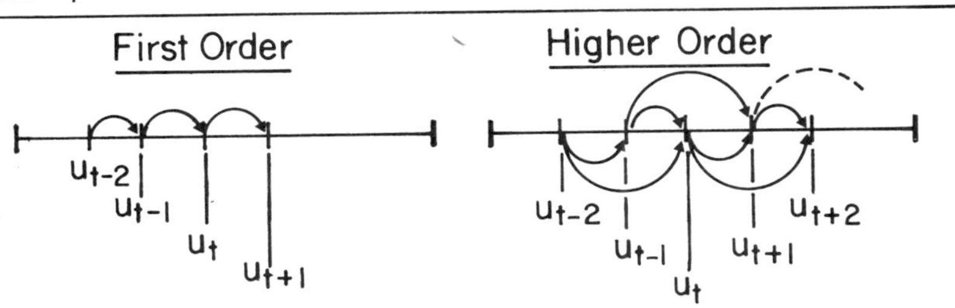

Figure 3.3 Autoregressive Schemes

Durbin and Watson (1950,1951) proposed a test to track down first order autocorrelation by examining the successive errors according to a test statistic

[2]We have not touched upon tests of joint significance in this text. See (Maddala, 1977, p. 111) for such tests.

[3]$u_t = \rho_1 u_{t-1} + \rho_2 u_{t-2} + \varepsilon_t$ is an example of a higher-order scheme.

[4]ρ is the first-order autocorrelation coefficient only if ε_t follows the basic assumption about error terms.

$$d = \frac{\sum_{t=2}^{n} (e_t - e_{t-1})^2}{\sum_{t=1}^{n} e_t^2} \qquad (3.1)$$

where e_t are the residuals from the regression. For large samples

$$d \cong 2(1 - \hat{\rho})$$

where ρ is the first-order autocorrelation coefficient. If there were no autocorrelation $\hat{\rho} = 0$, d should be approximately equal to 2. For positive correlation (i.e., $\rho > 0$), d will be less than 2, and for negative correlation ($\rho < 0$) d will be greater than 2, with d approximately equal to 4 for perfect negative correlation.

The modus operandi for systematically identifying the absence of autocorrelation can be stated thus:

H_0: $\rho = 0$ (No autocorrelation)

H_1: $\rho \neq 0$

1. Compute d using equation (3.1)
2. Decision rules:
   a. Reject H_1 if $d < d_L$ or $d > 4-d_L$
   b. Accept H_0 if $d_U < d < 4 - d_U$
   c. Indecisive if $d_L \leq d \leq d_U$ or if $4-d_U \leq d \leq 4-d_L$

Table 5 provides the values of d_L and d_U (where L and U stand for lower and upper limits respectively) for 5% level of significance.

Incidentally, $d < d_L$ signals positive autocorrelation and $d > 4 - d_L$ signifies negative autocorrelation.

For example, in Chapter 2 (Table 2.1) we find that the Durbin-Watson statistic for the market model for IBM stocks is $d = 1.85$. Turning to Table 5, we find that $d_L = 1.65$ and $d_U = 1.69$ at $n = 100$ observations, $k = 1$ explanatory variables, and a 5% significance level.[5] Since 1.85 is

[5]Although n=240 in the IBM problem, n=100 is being used because the table only includes values to that number. This decision causes no problems because n=100 is a more restrictive assumption, and the final decision of no autocorrelation would still result if n=240 were assumed.

above 1.69 and below 2.31 (rule b above), we would conclude that autocorrelation was not a problem, i.e., H_0 (also, we could conclude this at the 1% level of significance).

Suppose that autocorrelation was found, what can be done to eliminate its impact when estimating $\hat{\alpha}$ and $\hat{\beta}$? Several methods are available (Maddala, 1977), and Appendix K presents the quasi-first-difference method proposed by Cochrane-Orcutt (1949).[6]

MEASUREMENT ERRORS IN THE VARIABLES

In Chapter 2 we naively assumed that the regression variables were measured without any errors. But, what if the measured value turns out to be different from what we intended to measure? For example, the "true" measure of

---

[6]Our text is intended as a short introduction to econometric concepts, and as such we have had to ignore some important topics. One such topic is estimation of time series relationships which can be estimated based upon only past observations of the same series; that is, the dependent variable is a function of past values of itself. Such a situation can admit complex patterns of autocorrelation, and various methods have been developed for estimating such relationships. These methods concentrate on specifying a model which will produce residuals that are free from autocorrelation, and the specification may combine terms that are either moving averages (MA) and/or lagged values of the series (AR for autoregressive), possibly integrated (I) with lagged k^{th} order differences of the original series. Such models are designated AR, ARMA, and ARIMA, depending on the individual specification that results in independent residuals.

An interesting use of such modeling is found in a study by Rogalski and Vinso (1977). Their attention was addressed to the problem of <u>causality</u>, and in particular, to the question of whether changes in the money supply cause changes in stock prices. They estimated an ARMA process or each of the two time-series, thereby developing a series of independent residuals for each series. Then, they examined these residuals for lead-lag patterns to determine if one series of residuals preceded the other in a statistically significant way. Based upon these tests, they rejected the hypothesis that changes in the money supply precede changes in stock prices (in fact, they find some evidence to the contrary). The interested reader should review their work for definitions and tests of causality in time-series data.

the market returns R_{mt} is still up for debate (Roll[1969, 1977, 1978]). Market indices such as S&P, etc., are generally used as measures or proxies for the "true" market index R_{mt}, but clearly a number of assets are excluded (e.g., home mortgages, diplomas, etc.) So we inevitably introduce an error in the measurement of R_{mt};[7] i.e., if r_{mt} is the observed index,

$$R_{mt} = r_{mt} + \delta_t$$

where δ_t is the error term which is taken to satisfy the basic linear assumptions. The market model now becomes

$$\begin{aligned} R_{jt} &= \alpha + \beta(r_{mt} + \delta_t) + u_t \\ &= \alpha + \beta r_{mt} + u_t + \beta\delta_t \\ &= \alpha + \beta r_{mt} + \pi_t \qquad (3.2) \end{aligned}$$

where $\pi = u_t + \beta\delta_t$. As shown in Appendix M-9, $\mathrm{Cov}(r_{mt}, \pi_t) \neq 0$. If we were to run a regression using equation (3.2), we would be violating one of the basic assumptions required to justify the LS estimates as BLUE. In brief, errors in variables lead to inconsistent estimators.[8] One of the highly recommended (but somewhat impracticable) methods to solve the errors in measurement problem is called the instrumental variable technique (Kmenta [1964]). The consequences of errors in variables in the use of simple linear models will be discussed in some detail in the last part of this chapter, and thus we will move on here to other violations of the assumptions.

OTHER VIOLATIONS

Non-normal errors. Dowell and Grube (1978) found that the daily returns of common stocks are distributed in a non-Gaussian fashion with a fat-tail. It can be proved, however, that, even when the errors are not normally distributed, the LS estimators are unbiased, although not necessarily efficient. The standard errors (equations 2.9

---

[7]Observe that error in the measurement of the individual stock returns is already taken care of by incorporating the disturbance term u_t in the regression model.

[8]Of course, assuming that the probability limit of the covariance between the explanatory variable and the error equals zero alleviates this problem. Probability limits and their implications will be taken up in the second half of this chapter.

a and b)of the estimators are still calculated the same,but because the confidence intervals and tests for significance of the coefficients are dependent on the distribution of the error term, these tests will be less valid although they are still useful if the distribution tends to a normal distribution. Furthermore, we can obtain asymptotically consistent and unbiased estimators for *large* samples irrespective of the distribution of the error term. Maddala (1977) provides a summary of procedures for determining if normality is a resonable assumption, but unless the actual distribution is known, little can be done except to try to transform the variables such that the residuals appear normally distributed.[9]

Outliers. Point N in Figure 3.4 appears to be 'freaky' in the sense that it is farther away from the regression line than other points. Such points are called outliers. Analysis of residuals to detect outliers is a very *ad hoc* task, and usually one of two methods is tried: (1) classical statistical methods are used to compare outlier observations to the other observations, where outliers are classified by some arbitrary method (see Anscombe and Tukey, 1963); (2) arbitrary classification of outliers, and deletion of these from the regression analysis. Ultimately, the chosen procedures should rest upon the purpose and implicit logic of the model being estimated, although the actual classification of outliers must be regarded as an 'ad hoc' procedure.

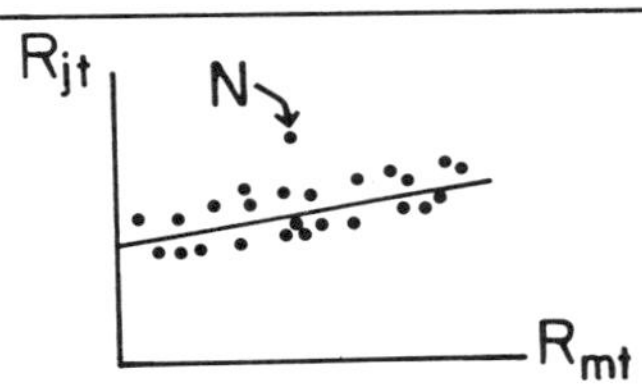

Figure 3.4 Outlier

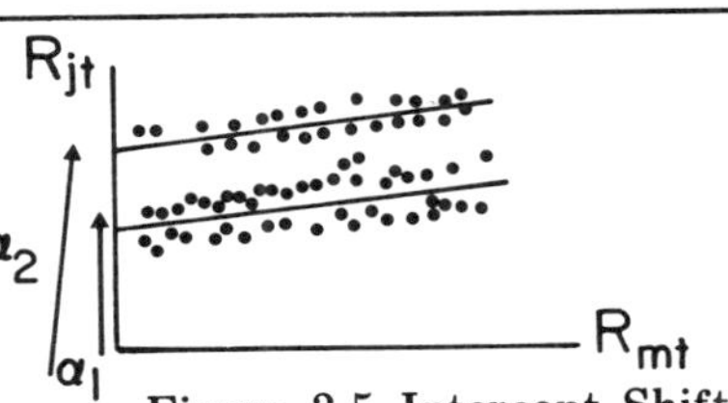

Figure 3.5 Intercept Shift

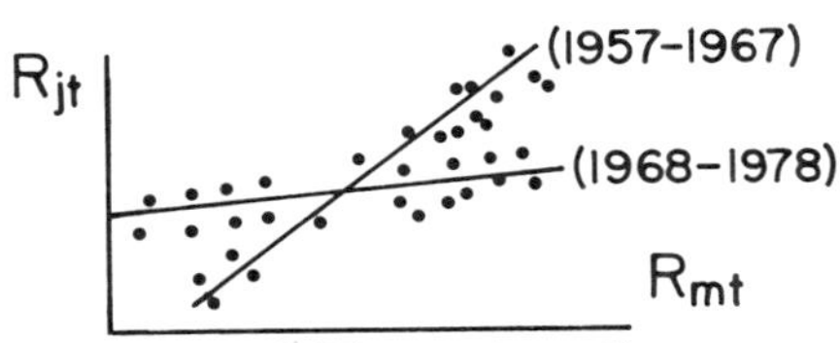

Figure 3.6 Nonstationarity

[9]Non-normal residuals may be important for research on common stock returns as return (but not residual) distributions have been found to have "fat tails" compared to normal distributions (Fama, 1965), as well as being skewed (Kraus and Litzenberger, 1976; Simkowitz and Beetles, forthcoming). For a survey of research on this topic, see Fogler (1978).

Dummy Variables. Figure 3.5 raises the possibility of two linear relationships between the variables concerned. Typical questions that one may ask are: Are the linear functions dependent on the state of the market, bear versus bull? Does the intercept change? What happens to the slope -- is there a parallel shift?

Assume for expository purposes, that there are two linear relationships such as:

$$R_{jt} = \alpha_1 + \beta R_{mt} + u_t \quad \text{(bear market)}$$

$$R_{jt} = \alpha_2 + \beta R_{mt} + u_t \quad \text{(bull market)}$$

These two equations can be combined into one as

$$R_{jt} = \alpha_1 + (\alpha_1 - \alpha_2)D + \beta R_{mt} + u_t$$

$$D = 0 \text{ (bear)}$$
$$= 1 \text{ (bull)}$$

where D is called the 'Dummy Variable'. We will develop this subject further in Chapter 4.

Nonstationarity. Kon and Jen (1978) examined the issue of whether a mutual fund's systematic risk remained constant over time. In other words, their goal was to determine whether the slope coefficient β exhibited any nonstationarity. This is depicted in Figure 3.6.[10] Our purpose here is to point out the existence of such possibilities, known as 'switching' regimes. In another study, Blume (1975) pointed out that, although portfolio betas do exhibit nonstationarity, part of the nonstationarity can be attributed to nonstationarity in the security betas rather than to the portfolio selection design (order bias). Nonstationarity is very difficult to deal with unless a specific type of functional change can be specified a priori (e.g., trend, cyclical, etc.), and the interested reader would do well to review Kon and Jen's study carefully.

Other studies have considered the fact that beta coefficients themselves may be random over time, and therefore that betas should be estimated by what is called the "random coefficients model" (e.g., Fabozzi and Francis [1978], Lee and Chen [1980], and Sunder [1980]). Interestingly, these studies produce betas which are quite different for some stocks. Yet, there are numerous other ways to handle beta nonstationarity as discussed in Maddala's (1977) Chapter 17 on "Varying Parameter Models."

---

[10] In Figure 3.6, R_{mt} = excess market returns and R_{jt} = excess stock returns to draw a one-to-one correspondence with Kon and Jen's article. Excess returns are the resulting return after subtracting out the risk-free rate of return.

Nonlinearity. Is the assumption of linearity between variables valid? For example, can the return (R_j) be related to risk (β_j) in a nonlinear fashion. To test this, Professors Fama and MacBeth (1973) tested the following model of return-to-risk:

$$R_j = a + b\beta_j + d\beta_j^2 + u_j$$

where β_j was the beta coefficient from a regression of the jth portfolio's return regressed against the market return. And interestingly, they found nonlinearity for short periods of time. Sometimes linear segments can be fit to such relationships, and discussion of treating such nonlinearity can be found in Kmenta (1964).

Variables can always be transformed into a nonlinear form and then entered into the regression equation. Thus, as long as the regression coefficients are assumed constant (linear), nonlinearity in the variables is not a problem if there is a suitable transformation. In the above relationship, however, $\hat{\beta}$ and $\hat{\beta}^2$ will not be linearly independent, and Chapter 4 will discuss such a situation (i.e., nonindependence of explanatory variables.)

Simultaneity. Consider two hypothetical equations,

$$\text{Dividends} = a + b(\text{External borrowing}) + c(\text{profit}) + d(\text{liquidity})$$

$$\begin{matrix}\text{External}\\ \text{Borrowing}\end{matrix} = \alpha + \beta(\text{Dividends}) + \gamma(\text{profit}) + \delta(\text{depreciation})$$

It is conspicuous that Dividends and External borrowing are dependent on each other. Thus running a regression of the former model independent of the latter causes what is commonly known as 'Simultaneity Bias' in our estimation of the model. This is the subject of our discussion in Chapter 5.

Omitted Variables. In discussing the error term u_i, omitted variables were suggested as a causal factor in the error term. When variables have a continuous and statistically significant relationship to the dependent variable, however, they should be included in the equation to be estimated; that is, if such variables would prevent the error term from having the desired properties, these variables must be specified as part of the equation.[11]

---

[11]There are two interesting cases that arise when inferences are to be drawn about the intercept term; while these cases arise because of inadequate specification, rather than omission of variables in the strict sense, this seems to be the most appropriate place to discuss these cases. Although the Capital-Asset-Pricing-Model specifies an intercept term such as the riskless rate, less rigorous models often specify only a series of independent variables and a general linear relationship with an admissible intercept term;

ROLL'S 1969 STUDY OF TIME SERIES BIAS IN THE CAPM

To appreciate the incredible problems that can arise when assumptions are violated, let us review an early study by Professor Richard Roll. In contrast to some of the foregoing violations that were immediately understandable at an intuitive level, the impact of measurement error may be less obvious. In fact, to reduce the problem to an understandable framework, the reader will have to be introduced to the concept of a "probability limit." Because

---

11 continued

subsequent interpretation of the intercept requires explicit knowledge of its "dimension" (see: Chapter 4, footnote 6). Second, in cross-sectional studies, the use of per share data will cause both the intercept and slope coefficients to be dependent on each company's number of shares outstanding, unless the intercept is hypothesized to pass through the origin. This latter problem can be understood by way of the following example. Assume that a stock's price per share (P_i) is specified to be ten times its earnings per share (E_i) plus $2. Then, assume the following data:

	E_i	P_i
Stock #1	1	12
Stock #2	2	22
Stock #3	3	32

Although the above will produce a regression line of $P = 2 + 10E$, if Stock #1 had a 2-for-1 split, this would no longer be true because the hypothesized population intercept of $2 would implicitly be reduced to $1 for Stock #1 (this problem is raised in E. G. Davis, D. M. Dunn, and W. H. Williams, "Ambiguities in Cross-Section Analysis of Per Share Financial Data," Journal of Finance, Volume XXVIII (December 1973), pp. 1241-1248). In such a case, either per share measurements must not be used or the intercept must be specified in a manner such that it will not be dependent on each company's per share weights. One method might be to specify the intercept term as a function of another variable such as book value, and then to assume any additional intercept effect is nonexistent, thereby specifying that the regression passes through the origin. This is a difficult but important consideration, and certainly you should be careful to hypothesize and specify the intercept explicitly.

this is a concept which you will not have had previously if you have only had elementary statistics, we believe that you will find this one of the most exciting parts of this text.

To examine how measurement errors might arise in testing the capital-asset-pricing model (CAPM), Roll asked what would happen when real-world markets violated the theoretical assumptions in the following three ways:

(i) Riskless rate is not a constant.

(ii) Observed market return is different from the 'true' market.

(iii) Riskless rate is measured with error.

Since the CAPM equation hypothesizes that the <u>expected</u> return of any asset i, $E(R_i)$, will be equal to the riskless rate, R_f, plus a risk premium equal to the asset's beta, β_i, multiplied against the <u>expected</u> excess return of a mean-variance efficient market portfolio, $E(R_m-R_f)$, the hypothesized relationship is

$$E(R_i) = R_f + \beta_i[E(R_m)-R_f] \tag{3.3}$$

Because the CAPM is a static equilibrium model, it implicitly assumes one time period; further, it is based upon <u>expectations</u> with no allowance for actual deviations from the expected values. These conditions are important to the model's validity, and numerous investment managers have been extremely critical of its use as a basis for measuring their performance -- in fact, many such managers have raised exactly Roll's three questions.

To go about examining the impact of these questions, it is necessary to realize that estimators are of two types, depending on the impact of sample size(n):

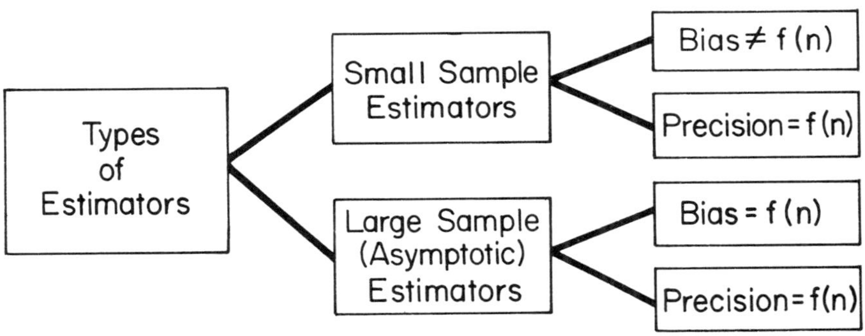

[14]The true model for equation (3.4b) is: $R_{it} = \beta R_{mt} + v_t$. That is, it is hypothesized that $\alpha = 0$ in equation (3.4b).

As indicated, if an estimator has finite or small-sample properties, then its unbiasedness does not require larger and larger samples; larger sample size, however, will decrease potential dispersion from the population parameter (Figure 3.7a). An example of this is illustrated in Appendix E for the sample mean. In contrast to the mean, the sample variance is a large-sample estimator; as such, both its unbiasedness and potential dispersion are affected by the sample size (Figure 3.7b). As shown in Figure 3.7b, the large-sample estimator is said to "approach" this true parameter "asymptotically"; since such an estimator's bias can only approach zero, however, its potential precision depends on how rapidly it converges on the asymptotic probability limit (denoted "plim"). Keeping the effects of sample size in mind, we now proceed to discuss Roll's article in detail.

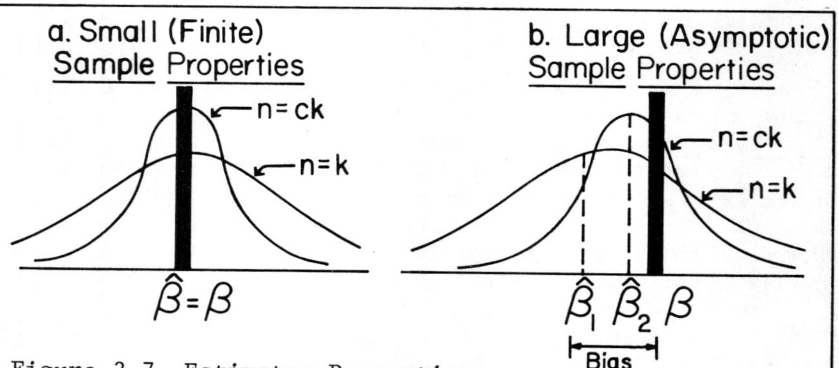

Figure 3.7 Estimator Properties

Case (i): The Effect of Erroneously Assuming a Constant Riskless Rate. One of the main assumptions of the CAPM is that dealers in capital markets can borrow and lend freely at a constant riskless rate, R_f. If, however, the R_f varies over time and if it is correlated with R_m over time, biased results will occur in the estimation of the regression coefficients of the market model.

Let us say, contrary to the assumptions of the CAPM, that the riskless rate is correlated with the market returns i.e., $Cov(R_{ft}, R_{mt}) \neq 0$. No bias occurs even if R_{ft} fluctuates over time, as long as $Cov(R_{ft}, R_{mt}) = 0$.[12]

Consider the market model[13]

[12]The implicit assumption is that $Cov\ (R_{ft}, u_t) = 0$.
[13]The original equation for equation (3.4a) is: $R_{jt} = \alpha + \beta R_{mt} + u_t$ and using the CAPM $\alpha = (1 - \beta)R_{ft}$. Hence (3.4a).

$$R_{jt} = (1 - \beta)R_{ft} + \beta R_{mt} + u_t \qquad (3.4a)$$

By setting $v_t = (1 - \beta)R_{ft} + u_t$, the fitted regression[14] is,

$$R_{jt} = \hat{\alpha} + \hat{\beta}\, R_{mt} + \hat{v}_t \qquad (3.4b)$$

Since v_t is a function of R_{ft} we can see that,

$$\mathrm{Cov}\,(\tilde{R}_{mt}, \tilde{R}_{ft}) \neq 0 \Rightarrow \mathrm{Cov}\,(R_{mt}, v_t) \neq 0$$

which violates the assumption that the explanatory variable is independent of the error term. Under such conditions, by looking at the asymptotic estimates of $\hat{\alpha}$ and $\hat{\beta}$ (Appendix M.10), the 'latent' bias quickly surfaces:

$$\operatorname{plim} \hat{\beta} = \underbrace{\beta}_{\text{true value}} + \underbrace{(1-\beta)\,\frac{\mathrm{Cov}\,(\tilde{R}_{mt}, \tilde{R}_{ft})}{V(\tilde{R}_{mt})}}_{\text{latent bias}} \qquad (3\text{-}5a)$$

$$\operatorname{plim} \hat{\alpha} = \underbrace{(1-\beta)\, E\,(\tilde{R}_f)}_{\text{true value}} - \underbrace{(1-\beta)\, E\,(\tilde{R}_m)\,\frac{\mathrm{Cov}\,(\tilde{R}_{mt}, \tilde{R}_{ft})}{V(\tilde{R}_{mt})}}_{\text{latent bias}} \qquad (3\text{-}5b)$$

where $V(\cdot)$ represents variance. Thus, in constrast to Chapter 2 where we saw that $E(\hat{\beta}) = \beta$ and $E(\hat{\alpha}) = \alpha = (1-\beta)R_f$ if R_f were constant, a stochastic R_{ft}, when correlated with R_{mt}, leads to biases in the estimation of α and β.

Some of the main implications of equations (3-5a) and (3-5b) can be summarized as follows:

1. $\hat{\alpha}$ and $\hat{\beta}$ will be biased in opposite directions.
2. direction of bias in $\hat{\beta}$:

$\mathrm{Cov}(\tilde{R}_{mt}, \tilde{R}_{ft})$	β >1	β <1
>0	↓	↑
<0	↑	↓

where '↓' indicates downward bias and '↑' indicates upward bias.

---

[14]The true model for equation (3.4b) is: $R_{jt} = \beta R_{mt} + v_t$. That is, it is hypothesized that $\alpha = 0$ in equation (3.4b).

3. Since an estimate of R_f is derived from $\tilde{\alpha}$ and $\hat{\beta}$ as

$$\hat{R}_f = \frac{\hat{\alpha}}{1-\hat{\beta}}$$

it can be shown (Appendix M.11) for a risk-averse market (Levy and Sarnat, 1972), that

$$\text{plim } \tilde{R}_f \begin{cases} < E(\tilde{R}_f) & \text{if } Cov(\tilde{R}_{mt}, \tilde{R}_{ft}) > 0 \\ > E(\tilde{R}_f) & \text{if } Cov(\tilde{R}_{mt}, \tilde{R}_{ft}) < 0 \end{cases}$$

Thus, the effect of assuming a constant R_f when it is not truly so, and when it is correlated with the market return, is to cause bias in the estimators of $\hat{\alpha}$, $\hat{\beta}$ and $\hat{R}_f$.

Case (ii): <u>The Effect of Measuring the Market Return With Error and Erroneously Assuming a Constant Riskless Rate</u>. Financial analysts commonly assume that the returns on any of the S&P, Dow Jones, Amex, etc., adequately represent the market returns. But, none of the indices can accurately represent the market portfolio of <u>all</u> assets (for an analysis of the implications of this, see Roll 1977, 1978). Thus, there is an inherent error in the measurement of R_{mt}.

To examine the impact of potential bias from this measurement error, Roll again turned to well-proven plim statements (Goldberger, 1964). To do this, he labelled r_{mt} as the observed market return and related this observed return to the true return (R_{mt}) via a model resembling equation (3.4a) i.e.,

$$r_{mt} = R_{ft}\ (1-\beta_m) + \beta_m R_{mt} + \varepsilon_{mt} \qquad (3\text{-}6)$$

The ideal situation is where $\beta_{mt} = 1$ because there would be no measurement error in r_{mt}. As shown in Appendix M.12, the market model then becomes:

$$R_{jt} = \alpha + \beta r_{mt} + \mu_j \qquad (3\text{-}7)$$

If we go through the procedure outlined in M.10, but applied this time to equation (3-7), we arrive at the following equations:[15]

$$\text{plim } \hat{\alpha} = (1 - \frac{\beta}{\beta_m})\quad [E(\tilde{R}_{ft}) - E(\tilde{r}_{mt})\ \frac{Cov(\tilde{r}_{mt}, \tilde{R}_{ft})}{V(\tilde{r}_{mt})}] +$$

[15]These equations could be skipped without loss of continuity and information.

$$\frac{\beta}{\beta_m}\,[E(\tilde{r}_{mt})(1-\rho_m^2)]$$

and

$$\text{plim}\ \hat{\beta} = \frac{\beta}{\beta_m} + \left(1 - \frac{\beta}{\beta_m}\right)\frac{\text{Cov}(\tilde{r}_{mt}, \tilde{R}_{ft})}{V(\tilde{r}_{mt})} - \frac{\beta}{\beta_m}(1-\rho_m^2)$$

where

$$\rho_m^2 = 1 - \frac{V(\tilde{\varepsilon}_{mt})}{V(\tilde{r}_{mt})}$$

So, what is the moral of our latest story? Measurement of market returns with error causes an additional bias (called 'attenuation bias') in the estimates of the regression coefficient, besides the bias attributable to correlation with a "non-constant" R_{ft}, and this additional bias is a function of the last term on each of the above equations.[16]

Case (iii): Errors in the Measurement of Both Riskless and Market Returns. Similar to the errors committed in the measurement of market returns, the riskless rate might be measured with error. By the same token, as in case (ii), we can show that R_{jt} would be a function of both r_{mt} and r_{ft}, i.e.,

$$R_{jt} = \gamma_0 + \gamma_1 r_{ft} + \gamma_2 r_{mt} + \mu_t \qquad (3.8)$$

with concomitant biases. Because such a model contains two explanatory variables which takes us into the realm of multivariate regressions (Chapter 4), we will not present the plim statements here. Even without going into Chapter 4, however, an intuitive grasp of Roll's results is possible and important; in particular, his results indicated inadquacies in estimates of the market model, and this warrants at least the following paragraph is deserved.

[16]Similar analyses of measurement errors are also found in the classic articles by Miller and Scholes and Black, Jensen and Scholes, as well as a recent article by Lee and Jen (1978).

Table 3.1 contains the estimates of γ_0, γ_1, and γ_2 obtained by Roll for the model represented by our equation 3.8, using logarithms of the price relatives on Treasury Bills and the Dow Jones Stock Index for the 793 weekly periods beginning October 4, 1949, for horizons going from 1 to 11 weeks. Two results are clear. First, most of the explanatory power is due to the relationship of the securities return to the riskfree rate (this statement is based upon visually comparing the estimates of the coefficients to their standard errors, although Roll has warned us that the standard errors are biased because slight positive autocorrelation and fat tails were evident in the residuals. Second, and most importantly, the coefficients show considerable variation over the subperiods, and thus do not appear reliable.

Roll went further and ingeniously derived two measures of the correlation of the measured variables to their unobserved counterparts, based upon plim properties [Roll 1969, p. 278]. He then used the results of regressions to examine these correlations, as well as their indicated stability under several alternative assumptions. Based upon this analysis he concluded that the data suggest that "...(a) the model's parameters are not temporarily constant, and (b) some non-portfolio motives for holding Treasury bills are not accounted for by the model (p. 287)." The latter result seems plausible, given the Federal Reserve Board's objective of monetary policy versus wealth maximization. Also, Roll noted that, under reasonable assumptions about his data, the Dow-Jones Composite bears little relation to the market portfolio. Clearly, this work is a magnum opus of econometric technique, as well as an indicator of the data sensitivity of the estimators over different periods; as such, the original article should be read by those desiring a thorough grasp of econometric procedures.

Since one is handicapped without knowledge of multiple regression analysis, we now move to Chapter 4 for this topic.

Table 3.1

ROLL'S TEST OF THE SHARPE MODEL ON TREASURY BILLS

Maturity, j (Weeks)	Total Sample (792 weeks)			SUB-PERIODS (198 WEEKS EACH) 1 Weeks 1-198			2 Weeks 199-396			3 Weeks 397-594			4 Weeks 595-792		
	$\hat{\gamma}_0$	$\hat{\gamma}_1$	$\hat{\gamma}_2$	$\hat{\gamma}_0$	$\hat{\gamma}_1$	$\hat{\gamma}_2$	$\hat{\gamma}_0$	$\hat{\gamma}_1$	$\hat{\gamma}_2$	$\hat{\gamma}_0$	$\hat{\gamma}_1$	$\hat{\gamma}_2$	$\hat{\gamma}_0$	$\hat{\gamma}_1$	$\hat{\gamma}_2$
1	.0353	.9943	$-.0^{4}400$	-.104	1.108	$.0^{4}2009$	-.0201	1.020	$.0^{3}347$	-.0136	1.017	$-.0^{3}1022$	.193	.9336	$-.0^{3}257$
	.9948	$.0^{2}831$	$.0^{4}885$	.8074	.0372	$.0^{3}143$	.9339	.0173	$.0^{3}167$	.9096	.0214	$.0^{3}209$	.8876	.0221	$.0^{3}171$
3	.0827	1.046	$-.0^{4}480$	-.245	1.265	$-.0^{3}160$	.0271	1.067	$.0^{3}682$	.0175	1.116	$.0^{4}889$	.622	.8299	$-.0^{3}435$
	.7876	.0193	$.0^{3}205$	.5097	.0879	$.0^{3}338$	.7693	.0408	$.0^{3}393$	.6908	.0531	$.0^{3}518$	.6797	.0398	$.0^{3}378$
5	.130	1.102	$.0^{4}688$	-.218	1.302	$.0^{4}378$	.0649	1.110	$.0^{3}865$	.0515	1.243	$.0^{3}348$	1.09	.7036	$-.0^{3}308$
	.6506	.0288	$.0^{3}306$	.3714	.120	$.0^{3}461$	.6401	.0587	$.0^{3}566$	.5386	.0823	$.0^{3}802$	.4874	.0509	$.0^{3}393$
7	.130	1.139	$-.0^{4}159$	-.302	1.376	$.0^{4}209$	.0240	1.177	$.0^{2}117$	.109	1.285	$.0^{4}178$	1.19	.6880	$-.0^{4}411$
	.5470	.0370	$.0^{3}394$	.3060	.147	$.0^{3}565$	.5526	.0749	$.0^{3}722$	.4090	.111	$.0^{2}109$	.4416	.0547	$.0^{3}478$
9	.0744	1.191	$-.0^{3}120$	-.422	1.452	$.0^{3}419$	$.0^{4}945$	1.191	$.0^{2}132$	.127	1.358	$-.0^{3}580$	1.12	.7208	$-.0^{3}552$
	.4679	.0454	$.0^{3}483$	.2766	.166	$.0^{3}640$	.4667	.0901	$.0^{3}869$	.3324	.140	$.0^{2}137$	.4050	.0618	$.0^{3}478$
11	.0910	1.174	$-.0^{3}345$	-.473	1.495	$.0^{3}423$	.0115	1.193	$.0^{2}174$	.0703	1.356	$-.0^{2}142$	1.03	.7407	$-.0^{3}852$
	.3899	.0526	$.0^{3}560$	.2248	.197	$.0^{3}757$	.3932	.105	$.0^{2}101$	.2671	.167	$.0^{2}163$	.3965	.0649	$.0^{3}501$

*Coefficients are given in the first row of each panel. Standard errors are given below $\hat{\gamma}_1$ and $\hat{\gamma}_2$. Multiple R^2 adjusted for degrees of freedom is given below $\hat{\gamma}_0$. Week number 1 starts October 4, 1949.

Source: Richard Roll, "Bias in Fitting the Sharpe Model to Time Series Data," Journal of Financial and Quantitative Analysis, Volume IV, September 1969, Table 1.

UNIVERSITY OF BRISTOL

4

multivariate regression models

Almost all finance questions are complex enough to require several independent variables. For example, while Chapter 2 showed that a market model for IBM (i.e., $R_{jt} = .007 + 1.06 R_{mt} + e_t$) had $R^2 = 0.47$, other variables might be expected to explain the remaining 53% of IBM's variation in return. In Chapter 1, Farrell's work showed that cyclical-stable-growth-and-oil variables affected a stock's return, and this may be part of the remaining 53%. Similarly, in the preceding chapter, Roll's study indicated that both the riskless rate and the market return were related to stock returns. In addition to Roll, others have noted the possibility of an interest rate variable, and in 1977, William Lloyd and Richard Shick tested a model proposed by Bernell Stone; viz., that stock returns over time (R_t) were a function of returns on both an equity index (R_{Et}) and a bond index (R_{Bt}):

$$R_t = B_0 + B_1 R_{Et} + B_2 R_{Bt} + e_t$$

Before we can discuss their results, however, the basics of multiple regression must be presented.*

---

*Multivariate generating processes are an important, but poorly understood, area of research. The finding that ex post multivariate relationships exist between asset returns and variables other than the market portfolio's return is not inconsistent with the ex ante capital-asset-pricing model's assumptions. In particular the CAPM's assumption of a covariance matrix with non-zero off-diagonal terms explicitly indicates the ex ante expectation of such relationships. For further discussion and clarification of the relationships, readers should refer to the "multi-beta" references on Sharpe (1978), Rosenberg (1974), as well as Section II of the paper by Fogler, John, and Tipton (1981). Also, the confusion even in simple tests is shown by the recent critiques of Lloyd and Shick's work which is used here because of its expository simplicity (see: two comments entitled "Comment: A Test of Stone's Two-Index Model of Returns," by N. Bulent Gultekin and Richard J. Rogalski and also the other by Don M. Chance, Journal of Financial and Quantitative Analysis, Volume XIV (September 1979), pp. 629-639, pp. 641- 644.)

As can be seen from our diagram below, virtually all of the material in this chapter has been discussed before in Chapter 2, with minor topics from Chapter 3.

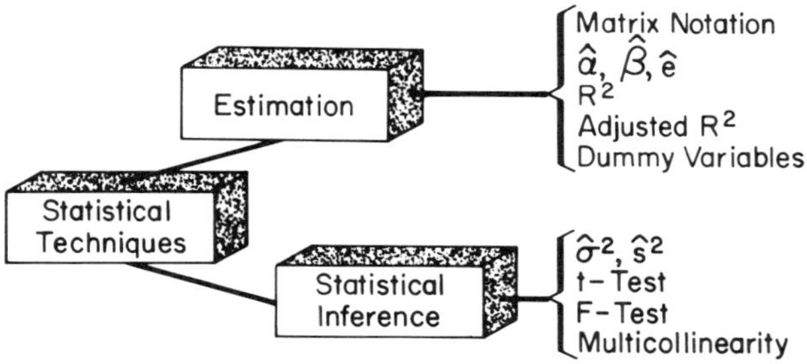

The two main differences in this chapter are: (1) there are several independent explanatory variables and (2) matrix algebra notation is used to condense the presentation (the basics of matrix algebra are reviewed in Appendix L). Most readers will find the material rather straightforward, once the notation is accepted, especially if it is remembered that the results are merely n-dimensional extensions of the mathematics already covered in Chapter 2.

1. MULTIVARIATE FORMAT

Dealing with models involving two or more explanatory variables requires an understanding of multiple regression analysis. Let us suppose initially that there are m variables (X_1, X_2, $...X_m$) that we think are capable of explaining the movements in the independent variable, i.e., $Y = f(X_1, X_2, ...X_m)$. Let us also say that we have n observations for each one of the variables. If we assume a linear relation between Y and the explanatory variables, we have[1]

$$Y_t = \beta_1 X_{1t} + \beta_2 X_{2t} + ...\beta_m X_{mt} + u_t \qquad t = 1, 2, ...n \qquad (4.1)$$

$$= \Sigma\beta_k X_{kt} + u_t \qquad k = 1, 2, ...m$$

which, in the matrix form, can be written as,

$$y = XB + u \qquad (4.2)$$

where lowercase letters represent vectors and capital letters represent matrices. The expanded version of eqn. (4.1) and the definitions of y, X, b and u in eqn. (4.2) are shown in Table 4.1.

Before we discuss how to estimate the regression coefficients, two assumptions about the multivariate models are needed in addition to the ones outlined in Chapter 2.

Table 4.1
TWO EQUIVALENT "FORMATS"

Original Format	Matrix Format
True Model $Y_1 = \beta_1 X_{11} + \beta_2 X_{21} + \ldots. \beta_m X_{m1} + u_1$ $Y_2 = \beta_1 X_{12} + \beta_2 X_{22} + \ldots. \beta_m X_{m2} + u_2$ $\vdots$ $Y_t = \beta_1 X_{1t} + \beta_2 X_{2t} + \ldots. \beta_m X_{mt} + u_t$ $\vdots$ $Y_n = \beta_1 X_{1n} + \beta_2 X_{2n} + \ldots. \beta_m X_{mn} + u_n$	**True Model** $Y = X\beta + U$ where $y = \begin{bmatrix} Y_1 \\ Y_2 \\ \vdots \\ Y_t \\ \vdots \\ Y_n \end{bmatrix} \quad X = \begin{bmatrix} X_{11} & X_{21} \ldots X_{m1} \\ X_{12} & X_{22} \ldots X_{m2} \\ & \vdots \\ X_{1t} & X_{2t} \ldots X_{mt} \\ & \vdots \\ X_{1n} & X_{2n} \ldots X_{mn} \end{bmatrix} \quad u = \begin{bmatrix} u_1 \\ u_2 \\ \vdots \\ u_t \\ \vdots \\ u_n \end{bmatrix}$
Regression Model $Y_1 = \hat{\beta}_1 X_{11} + \hat{\beta}_2 X_{21} + \ldots. \hat{\beta}_m X_{m1} + e_1$ $Y_2 = \hat{\beta}_1 X_{12} + \hat{\beta}_2 X_{22} + \ldots. \hat{\beta}_m X_{m2} + e_2$ $\vdots$ $Y_t = \hat{\beta}_1 X_{1t} + \hat{\beta}_2 X_{2t} + \ldots. \hat{\beta}_m X_{mt} + e_t$ $\vdots$ $Y_n = \hat{\beta}_1 X_{1n} + \hat{\beta}_2 X_{2n} + \ldots. \hat{\beta}_m X_{mn} + e_n$	**Regression Model** $y = X\hat{\beta} + e$ where $\hat{\beta} = (\hat{\beta}_1 \ \ \hat{\beta}_2 \ \ldots. \hat{\beta}_m) \qquad e = \begin{bmatrix} e_1 \\ e_2 \\ e_t \\ e_n \end{bmatrix}$

The first assumption is that the explanatory variables are independent of each other; this independence is necessary for accurately estimating the size of standard errors, although the estimated beta coefficients will still be unbiased. The second assumption is that the number of observations, n, will be greater than the number of explanatory variables m (i.e., that the rank of X = m), which reflects the need for m independent equations to estimate the m unknown coefficients.

Estimating the coefficients is straightforward. The estimated regression model for eqn. (4.2) is [see Table (4.1)].

$$y = X\hat{\beta} + e \tag{4.3}$$

The $\hat{\beta}$ coefficients are obtained by using the familar least-squares procedure (Appendix M-13). The sum of squared errors (SSE) can be written using the matrix notation as $SSE = \Sigma e_t^2 = e'e$, where the prime (') indicates the transpose. Minimizing SSE with respect to β we get

$$\hat{\beta} = (X'X)^{-1}X'y, \tag{4.4}$$

The <u>variance-covariance matrix</u> of $\hat{\beta}$ can be shown (Appendix M-14) to be

$$V(\hat{\beta}) = \sigma_u^2\,(X'X)^{-1} \tag{4.5}$$

For a model with three explanatory variables, the variance-covariance matrix is as represented below:

$$\begin{bmatrix} V(\hat{\beta}_1) & cov(\hat{\beta}_1,\hat{\beta}_2) & cov(\hat{\beta}_1,\hat{\beta}_3) \\ cov(\hat{\beta}_1,\hat{\beta}_2) & V(\hat{\beta}_2) & cov(\hat{\beta}_2,\hat{\beta}_3) \\ cov(\hat{\beta}_1,\hat{\beta}_3) & cov(\hat{\beta}_2,\hat{\beta}_3) & V(\hat{\beta}_3) \end{bmatrix}$$

This symmetric matrix contains all combinations of the variance and covariance relationships within the three variables. The square roots of the diagonal elements of the variance-covariance matrix are the standard errors of the corresponding regression coefficients. Relating this to Chapter 2 may help to enforce your level of understanding; remember that β_1 here is equivalanet to α there, and thus the corresponding matrix there was

---

[1]Letting $X_{1t} = 1$ for all t observations is equivalent to causing β_1 to be the intercept for the linear relationship in equation (4.1)

$$\text{Var }(\hat{\beta}) = \begin{bmatrix} V(\alpha) & \text{cov}(\hat{\alpha},\hat{\beta}) \\ \text{cov}(\hat{\alpha},\hat{\beta}) & V(\hat{\beta}) \end{bmatrix}$$

$$= \begin{bmatrix} \sigma_u^2 \Sigma R^2_{mt} / n\Sigma(R_{mt}-\bar{R}_m)^2 & -\bar{R}_m \sigma_u^2 / \Sigma(R_{mt}-\bar{R}_m)^2 \\ -R_m \sigma_u^2 / \Sigma(R_{mt}-\bar{R}_m)^2 & \sigma_u^2 / \Sigma(R_{mt}-\bar{R}_m)^2 \end{bmatrix}$$

$$= \sigma_u^2 \begin{bmatrix} \Sigma R^2_{mt} / n\Sigma(R_{mt}-\bar{R}_m)^2 & -\bar{R}_m / (R_{mt}-\bar{R}_m)^2 \\ -\bar{R}_m / \Sigma(R_{mt}-\bar{R}_m)^2 & 1 / \Sigma(R_{mt}-\bar{R}_m)^2 \end{bmatrix}$$

As in Chapter 2, derivation of the variance-covariance matrix is not possible without estimation of σ_u^2, the variance of the error term. It can be proved that the sample variance is given by

$$s^2 = \frac{e'e}{n-m} \tag{4.6}$$

(where n is the number of observations and m is the number of explanatory variables), and this estimate is an unbiased estimator of σ_u^2. When k = 2, $\hat{s}^2 = e'e/n-2$, which is a result familiar to us from Chapter 2.

2. EXPLAINED VARIATION AND R^2

Another result that is similar to Chapter 2 is that R^2 is a ratio of the explained variation to the total variation in the dependent variable Y. That is,

$$R^2 = \frac{\text{Explained Variation}}{\text{Total Variation}}$$

$$= \frac{\hat{\beta}'X'y - \frac{1}{n}(\Sigma Y_t)^2}{y'y - \frac{1}{n}(\Sigma Y_t)^2}$$

While the above expression may look imposing at first,[2] its components are easily understood when it is

---

[2]Since y is order (nx1), y'y is a matrix of order (1x1); i.e., y'y is a scalar quantity equal to ΣY_t^2.

remembered that the total variation in the dependent variable, Y, can be divided into two parts: (1) that explained by the regression estimate; (2) the unexplained portion. This description is equivalent to

$$\text{Total Variation} = \text{Explained Variation} + \text{Unexplained Variation}$$

$$\Sigma(Y_t-\bar{Y})^2 = \Sigma(\hat{Y}_t-\bar{Y})^2 + \Sigma e_t^2$$

Further, the total variation can be broken into smaller parts for calculation purposes; e.g.,

$$\begin{aligned}\Sigma(Y_t-\bar{Y})^2 &= \Sigma Y_t^2 - 2\bar{Y}\Sigma Y_t + \Sigma\bar{Y}^2 \\ &= \Sigma Y_t^2 - 2/n(\Sigma Y_t)^2 + 1/n\ (\Sigma Y_t)^2 \\ &= \Sigma Y_t^2 - 1/n(\Sigma Y_t)^2 \\ &= y'y - 1/n(\Sigma Y_t)^2\end{aligned}$$

Deriving the explained variation (i.e., the numerator in the R^2 ratio) is straightforward but longer, and therefore it has been placed in Appendix M-15.

As in simple regression, R^2 provides a measure of the goodness of fit. This statistic should be adjusted for the degrees of freedom, as can be seen by reviewing the R^2 equation that was used in Chapter 2.

$$R^2 = \frac{SSR}{SST} = 1 - \frac{SSE}{SST} = 1 - \frac{\Sigma(Y_t-\hat{Y}_t)^2}{\Sigma(Y_t-\bar{Y})^2} = 1 - \frac{\Sigma e_t{}^2}{\Sigma(Y_t-Y)^2}$$

The adjustment is needed because, with the addition of more explanatory variables, the sum of the squared errors (Σe_t^2) decrease while $\Sigma(Y_t-Y)^2$ will be constant -- thus, the R^2 values will be boosted, regardless of whether the additional variables are significant or not.[3] This boosting of

[3]This type of artificial "boosting" is best illustrated by the extreme case -- <u>if the number of variables is increased to the point where the variables equal the observations, R^2 must equal 1</u>. This is shown by elementary mathematics in Appendix M-17, and results from the fact that each additional variable allows you to "bend" the explanatory plane in a new dimension to better fit the observations. Such a procedure merely "force fits" the estimates to the <u>sample</u> data, and thus the estimates become very <u>sample-sensitive</u>, versus population parameter oriented.

R^2 is because the above equation does not take into account the degrees of freedom associated with Σe_t^2.[4] If we were to adjust for the degrees of freedom (which nullifies the boosting effect referred to above), we would obtain what is widely known as the 'Corrected Multiple Coefficient of Determination' or 'corrected R^2', i.e.,

$$R^2 = 1 - \frac{(\Sigma e_t^2)/n-m}{\Sigma(Y_t-\overline{Y})^2/n-1} \qquad \text{i.e.,} = 1 - \frac{n-1}{n-m}(1-R^2)$$

If $(1-R^2)$ decreases slower than $(n-m)$ due to the addition of more variables, R^2 will actually decline, indicating that the extra variables do not provide any further information.

3. SIGNIFICANCE TESTS[5]

The t-tests that we developed in Chapter 2 for the regression coefficients, and the F-test to examine the validity of the model as a whole, are still valid for the multiple regression model. An adjustment, however, is necessary to account for the degrees of freedom associated with the multiple regression estimates. This adjustment for degrees of freedom will become clear from the following discussion.

t-test for the Significance of Regression Coefficients. To test whether a regression coefficient is different from zero is to establish the hypothesis that

$$H_0: \hat{\beta}_j \neq 0$$

The appropriate t statistic is

$$t = \frac{\hat{\beta}_j - 0}{V(\hat{\beta}_j)} = \frac{\hat{\beta}_j}{V(\hat{\beta}_j)}$$

---

[4]Σe_t^2 has $(n-m)$ degrees of freedom since the sum is obtained from n values of Y and m estimates of β. Similarly, degrees of freedom for $\Sigma(Y_t-\overline{Y})$ are $(n-1)$.

[5]The tests discussed here parallel those in Chapter 2. An additional test, which may be of interest, is whether the coefficients from two different regressions are significantly different. Such a test is discussed in many econometric texts, and is based upon an article by Gregory C. Chow, "Tests of the Equality Between Sets of Coefficients in Two Linear Regressions," Econometrics, Volume 28, 1960, pp. 591-605.

To obtain $V(\hat{\beta}_j)$ we have to look for the relevant diagonal element in the variance-covariance matrix for β. The degrees of freedom are equal to the number of observations minus the number of explanatory variables (including the intercept as one of the variables). The decision rests on the level of significance the investigator is willing to assume.

F tests. Instead of testing each one of the coefficients independently, an F test can be used to test the overall linear relation. To do this, we would use the test statistic (Johnston, 1972)

$$F_{m-1,\ n-m} = \frac{R^2/m-1}{(1-R^2)/(n-m)} = \frac{\hat{\beta}X'y/m-1}{e'e/(n-m)}$$

where n is the number of observations and m is the number of explanatory variables (including the intercept term, if any). Naively stated, the F ratio in this case enables us to compare the explained variations with the unexplained. To prove that an overall relation exists is equivalent to proving that the explained variation is considerably greater than the unexplained portion.

The F test is very general, in that many problems can be reduced to the question of whether the explained variation is considerably greater than the unexplained. For example, consider the question of comparing the following two linear models:

Model I: $$Y_t = \beta_1 X_1 + \beta_2 X_2 + \beta_3 X_3 + \ldots + \beta_m X_m;$$

$$(SSE)_I = \Sigma e^2_{t,I}$$

Model II: $$Y_t = \alpha_1 X_1 + \alpha_2 X_2 + \alpha_3 X_3 + \ldots + \alpha_m X_m + \alpha_{m+1} X_{m+1} + \ldots + \alpha_{m+q} X_{m+q};$$

$$(SSE)_{II} = \Sigma e^2_{t,II}$$

Model II has q more explanatory variables than Model I. To test whether the additional variables, X_{m+1} through X_{m+q}, in model II add any significant explanatory power over variables X_1 through X_m, we can use the following F statistic (see Appendix M-24)

$$\frac{[(SSE)_I - (SSE)_{II}]/q}{(SSE)_{II}/(n-m-q)} \sim F_{q,(n-m-q)}$$

The bracketed term $[(SSE)_I - (SSE)_{II}]$ represents the reduction in Model I's unexplained variation (or conversely, improvement in explained variation). Thus, this test captures any significant reductions in unsystematic variations due to the extra variales (or conversely, any significant additions to the systematic variations).

4. MULTIPLE REGRESSION: SUMMARIZED AND APPLIED

Table 4.2 summarizes the foregoing results.[6] These results will now be applied to study a two-variable model of stock price returns for IBM's stock.

As indicated, previously, Lloyd and Shick (1977) were testing whether bond returns might be a significant variable in explaining stock returns; thus, their equation was

$$R_{jt} = \hat{\beta}_0 + \hat{\beta} R_{Et} + \hat{\beta}_2 R_{Dt} + e_t \qquad t = 1, 2, \ldots, n$$

where j is the subscript for a particular security, R_{Et} is the return from the equity market index (CRSP) and R_{Dt} is the return from a debt market index (Salomon Brothers Long Bond Index), and each return is for period t.

[6]Although we do not discuss it above, readers should be careful about their interpretation of the intercept term in a multiple regression. The scale of the estimated intercept will be a function of one or more of the dependent variables. That is, the intercept will not be a "dimensionless" number unless it is hypothesized to be zero (that is, the plane is hypothesized to pass through the origin). Further, to avoid comparing "apples versus oranges" it is necessary for the dimension (dollars, quantity, per share, and so on) to be the same for both the intercept and the dependent variable. For studies whose hypotheses rely on interpretation and inference about the intercept, see Craig G. Johnson, "Dimensional Analysis and the Interpretation of Regression Coefficients," Journal of Financial and Quantitative Analysis, Volume VII (January 1972), pp. 1399-1406, as well as introductory textbook in Physics such as David Halliday and Robert Resnick, Fundamentals of Physics, (John Wiley and Sons: New York, 1974), pp. 35-36. Slope coefficients also have dimensions implicitly, although their dimension will be more obvious as it is based on the relative sensitivity of the dependent variable to the independent variable.

Table 4.2
MULTIPLE REGRESSION IN A 'NUTSHELL'

Regression Equation

$$Y_t = \hat{\beta}_1 X_{1t} + \hat{\beta}_2 X_{2t} + \ldots . \hat{\beta}_m X_{mt} + e_t$$

m = # of variables

t = 1, 2,...n

Estimated Coefficients

$$\hat{\beta} = (X'X)^{-1}X'y = (\hat{\beta}_1 \; \hat{\beta}_2 \; \ldots\ldots\ldots \hat{\beta}_m)$$

Variance of Coefficient Estimates

$$V(\hat{\beta}) = \sigma^2{}_u (X'X)^{-1} = \hat{s}^2 (X'X)^{-1}$$

Unbiased Estimator of σ^2

$$\hat{s}^2 = \frac{\Sigma e_t^2}{n-m} = \frac{e'e}{n-m}$$

Standard Error of Coefficient Estimates

$$SE(\hat{\beta}_i) = \sqrt{V(\hat{\beta}_i)}$$

R^2 and Adjusted R^2

$$R^2 = \frac{\hat{\beta}'X'y - \frac{1}{n}(\Sigma Y_t)^2}{y'y - \frac{1}{n}(\Sigma Y_t)^2}$$

$$\text{corrected } R^2 = 1 - \frac{n-1}{n-m}(1-R^2)$$

t-Test Coefficients -- H_0: $\hat{\beta}_i \neq 0$

$$\frac{\hat{\beta}_i}{SE(\hat{\beta}_i)} \sim t_{n-m}$$

F-Test for Explanatory Significance of Linear Model

$$\frac{R^2/m-1}{(1-R^2)/n-m} \sim F_{m-1,n-m}$$

Table 4.3 includes (1): the data; (2) the results for both single and multiple index models; and (3) the major computations. Several points are worth mentioning. First, the addition of the bond index reduced the t-statistic for the coefficient of the market return rather sharply, from 5.82 to 3.35, suggesting that interest rate effects may be an important variable (which would be expected). The significance of the coefficient on the bond index was rather low, however, and also the adjusted R^2 was only .60 versus .59 for the single equation model. Thus, this low additional explanatory power suggests that the overall market return contains most of the interest rate effect.[7]

Finally, the above results suggest that there is multicollinearity between the stock index and the bond index. This means, equivalently stated, that the correlation coefficient between the two indexes is not zero -- i.e., there is some relationship. The joint fact that the significance of the stock index coefficient dropped so much, while the bond index did not add much explanatory power, suggests that the stock index's returns "moved" with ("were correlated with") the returns of the bond index. Fortunately, as discussed in Chapter 2 under multicollinearity, the coefficients are still unbiased estimators, although their standard errors are not accurately estimated. The tests of significance, therefore, are no longer valid because independence is assumed between the explanatory variables when calculating standard errors for the coefficients. Because multicollinearity is a common problem in multiple regressions, the next section is devoted to discussing its effect.

5. MULTICOLLINEARITY

As indicated above, multicollinearity arises due to the negation of the assumption that the m explanatory variables are independent of each other (or stated equivalently, rank $X < m$). There are two ways that this can

---

[7]The exact role of interest rate variables is still in the conjectural stage for two reasons: (1) no theory is available that adequately ties stock returns to interest rates, and (2) the empirical studies have produced mixed results. For example, Lloyd and Schick found the bond index had only a small incremental effect in explaining the returns of bank stocks (although it was more significant than the equity index), while it was more successful as an explanatory variable for some of the Dow-Jones stocks. Friend, Westerfield, and Granito (1978) also found that an independent bond factor influenced returns, although its influence varied considerably by sample period.

Table 4.3
MULTIPLE REGRESSION

a. Data

IBM/100 R_j	MKTRET R_E	SOLY R_D
-0.023220	-2.40	5.02
-0.094787	-19.83	-4.08
0.054493	17.80	8.09
0.030261	9.76	8.72
0.041409	11.20	4.07
-0.038014	0.09	-2.90
-0.012728	-0.66	4.21
0.036185	4.62	5.42
0.044680	6.50	0.98
0.009569	0.06	1.29
0.013293	2.85	11.34
-0.002559	7.12	3.48
0.024991	-6.93	0.15
-0.026856	-7.24	-0.35
-0.065187	7.48	2.14
-0.013366	-10.60	-0.78
-0.013323	-2.20	-3.50
-0.031703	-9.67	-5.16
-0.090151	-24.45	-3.07
0.021387	9.48	9.29
0.073895	23.75	4.76
0.006145	16.08	3.59
-0.031239	-11.55	-3.28
0.062789	8.18	9.22

b. Single and Multiple Index Returns

INDEPENDENT VARIABLE	ESTIMATED COEFFICIENT	STANDARD ERROR	T-STATISTIC
C	-0.466785	0.590830	-0.790049
MKTRET	0.300932	0.517362E-01	5.81666

R-SQUARED = 0.6060

F-STATISTIC(1, 22) = 33.8335

DURBIN-WATSON STATISTIC (ADJ. FOR 0 GAPS) = 2.1250

NUMBER OF OBSERVATIONS = 24

SUM OF SQUARED RESIDUALS = 182.216

STANDARD ERROR OF THE REGRESSION = 2.87794

ESTIMATE OF VARIANCE-COVARIANCE MATRIX OF ESTIMATED COEFFICIENTS

```
 0.349E 00 -0.326E-02
-0.326E-02  0.268E-02
```

CORRECTED R-SQ=0.5881

INDEPENDENT VARIABLE	ESTIMATED COEFFICIENT	STANDARD ERROR	T-STATISTIC
C	-0.935264	0.683757	-1.36783
MKTRET	0.300932	0.509336E-01	5.90832
SOLNEW	0.223653	0.171593	1.30339

R-SQUARED = 0.6355

F-STATISTIC(2, 21) = 18.3035

DURBIN-WATSON STATISTIC (ADJ. FOR 0 GAPS) = 2.1054

NUMBER OF OBSERVATIONS = 24

SUM OF SQUARED RESIDUALS = 168.579

STANDARD ERROR OF THE REGRESSION = 2.83330

ESTIMATE OF VARIANCE-COVARIANCE MATRIX OF ESTIMATED COEFFICIENTS

```
 0.468E 00 -0.316E-02 -0.617E-01
-0.316E-02  0.259E-02  0.209E-07
-0.617E-01  0.209E-07  0.294E-01
```

CORRECTED R-SQ=0.6007

c. Some Basic Calculations

$$(X'X) = \begin{bmatrix} 24.00 & 29.24 & 58.65 \\ 29.24 & 3130.02 & 958.06 \\ 58.65 & 958.05 & 669.99 \end{bmatrix} \quad \begin{bmatrix} \hat{\beta}_1 \\ \hat{\beta}_2 \\ \hat{\beta}_3 \end{bmatrix} = [X'X][X'y] = \begin{bmatrix} -.94 \\ .24 \\ .23 \end{bmatrix}$$

$$\hat{s}^2 = \frac{\Sigma e^2_t}{n-3} = \frac{168.58}{24-3} = 8.0$$

happen: either two variables are directly correlated with each other, or alternatively, some combination of a few variables may be correlated with another variable.[8] In such situations we find that the data matrix X has linearly dependent columns and hence the determinant of X, $|X|$, is zero.[9] As shown in Appendix L, $(X'X)^{-1}$ does not exist when $|X| = 0$, with the result that the vector $\hat{\beta}$ is not defined. But, rarely do we find instances where perfect correlation exists; instead, as the correlation coefficient between variables i and j approaches one, i.e., $r_{ij} \to 1$, $|X|$ approaches zero. As $|X|$ approaches zero, $(X'X)^{-1}$ increases and the $\hat{\beta}$ estimates become very imprecise in the sense that they can vary greatly from sample to sample -- i.e., extreme sample sensitivity becomes a problem. That is, as $(X'X)^{-1}$ increases with multicollinearity, the standard errors of the coefficients tend toward infinity since $V(\hat{\beta}) = \sigma^2 (X'X)^{-1}$.

Unfortunately, detection of the impact of multicollinearity can be very difficult. The existence of both a high R^2 and t statistics that are low (because the standard errors have been increased) suggests that multicollinearity may be present. The exact source of the multicollinearity, however, may be difficult to find if there are several variables. One possibility is to examine the matrix of partial correlation coefficients among the explanatory variables, but no definite set of rules exist for isolating the exact relationships causing the collinearity, unless there are only two explanatory variables and then the correlation will be the only one possible. Finally, even if the source of multicollinearity is detected, the degree of 'seriousness' is in the eyes of the beholder, as there is no specific cutoff point to identify multicollinearity. Both Gujararti (1978) and Maddala (1977) present excellent discussions and examples of this problem, and the interested reader should refer to them.

To further compound the problem, correction for multicollinearity is 'ad hoc' at best (this is not surprising, since it is hard to be exactly sure of its cause). The procedures include dropping highly correlated variables, adding uncorrelated variables, combining cross-sectional and time series data, and transforming the highly correlated variables. Recently, several finance studies have utilized "orthogonalization" to isolate the separate influence of multicollinear variables; however, as discussed below, while separation is achieved, no real additional information is gained.

---

[8]Technically, the former is a special case of the latter.

[9]For an example of linear dependence in a matrix, see Appendix L.

Table 4.4a contains the simple correlation coefficients between IBM (STKRET) and several indexes. As can be seen, the simple correlation coefficient between the stock market index and the bond index is approximately .69, thereby confirming our earlier suspicion of multicollinearity, as well as explaining why the addition of the bond index added so little explanatory power.

In order to separate the influence of the bond index from that of the stock index, Lloyd and Shick decided to create an "orthogonal" bond index (for another example of this methodology see Friend, Westerfield and Granito [1978]), i.e., a bond index which would be uncorrelated with the stock market index. This bond "factor," R_{Dt}, is obtained (see Appendix M-17) as follows:

$$R^*_{Dt} = R_{Et} - [cov(R_{Et},R_{Dt})/V(R_{Et})]^*R_{Et}$$

such that $cov(R_{Et},R^*_{Dt}) = 0$, where R^*_{Dt} is the orthogonal factor.[10] In effect, R^*_{Dt} is equivalent to the residual errors from a linear regression of R_{Dt} against R_{Et} with the intercept constrained to zero. Similarly, an independent stock market index could be created by $R^*_{Et} = R_{Dt} - [cov(R_{Et},R_{Dt})/V(R_{Dt})]^*R_{Dt}$.

The use of orthogonalized factor variables allows one to establish the additional gain from the inclusion of the new variable. As Lloyd and Shick put it, "The coefficient of the orthogonalized bond index will measure the sensitivity of a security's return beyond that already reflected by the stock index." Also, the t-statistic will indicate whether the "new variable" has a statistically significant influence. It should be noted, however, that the orthogonalizing process changes the original character of R_{Dt}; after orthogonalizing, R^*_{Dt} is not the returns from the bond

[10]The term 'factor' is used here because it is similar to an orthogonal factor obtained in factor analysis (see Statistical Package for the Social Sciences [1975] and Johnston [1972]). If the stock index had been obtained as the first principal component, then the new bond index would be equivalent to the second principal component; principal components are variables which are orthogonal to each other, and a linear combination of which explains the maximum amount of variation in a normalized variance-covariance matrix of the explanatory variables. Because the linear combination does not generally include an intercept term, excess returns (after substracting the market's riskless rate intercept) should be used for analyses of stock returns.

Table 4.4

USE OF ORTHOGONAL INDEXES

a. Correlation Matrix

	STKRET	MKTRET	SOLY	SOLNEW	MKTNEW
STKRET	1.0000	0.77844	0.66419	0.17172	0.44082
MKTRET	0.77844	1.0000	0.69450	-0.23762E-05	0.71949
SOLY	0.66419	0.69450	1.0000	0.71949	-0.31376E-05
SOLNEW	0.17172	-0.23762E-05	0.71949	1.0000	-0.69451
MKTNEW	0.44082	0.71949	-0.31376E-05	-0.69451	1.0000

b. Variance-Covariance Matrix

	STKRET	MKTRET	SOLY	SOLNEW	MKTNEW
STKRET	20.106	40.487	14.251	2.6511	16.496
MKTRET	40.487	134.54	38.548	-0.94892E-04	69.646
SOLY	14.251	38.548	22.898	11.854	-0.12530E-03
SOLNEW	2.6511	-0.94892E-04	11.854	11.854	-19.955
MKTNEW	16.496	69.646	-0.12530E-03	-19.955	69.646

c. Multiple Regression with Orthogonal Bond Index

INDEPENDENT VARIABLE	ESTIMATED COEFFICIENT	STANDARD ERROR	T-STATISTIC
C	-0.935264	0.683757	-1.36783
MKTRET	0.300932	0.509336E-01	5.90832
SOLNEW	0.223653	0.171593	1.30339

R-SQUARED = 0.6355

F-STATISTIC(2, 21) = 18.3035

DURBIN-WATSON STATISTIC (ADJ. FOR 0 GAPS) = 2.1054

NUMBER OF OBSERVATIONS = 24

SUM OF SQUARED RESIDUALS = 168.579

STANDARD ERROR OF THE REGRESSION = 2.83330

ESTIMATE OF VARIANCE-COVARIANCE MATRIX OF ESTIMATED COEFFICIENTS

0.468E 00	-0.316E-02	-0.617E-01
-0.316E-02	0.259E-02	0.209E-07
-0.617E-01	0.209E-07	0.294E-01

CORRECTED R-SQ=0.6007

index, but only those residual returns which are not correlated with the stock index.[11]

The foregoing process was applied to create two new indexes called SOLNEW for R^*_{Dt} and MKTNEW for R^*_{Et}. As Table 4.4a and Table 4.4b indicate, these new indexes were virtually uncorrelated (except for possible rounding error and the impact of forcing the intercept to zero) with the original indexes. Most interesting, however, are the results of the multiple regression of IBM's returns against the original stock index and the new orthogonalized bond returns -- the orthogonalization adds virtually nothing to the explanatory power, nor does it change the t-statistic on the bond index.[12] All that was accomplished was that the $\hat{\beta}$ coefficient on the stock index (Table 4.4c) was left very close to its original value in the simple regression of IBM's returns versus the stock market (it would have been exact except for the possible rounding and forcing the constant to zero in the orthogonalizing, as previously mentioned).

6. DUMMY VARIABLES

In contrast to multicollinearity which is a problem for all observations, many investment studies hypothesize a different functional relationship for some of the observations. For example, utility companies often are believed to have common characteristics among themselves, especially compared with riskier industrial companies -- and each reacts differently to the various economic environments. Bond classifications such as AAA, AA, A, etc., are a result

[11]It is important to realize that this is different than with principal components where all are determined simultaneously; thus the first principal component might itself be a linear combination of both the stock and bond effects, while the second principal component would be the orthogonal residuals from the first principal component. Thus the second principal component could also itself be a combination of both indexes. The sequential orthogonalization method, described above, at least allows one to isolate the statistical significance of the additional variable, although this can be done directly by the F test anyway.

[12]This is pointed out because potential users may feel that there is some statistical advantage in having independent variables. While this would be true if they are really independent, the variables derived from either orthogonalizing, principal components, or factor analysis are merely transformations of the original variables unless some new a priori information is used for the transforming.

of hypothesized group differences. In order to group such diverse companies together, thereby gaining more degrees of freedom, some new variables are needed to reflect the nominal differences, and this is where dummy variables come in.

To see how dummy variables are used, consider a model where Y_t represents the stock price at time t and X_{it} are the earnings per share for the ith firm at time t. Considering only two firms, and assuming that their prices <u>follow the same generating process except for the intercept level</u>, the prices could be represented as

$$Y_{1t} = \alpha_1 + \beta_1 X_{1t} + u_t \qquad \underline{\text{Firm 1:}}$$

$$Y_{2t} = \alpha_1 + \alpha_2 + \beta_1 X_{1t} + u_t \qquad \underline{\text{Firm 2:}}$$

These two equations can be combined to give

$$Y_{2t} = \alpha_1 + \alpha_2 D + \beta_1 X_{it} + u_t$$

where

$$D = \begin{cases} 0 & \text{if } i = 1 \\ 1 & \text{if } 1 \neq 1 \end{cases}$$

The variable D in the equation is called the dummy variable which, in this case, serves to capture the differences in stock prices based on firm specifics (which could be due to being in different industries, and so on). The implicit assumption in the above model is that the slope coefficients remain the same for both firms; in other words, the impact of earnings per share on stock price is taken to be of the same degree regardless of the firm.[13]

Besides being useful in capturing 'firm effects', dummy variables can also serve to detect 'time effects' (e.g., variations in stock prices attributed to time alone), industry effects, other effects arising out of various classification schemes (e.g., classifying stocks of comparable risks together), and/or any other desired combination of these effects.

---

[13]This assumption, however, is not necessary. If the slope coefficient were thought to be different for one of the firms, then the earnings variable could be entered again as another explanatory variable which was multiplied by the same type of dummy variable. Such a test would allow one to determine if the stocks had significantly different slope coefficients. For a simple discussion of this, see Gujarati (1978).

An interesting example of the use of dummy variables is provided by Wippern's (1966) cross-sectional analysis of the earnings/price (E/P) ratios of companies in seven different industries, for the years 1956, 1958, 1961 and 1963. His model used four explanatory variables: leverage (L), earnings growth (G), dividend payout (P), and the size (S) of the firm. He then grouped all firms in the same industry together, and used dummy variables to isolate the 'industry effects'. The set of seven equations, one for each industry, were then reduced to a single equation for the cross-section data:

$$E/P = a + \beta_1 L + \beta_2 G + \beta_3 P + \beta_4 S^* + \beta_5 D_1 + \beta_6 D_2 + \ldots + \beta_{10} D_6$$

where $S^* = \log(S)$ and D_1 through D_6 are the industry dummy variables.

In the above equation, there are only six dummy variables and a constant (a). Using seven dummy variables plus a constant term would lead to what is known as a 'dummy variable trap'. To understand why this happens, let us turn to Table 4.5, which contains the partial X matrix. We can see from the matrix that column 1 is a linear combination of the rest of the columns thus giving rise to a singular X matrix. As pointed out in the earlier section on multicollinearity, we cannot calculate $(X'X)^{-1}$ if $\underset{\sim}{X}$ is singular, and $\hat{\beta}$ will be undefined (recall that $\hat{\beta} = (X'X)^{-1}X'y$) if X is singular. So, in order to avoid the trap in a regression model with $\underline{d}$ groups (or classifications), use either $\underline{d}$ dummy variables and no constant term or (d-1) dummy variables with a constant.

Wippern's regression results are presented in Table 4.6a, with the t-statistics in parenthesis. The Drug (and maybe Paper and Oil) industry dummy variables have coefficients that are significantly different from the overall intercept. For example, X_5 was the dummy variable for the second industry, and its the t-statistic of .065 indicates that its coefficient of .0008 is not significantly different from zero; therefore you would not reject the hypothesis that the first industry's intercept (β_0 was labelled 'a' by Wippern) of 0.1441 was applicable to this industry also.[14] The foregoing test is different from testing the significance of each industry intercept from

[14]The significance of the coefficients was tested further as shown in part b of Table 4.6; here the four separate years of data were "pooled" together, and this approach will be discussed further in the next chapter. Here in part b, both the Paper and Drug industry dummy variables had significant coefficients at the 5% level.

Table 4.5

DUMMY VARIABLE TRAP

	β_0	D_1	D_2	D_3	D_4	D_5	D_6	D_7
Industry # 1	1	1	0	0	0	0	0	0
	1	1	0	0	0	0	0	0
	.	.	.	.	.	.	.	.
	.	.	.	.	.	.	.	.
	.	.	.	.	.	.	.	.
	.	.	.	.	.	.	.	.
Industry # 2	1	0	1	0	0	0	0	0
	1	0	1	0	0	0	0	0
	.	.	.	.	.	.	.	.
	.	.	.	.	.	.	.	.
	.	.	.	.	.	.	.	.
	.	.	.	.	.	.	.	.
Industry # 7	1	0	0	0	0	0	0	1
	1	0	0	0	0	0	0	1
	.	.	.	.	.	.	.	.
	.	.	.	.	.	.	.	.
	.	.	.	.	.	.	.	.
	.	.	.	.	.	.	.	.

Note: Column No. 1 Minus Other Columns = 0

zero. For example, for the second industry, the intercept is the sum of both the first industry's intercept plus the coefficient of the corresponding dummy variable, i.e., β_0 + β_5 (see Table 4.7a); to test the significance of this, the appropriate standard error is

$$SE(\hat{\beta}_0 + \hat{\beta}_5) = \sqrt{V(\hat{\beta}_0) + V(\hat{\beta}_5) + 2Cov(\hat{\beta}_0,\hat{\beta}_5)}$$

We can also raise several other important questions about the model. If instead of only studying one time period, we were to consider more than one period, we might want to evaluate the temporal effects, i.e., to see whether the coefficients are nonstationary over time. To see how this would be done, consider a hypothetical model that incorporates time effects such as,

Table 4.6
WIPPERN'S RESULTS

a. Regression Equations (t Ratios in Parentheses)

Cross Section Year	a	X_1 Leverage	X_2 Growth	X_3 Payout	Log X_4 Size	X_5 Oil
1956	.1441	.0878 (1.794)a	-.0491 (1.719)a	-.0438 (2.080)a	-.0076 (1.810)a	.0008 (.065)
1958	.0990	.0717 (1.972)a	-.0612 (2.132)a	-.0522 (2.961)a	-.0007 (.2723)	-.0029 (.356)
1961	.0990	.0321 (.7627)c	-.1116 (5.847)a	-.0268 (1.888)a	-.0046 (2.202)a	-.0215 (2.825)a
1963	.0865	.1130 (2.338)a	-.0562 (1.856)a	-.0170 (1.312)b	-.0042 (2.233)a	.0128 (1.720)a

Cross Section Year	X_6 Machinery	X_7 Paper	X_8 Drugs	X_9 Rubber	X_{10} Containers	R^2
1956	-.0191 (1.834)[a]	-.0162 (1.555)[b]	-.0222 (1.818)[a]	-.0046 (.343)	-.0074 (.5116)	.533
1958	.0063 (.0921)[c]	-.0167 (2.432)[a]	-.0246 (2.737)[a]	-.0128 (1.422)[b]	-.0048 (.570)	.604
1961	.0028 (.4296)	-.0080 (1.275)[c]	-.0195 (2.950)[a]	-.0007 (.902)[c]	-.009 (.1276)	.693
1963	.0052 (.8701)[c]	-.0076 (1.268)[b]	-.0149 (2.207)[a]	-.0030 (.4129)	.0003 (.0435)	.624

[a]Significant at the .05 level.
[b]Significant at the .10 level.
[c]Significant at the .25 level.

b. Regression Equations--Pooled Estimates (t Ratios in Parentheses)

Year	a*	X_1 Leverage	X_2 Growth	X_3 Payout	Log X_4 Size	X_5 Oils
1956	.1172					
1958	.0995					
		.0773 (3.474)[a]	-.0825 (5.368)[a]	-.0318 (3.769)[a]	-.0039 (3.078)[a]	.0065 (1.466)[d]
1961	.1020					
1963	.1000					

Year	Machinery	Paper	Drugs	Rubber	Containers	R2
1956						
1958						
	.0012 (.324)	-.0019 (3.298)[a]	-.0176 (4.402)[a]	-.0044 (.981)[e]	.0021 (.463)	.589
1961						
1963						

*Intercepts determined from the values of dummy variables for three of the four cross section years as follows:

1958	-.0177 (6.921)[a]
1961	-.0152 (5.730)[a]
1963	-.0172 (6.568)[a]

[a]Significant at the .005 level.
[b]Significant at the .01 level.
[c]Significant at the .05 level.
[d]Significant at the .10 level.
[e]Significant at the .20 level.

Ronald Wippern, "Financial Structure of the Value of the Firm," Journal of Finance, Volume XXI (December 1966), Tables 1 and 2, pp. 622, 623.

Table 4.7

USING DUMMY VARIABLES
(a) Industry Effects

	Industry						
	1	2	3	4	5	6	7
	$D_0=1$	$D_1=1$	$D_2=1$	$D_3=1$	$D_4=1$	$D_5=1$	$D_6=1$
Intercept	$\beta_0=a$	$\beta_0+\beta_5$	$\beta_0+\beta_6$	$\beta_0+\beta_7$	$\beta_0+\beta_8$	$\beta_0+\beta_9$	$\beta_0+\beta_{10}$

USING DUMMY VARIABLES
(b) Both Time and Industry Effects

Industry \ Time	1	2	3
1	β_1	$\beta_1 + \beta_6$	$\beta_1 + \beta_7$
2	$\beta_1 + \beta_4$	$\beta_1+\beta_4+\beta_6$	$\beta_1+\beta_4+\beta_7$
3	$\beta_1 + \beta_5$	$\beta_1+\beta_5+\beta_6$	$\beta_1+\beta_5+\beta_7$

$$Y = \beta_1 + \beta_2X_2 + \beta_3X_3 + \beta_4D_1 + \beta_5D_2 + \beta_6T_1 + \beta_7T_2 + u$$

where D's are dummy variables for industries (three in all) and the T's are dummy variables for alternative time periods (three in all). We have carefully avoided the dummy variable trap by using only 2 dummy variables for each effect. Table (4.7b) shows the intercept term for various combinations of industries and time periods.

Analyses might extend the use of dummy variables further. In addition to determining if intercepts vary between industries and over time, the variation in slope coefficients might be assessed. By associating dummy variables with the slope coefficients, it is possible to isolate whether slopes differ by either their industry affiliation or time period of measurement. Such issues can be systematically tackled by using the analysis of covariance approach, and the interested reader is referred to Gujarati (1978) for a clear summary of this.

5

the general linear model

"Residuals are not all that residual"
-- Ganapathy and Fogler

This chapter is concerned with violations of two assumptions required by OLS to ensure BLUE estimators--homoscedasiticty of the error term and independence of the explanatory variables from the error term. Homoscedasticity is lost when the error term's variance changes either across time or across categories (e.g., one company versus another, one industry versus another). Independence of the explanatory variable from the error term may not exist for several reasons, but we will be interested in the situation where independence is lost because the equation being estimated is part of a larger set of equations.

Some possible reasons to expect these violations in financial models are illustrated in Figure 5.1a. This "general model" indicates that stock returns on the ith stock in period t, R_{it}, can be a function of five types of variables:

(1) R_{jt}, returns on other stocks,
(2) R_{mt}, return of the whole market and other macroeconomic variables,
(3) X_{it}, X_{jt}, microeconomic variables unique to the various companies,
(4) u_t, the error terms from all securities, and
(5) t, time.

Further, the return equations themselves are not independent because: (1) the return variables in one equation may be dependent variables in some other stock's return equation; (2) the error terms between equations may be related.

Figure 5.1 presents a rather complete view of what may determine stock returns, and it indicates that simple beta measures may be only rough summaries. Three assumptions suffice, for example, to reduce the general model to the standard Sharpe diagonal model of capital-asset pricing theory: (1) that the residual error matrix be diagonal; (2) that no nonmarket relationship exist between security returns, $r_{ij} = 0$ if $i \neq j$ (for further detail, see the note on the bottom of page 48); and (3) that no non-market relationship exists between returns and other microeconomic variables, $b_{jk} = 0$. Of course, if these assumptions are

Figure 5.1
The Simultaneous Picture Revisited

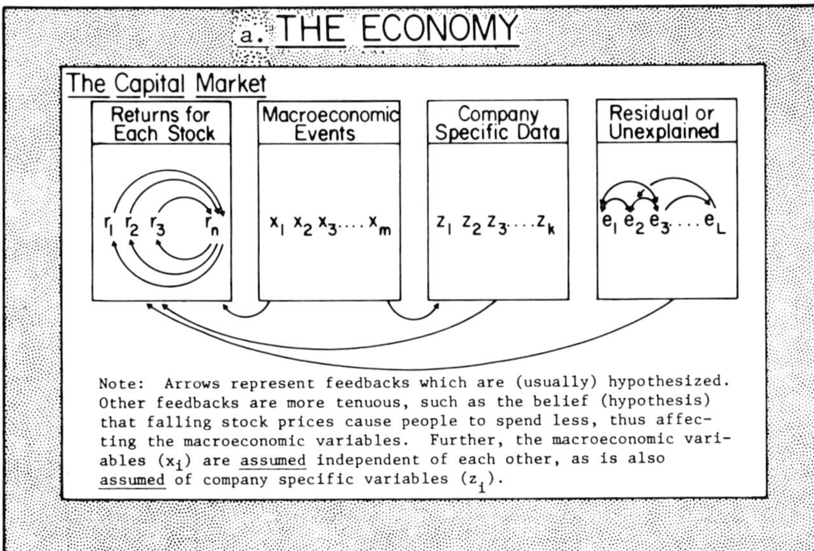

b. THE EQUATIONS

Security 1: $R_{1t} = \alpha_1 + \gamma_{12}R_{2t} + \gamma_{13}R_{3t} + \dots + \gamma_{17}R_{7t} + b_{11}X_{11t} + b_{12}X_{12t} + b_{13}X_{13t} + b_{1m}R_{mt} + \varepsilon_{1t}$

$\vdots$

Security k: $R_{kt} = \alpha_k + \gamma_{k1}R_{1t} + \gamma_{k2}R_{2t} + \dots + \gamma_{k6}R_{6t} + b_{k1}X_{k1t} + b_{k2}X_{k2t} + b_{k3}X_{k3t} + b_{km}R_{mt} + \varepsilon_{kt}$

c. MATRIX NOTATION

$$\Gamma R_i = BX + B_m R_m + E$$

or

$$R_i = \Gamma^{-1} BX + \Gamma^{-1} B_m R_m + \Gamma^{-1} E$$

d. CONDITIONS FOR SHARPE DIAGONAL MODEL

1. Γ^{-1} B is a null matrix
2. Variance-Covariance Matrix of Γ^{-1} is diagonal.

not valid, then estimated betas are likely to be biased because they will be linear functions of the "missing variables."

The importance of considering across time and type effects in error terms is evident from Table 5.1. This table presents the results of a study by Hui-shyong Chang and Cheng Lee on the common stock prices of 100 firms in the electric utility industry from 1963 to 1973. As indicated in the extreme left column, three alternative estimation procedures were used; OLS (Ordinary Least Squares - Chapter 2), LSDV (Least-Squares Dummy-Variable Technique - Chapter 4), and GLS (Generalized Least Squares). Each equation related the stock price with dividends and retained earnings per share, but the most notable aspect is that the R^2 statistic rises continually with refinements in LSDV and GLS formulations. While such increased explanatory power suggests that some relationships are being captured, the reader cannot assess the implications unless he knows GLS, which is a procedure which encompasses all cases that violate the assumption that $u \sim N(0, \sigma^2 I)$, i.e., that the term is normally distributed and homoscedastic over time. In addition to GLS which focuses on the error term directly, the second part of this chapter will address the effect of simultaneous feedbacks between both dependent and independent variables in systems of equations, as well as two basic estimating techniques (Two-Stage Least Squares, Indirect Least Squares) for such situations.

Finally, before proceeding, let us summarize the content of this chapter in our standard diagram:

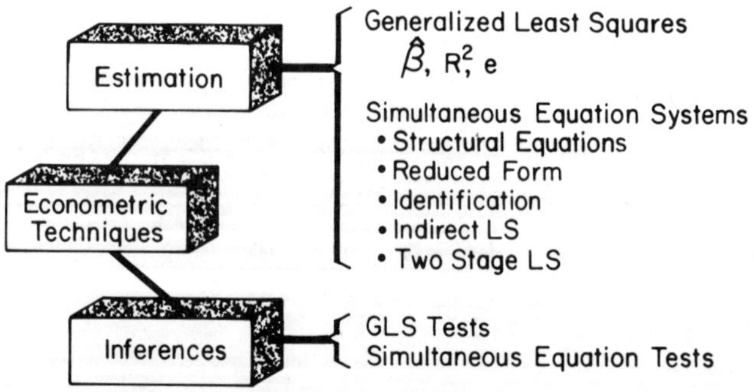

As can be seen, and as was stated above, this chapter does not add any new statistics but rather adjusts the previous material to recognize the impact of dependence between error terms of one or several equations, and how to calculate the estimators.

Table 5.1
CHANG AND LEE STUDY

ESTIMATED COEFFICIENTS FROM THE POOLED DATA (LINEAR FORM)

Based on	Constant	Coefficient for Dividend	Coefficient for (Earning-Dividend)	R^2
(a) OLS	9.64	8.65	12.01	0.31
	(0.99)	(0.78)	(0.93)	
(b) LSDV with	19.59	5.94	3.12	0.48
firm effects	(1.49)	(1.23)	(1.30)	
(c) GLS with	16.25	7.05	5.73	0.48
firm effects	(1.42)	(1.06)	(1.17)	
(d) LSDV with	2.87	12.67	13.97	0.74
time effects	(0.64)	(0.49)	(0.58)	
(e) GLS with	2.91	12.64	13.96	0.74
time effects	(2.54)	(0.49)	(0.58)	
(f) LSDV with	-2.44	20.72	6.18	0.91
both effects	(0.70)	(0.56)	(0.55)	
(g) GLS with	-1.70	19.83	6.82	0.91
both effects	(2.71)	(0.54)	(0.54)	

Note: Figures in parentheses are standard errors and LSDV is OLS with dummy variables.
Source: Hui-Shyong Chang and Cheng F. Lee, "Using Pooled Time-Series and Cross-Section Data to Test the Firm and Time Effects in Financial Analyses," Journal of Financial and Quantitative Analysis, September 1977, pp. 457-471. Table 1.

1. GENERALIZED LEAST SQUARES (GLS)

We now proceed to lay the groundwork for attacking the problems raised above. In Chapter 4 we assumed that $E(u) = 0$, and $E(uu') = \sigma^2 I$, i.e., the residuals have a constant variance and are not correlated. Now, we relax the latter assumption and replace it by saying that the residuals can have nonconstant variance and can be correlated among themselves i.e., $E(uu') = \Omega = \sigma^2 V$ where Ω represents the variance-covariance matrix of the residuals.

$$E(uu') = \Omega = \begin{bmatrix} \sigma_1^2 & \sigma_{12} & \cdots & \sigma_{1n} \\ \sigma_{21} & \sigma_2^2 & \cdots & \cdot \\ \sigma_{31} & \cdots & & \vdots \\ \vdots & & & \vdots \\ \sigma_{n1} & \cdots & \cdots & \sigma_n^2 \end{bmatrix} = \begin{bmatrix} E(u_1^2) & E(u_1,u_2) & \cdots & E(u_1,u_n) \\ E(u_2,u_1) & E(u_2^2) & \cdots & \cdot \\ E(u_3,u_1) & \cdots & \cdots & \vdots \\ \vdots & \vdots & & \vdots \\ E(u_n,u_1) & \cdots & \cdots & E(u_n^2) \end{bmatrix} = \sigma^2 V$$

The previous cases in Chapters 2 through 4 implicitly assumed that V = I. For the general linear model (y = XB + u), however, the least-squares estimators are not BLUE when the covariance matrix is not an identity matrix (or a scalar of it).[1] Thus, we need to transform the model in such a way that the L.S. estimators can again be BLUE.

The trick is to find a transformation for all the variables, such that the resultant error term can be expressed as a constant times an identity matrix. The necessary transformation is accomplished by expressing V in terms of a nonsingular matrix Q, such that V = QQ' and $Q^{-1}VQ^{-1\prime} = I$ (see Appendix L, which indicates that any symmetric positive definite matrix can be expressed in terms of another nonsingular matrix Q as QQ').[2] Premultiplying on both sides of the general linear model by Q^{-1} gives

$$Q^{-1}y = Q^{-1}XB + Q^{-1}u$$

Setting $y^* = Q^{-1}Y$, $X^* = Q^{-1}X$ and $u^* = Q^{-1}u$, the modified model becomes,

$$y^* = X^*B + u^* \tag{5.1}$$

which, as shown below, conforms to the requirements for ordinary least-squares estimation (thus, this is simply least-squares with the variables weighted first by multiplication by Q^{-1} which has weights which reflect the heterogeneous variances of each u_i; a common adjustment is to reweight the original observations to normalize them by dividing them by the standard deviation of the cross-section dispersion for the respective time period, although we will show other weighting schemes below). The new error term will be homogeneous because

---

[1]Such estimates still will be unbiased and linear, although not minimum variance.

[2]It can be proved that Ω is a positive definite matrix, and hence V is also a positive definite matrix.

$$E(u^*u^{*\prime}) = E(Q^{-1}uu'Q^{-1\prime})$$
$$= Q^{-1}E(uu')\,Q^{-1\prime}$$
$$= Q^{-1}\,\Omega\,Q^{-1\prime}$$
$$= \sigma^2 I \text{ (see footnote 2)}$$

So the transformed linear model (5.1) contains a residual vector that has a scalar covariance matrix, and thus, model (5.1) can be solved using the standard least-squares approach outlined in Chapter 4.

Thus, the beta coefficients of the transformed variables are

$$\hat{B} = (X^{*\prime}X^*)^{-1}\,X^{*\prime}y^*$$

and are BLUE. Now reverting back to the original matrices, and since it can be shown that $V^{-1} = Q^{-1\prime}Q^{-1}$, we obtain the equivalent solution vector (see Appendix L-18 for derivation)[3]

$$\hat{B} = (X'V^{-1}X)^{-1}(X'V^{-1}y) = (X'\Omega^{-1}X)^{-1}\,X'\Omega^{-1}y \tag{5.2}$$

which is called the <u>Aitken (1934) or GLS estimator</u>. The variance-covariance matrix is

$$V(\hat{B}) = \sigma^2(X'V^{-1}X)^{-1} = (X'\Omega^{-1}X)^{-1} \tag{5.3}$$

The problem now becomes one of estimating the elements of the $\Omega = \sigma^2 V$, which boils down to estimating V because an unbiased estimate of σ^2 is also a function of V, viz:

$$\hat{\sigma}^2 = \frac{1}{n-m}\,(e'V^{-1}e) \tag{5.4}$$

where $e = y - X\hat{B}$, n is the number of observations and m is the number of parameters to be estimated.

The reader may have already realized how difficult it would be to estimate the Ω matrix. For example, for a Ω matrix of order nxn we have to estimate $n(n + 1)/2$ elements (because Ω is a symmetric matrix).[4] By imposing certain restrictions it is possible to make the Ω matrix 'manageable.' To illustrate, suppose that the off-diagonal elements are zero; this condition provides a diagonal matrix.

[3] $\Omega = \sigma^2 QQ' \Rightarrow Q^{-1}\Omega = \sigma^2 Q' \Rightarrow Q^{-1}\Omega Q'^{-1} = \sigma^2 I$
$\Rightarrow Q^{-1}\Omega Q^{-1\prime} = \sigma^2 I.$

[4] $1+2+3+4+\ldots\ldots+n=n(n + 1)/2$

If the diagonal elements are not equal, we have the familiar case of heteroscedasticity (conversely, if all the diagonal elements are equal (to σ^2), we have homoscedastic disturbances). If the off-diagonal elements are non-zero, then other correlation is expected. Thus, we can see that GLS procedure is a generalized procedure encompassing cases that we considered in Chapters 2 through 4. So much for the groundwork. We will now consider specific cases.

HETEROSCEDASTIC DISTURBANCES

Consider a model of stock returns such as

$$R_i = \beta_1 + \beta_2(\text{Profit})_i + \beta_3(\text{Div})_i + \beta_4(\text{Debt})_i + u_i$$

$$i = 1,2,\ldots k$$
$$k = \text{number of firms}$$

where R_i stands for the return on the stock, and the remaining variables are the profits, dividends, and debt of the ith firm, as well as its error from the average cross-sectional relationship.

Suppose now that you hypothesized that the error term would be affected by the size of the firm's dividend (which seems intuitively plausible if lower dividend companies are less stable in their returns). Suppose further, that we tested this hypothesis and found that the equation $|e_k| = \hat{a}_1 + \hat{a}_2\ (\text{Div})_k$ turned out to be significant (see Rogalski and Vinso, 1978).[5] Then we can write the error term u_k as $u_k = \omega_k\ (a_1 + a_2\ (\text{Div})_k)$ with the hypothesis that $E(\omega) = 0$ and $V(\omega) = E(\omega^2) = \sigma^2$. Assuming that the off-diagonal elements are zero, we have

$$E\,(uu') = \sigma^2 V = \sigma^2 \begin{bmatrix} [a_1 + a_2(\text{Div})_1]^2 & 0 \;.\;.\;.\;.\;.\;.\;.\;.\;. & 0 \\ 0 & [a_1 + a_2(\text{Div})_2]^2 & \vdots \\ 0 \;.\;.\;.\;.\;.\;.\;.\;.\;. & . \;.\;. & [a_1 + a_2(\text{Div})_k]^2 \end{bmatrix}$$

The matrix V can be estimated once $\hat{a}_1$ and $\hat{a}_2$ are obtained from the equation $|e_k| = \hat{a}_1 + \hat{a}_2\ (\text{Div})_k$ and therefore, the coefficients β_1 through β_k can be estimated, i.e.,

[5]Rogalski and Vinso's article deals with time-series data, not cross-sectioned data, but the procedure is the same.

$$\hat{\beta} = \begin{bmatrix} \hat{\beta}_1 \\ \hat{\beta}_2 \\ \hat{\beta}_3 \\ \hat{\beta}_4 \end{bmatrix} = (X'V^{-1}X)\ (X'V^{-1}y) \tag{5.5}$$

where

$$X = \begin{bmatrix} 1 & \bar{\Lambda}_1 & (Div)_1 & (Debt)_1 \\ 1 & \bar{\Lambda}_2 & (Div)_2 & (Debt)_2 \\ \cdot & \cdot & \cdot & \cdot \\ \cdot & \cdot & \cdot & \cdot \\ \cdot & \cdot & \cdot & \cdot \\ \cdot & \cdot & \cdot & \cdot \\ 1 & \bar{\Lambda}_k & (Div)_k & (Debt)_k \end{bmatrix} \text{ and } y = \begin{bmatrix} R_1 \\ R_2 \\ \cdot \\ \cdot \\ \cdot \\ \cdot \\ R_k \end{bmatrix}$$

Similarly, we can also obtain $\hat{\sigma}^2$ and $V(\hat{B})$ using equations (5.4) and (5.3) respectively. The usual significance tests follow once B and V(B) are estimated. To see how such estimates are used, we will now return to the interesting study by Chang and Lee which was discussed at the beginning of this chapter.

POOLING, THE CHANG AND LEE STUDY, AND GLS ESTIMATES

The Chang and Lee study demonstrates the pooling of both cross-sectional and time series data to evaluate both firm and time effects in financial analyses. The model purports that there is a strong relationship between stock price per share (P) on the one hand, and dividends (Div) and retained earnings per share (R) on the other, i.e.,

$$P_{it} = \beta_1 + \beta_2(Div)_{it} + \beta_3 R_{it} + u_{it} \qquad i = 1,2,....k \quad (5.5a)$$

$$t = 1,2,...n$$

A general relationship for the above model can be written as

$$P_{it} = \sum_{j=1}^{m} \beta_j X_{jit} + u_{it} \tag{5.3b}$$

where $Xj(j = 1,2,...,m)$ are the explanatory variables. Because the error term could vary systematically either for the specific firm or over time, such influences are important to isolate. The procedure for accomplishing this isolation is relatively simple, although it requires a series of assumptions and matrix transformations that are explained in the next five paragraphs.

In what is known as an 'error components model,' Chang and Lee divided the error term u_{it} into three parts to isolate firm and time effects:

$$u_{it} = \nu_t + \omega_i + \mu_{it} \qquad \begin{array}{l} i = 1,2,\ldots,k \\ t = 1,2,\ldots,n \end{array}$$

where ν_t is considered to be cross-section invariant and would exemplify the unobserved time effects; ω_i, similarly, is associated with the firm effects (time invariant); and μ_{it} captures the mixed cross-section and time-series effects. Now, equation (5.5) can be written as

$$P_{it} = \sum_{j=1}^{m} \beta_j X_{jit} + \nu_t + \omega_i + \mu_{it} \qquad \begin{array}{l} i = 1,2,\ldots,k \\ t = 1,2,\ldots,k \end{array}$$

Certain assumptions have to be imposed on the error components so that we can derive some useful results. They are,

$$\nu_t \sim N(0,\sigma_\nu^2) \; ; \; \omega_i \sim N(0,\sigma_\omega^2) \; ; \; \mu_{it} \sim N(0,\sigma_\mu^2)$$

and hence

$$E(\omega_i \nu_t) = E(\nu_t \mu_{it}) = E(\omega_t \mu_{it}) = 0$$

$$E(\nu_t \omega_p) = 0 \quad t \neq p$$

$$E(\omega_i \omega_q) = 0 \quad i \neq q$$

$$E(\mu_{it} \mu_{qp}) = E(\mu_{it} \mu_{ip}) = E(\mu_{it} \mu_{qt}) = 0$$

$$(i \neq q \; ; \; t \neq p)$$

These assumptions enable us to derive the variance-covariance matrix of u_{it} along with $E(u_{it}) = 0$; i.e.,

$$\begin{aligned} &\mathrm{Var}(u_{it}) = \sigma_\nu^2 + \sigma_\omega^2 + \sigma_\mu^2 = \sigma^2 \\ &\mathrm{Cov}\,(u_{it}, u_{qt}) = \sigma_\nu^2 \qquad (i \neq q) \\ &\mathrm{Cov}\,(u_{it}, u_{qp}) = 0 \qquad (i \neq q,\; t \neq p) \\ &\mathrm{Cov}\,(u_{it}, u_{ip}) = \sigma_\omega^2 \qquad (t \neq p) \end{aligned} \tag{5.6}$$

Equation (5.6) can now be used to construct the Ω matrix.

To understand how this can be done, let us consider a simple model with just two explanatory variables, two firms and two time periods, i.e., m = 2, k = 2, n = 2. For purposes of illustration, let price per share (P) be a function of dividends alone. Then

$P_{it} = \beta_1 + \beta_2(\text{Div})_{it} + u_{it}$, where i = 1,...,m and t = 1,.n

can be expanded into

$$P_{11} = \beta_1 + \beta_2(\text{Div})_{11} + u_{11}$$

$$P_{12} = \beta_1 + \beta_2(\text{Div})_{12} + u_{12}$$

$$P_{21} = \beta_1 + \beta_2(\text{Div})_{21} + u_{21}$$

$$P_{22} = \beta_1 + \beta_2(\text{Div})_{22} + u_{22}$$

The error matrix u is

$$u = \left.\begin{bmatrix} u_{11} \\ u_{12} \\ u_{21} \\ u_{22} \end{bmatrix} \begin{matrix} \left.\vphantom{\begin{matrix} a \\ a \end{matrix}}\right\} k \\ \left.\vphantom{\begin{matrix} a \\ a \end{matrix}}\right\} k \end{matrix}\right] \rightarrow n$$

The order of u is (kn x 1) and is independent of the number of explanatory variables. In the present case, kn = 4. The variance-covariance matrix of u for the simple case is

$$E(uu') = E \begin{bmatrix} u_{11} \\ u_{12} \\ u_{21} \\ u_{22} \end{bmatrix} \begin{bmatrix} u_{11} & u_{12} & u_{21} & u_{22} \end{bmatrix}$$

$$= \begin{bmatrix} E(u_{11}^2) & E(u_{11}u_{12}) & E(u_{11}u_{21}) & E(u_{11}u_{22}) \\ E(u_{12}u_{11}) & E(u_{12}^2) & E(u_{12}u_{21}) & E(u_{12}u_{22}) \\ E(u_{21}u_{11}) & E(u_{21}u_{12}) & E(u_{21}^2) & E(u_{21}u_{22}) \\ E(u_{22}u_{11}) & E(u_{22}u_{12}) & E(u_{22}u_{21}) & E(u_{22}^2) \end{bmatrix} \qquad (5.7a)$$

Using the set of equations (5.6) and (5.7a) we get

$$\Omega = E(uu') = \begin{bmatrix} \sigma^2 & \sigma_\omega^2 & \sigma_\nu^2 & 0 \\ \sigma_\omega^2 & \sigma^2 & 0 & \sigma_\nu^2 \\ \sigma_\nu^2 & 0 & \sigma^2 & \sigma_\omega^2 \\ 0 & \sigma_\nu^2 & \sigma_\omega^2 & \sigma^2 \end{bmatrix} \tag{5.7b}$$

which can be partitioned into

$$\Omega = \left[\begin{array}{cc|cc} \sigma^2 & \sigma_\omega^2 & \sigma_\nu^2 & \\ \sigma_\omega^2 & \sigma^2 & & \sigma_\nu^2 \\ \hline \sigma_\nu^2 & & \sigma^2 & \sigma_\omega^2 \\ & \sigma_\nu^2 & \sigma_\omega^2 & \sigma^2 \end{array}\right] \tag{5.7c}$$

In a general case, we can see by way of induction that such a partitioning will give kxk submatrices with each submatrix of order nxn. Equation (5.7c) can again be modified as

$$\Omega = \left[\begin{array}{c|c} \sigma_\omega^2 \begin{pmatrix} \sigma^2/\sigma_\omega^2 & 1 \\ 1 & \sigma^2/\sigma_\omega^2 \end{pmatrix} & \sigma_\nu \begin{pmatrix} 1 & 0 \\ 0 & 1 \end{pmatrix} \\ \hline \sigma_\nu^2 \begin{pmatrix} 1 & 0 \\ 0 & 1 \end{pmatrix} & \sigma_\omega^2 \begin{pmatrix} \sigma^2/\sigma_\omega^2 & 1 \\ 1 & \sigma^2/\sigma_\omega^2 \end{pmatrix} \end{array}\right] \tag{5.7d}$$

The frightful looking equation (5.7d) can be written compactly as

$$\Omega = \begin{pmatrix} \sigma_\omega^2 A_2 & \sigma_\nu^2 I_2 \\ \sigma_\nu^2 I_2 & \sigma_\omega^2 A_2 \end{pmatrix}$$

where

$$A_2 = \begin{pmatrix} \sigma^2/\sigma_\omega^2 & 1 \\ 1 & \sigma^2/\sigma_\omega^2 \end{pmatrix}_{2x2} \qquad I_2 = \begin{pmatrix} 1 & 0 \\ 0 & 1 \end{pmatrix}_{2x2}$$

These results can be easily extended to the general case with

$$P_{it} = \sum_{j=1}^{m} \beta_j X_{jit} + u_{it} \qquad i = 1,2,\ldots,k$$

$$u_{it} = \nu_t + \omega_i + \mu_{jt} \qquad t = 1,2,\ldots,n$$

$$E(uu^1) = \begin{bmatrix} \sigma^2_\omega A_n & \sigma^2_\nu I_n & \cdots & \sigma^2_\nu I_n \\ \sigma_\nu^2 I_n & \sigma\omega^2 A_n & \cdots & \sigma_\nu^2 I_n \\ \vdots & & & \\ \sigma_\nu^2 I_n & \cdots & \cdots & \sigma_\omega^2 A_n \end{bmatrix}_{kxk}$$

where I_n is an Identity matrix of order nxn, and

$$A_n = \begin{bmatrix} \sigma^2/\sigma_\omega^2 & 1 & \cdots & 1 \\ 1 & \sigma^2/\sigma_\omega^2 & \cdots & 1 \\ \vdots & & & \\ 1 & 1 & \cdots & \sigma^2/\sigma_\omega^2 \end{bmatrix}_{nxn}$$

As we did in the case of heteroscedastic disturbances, we now have to estimate the Ω matrix for the pooling model also. This involves the estimation of σ^2_ω, $\sigma^2{}_\nu$ and σ^2_μ. The estimates can be obtained as follows (see Wallace and Hussain, 1969):

$$\hat{\sigma}_\mu{}^2 = \frac{1}{(k-1)\ (n-1)} \left[\sum_{i=1}^{k} \sum_{t=1}^{n} e_{it} - \frac{1}{n} \sum_{t=1}^{n} e_{it} - \frac{1}{k} \sum_{i=1}^{k} e_{it} \right]$$

$$\hat{\sigma}_\omega{}^2 = \frac{1}{n} \left[\frac{1}{(k-1)n} \sum_{i=1}^{k} \sum_{t=1}^{n} e_{it}{}^2 - \hat{\sigma}_\mu{}^2 \right] \qquad (5.7e)$$

$$\hat{\sigma}_\nu{}^2 = \frac{1}{k} \left[\frac{1}{k(n-1)} \sum_{t=1}^{n} \sum_{i=1}^{k} e_{it}{}^2 - \hat{\sigma}_\mu{}^2 \right]$$

where e_{it} are the residuals obtained by performing OLS on the pooled data.

Table 5.2 shows the relationship of GLS on pooled data, to both the LS dummy variable (LSDV) technique and OLS. From this table, we see that by using the GLS technique, the sample itself is capable of providing evidence to the presence or absence of time and/or firm effects. Returning to Table 5.1, which summarizes Chang and Lee's findings on the model,

$$P_{it} = \beta_1 + \beta_2(Div)_{it} + \beta_3 R_{it} + u_{it} \tag{5.5a}$$

going from OLS to GLS with both time and firm effects helped in improving the estimates of the coefficients of both Dividends and Retained Earnings and also in obtaining higher R-squared values. There appeared to be little interaction, however, between the specific firm and the specific time period effects. That is, since LSDV accounts for the variation within the dummy variables but not between them, the similar GLS results indicate very little sample interaction between the dummy variables. Nevertheless, GLS provides a thorough capability for correcting correlations within the residuals, as is shown in the next example below.

Table 5.2

RELATIONSHIP AMONG GLS, LSDV AND OLS TECHNIQUES

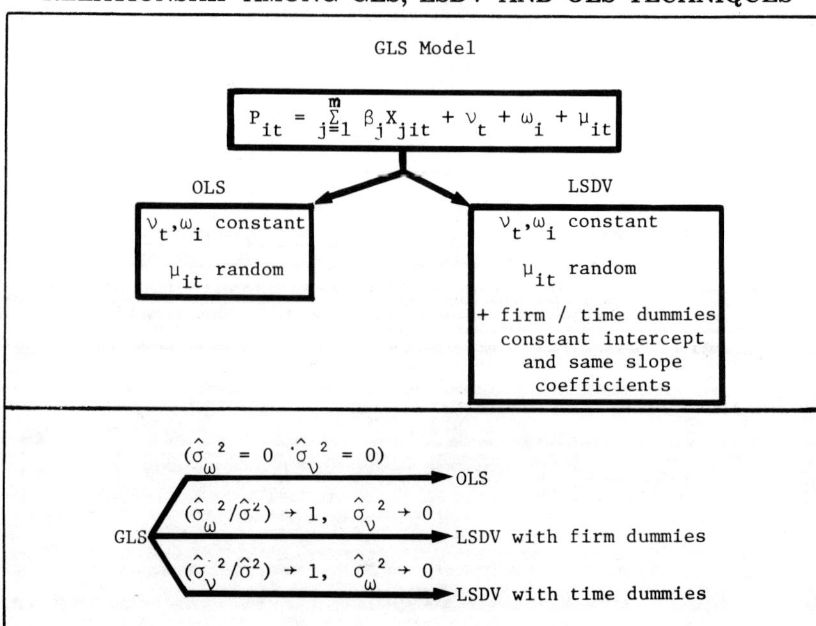

SEEMINGLY UNRELATED REGRESSIONS (SUR)

According to some theories (for example, Simkowitz and Logue [1973]), stock returns (R_{jt}) can be explained by the market index (R_{mt}) and the firm related variables, viz., a profitability index ($\bar{\pi}$) a leverage index (L), and a dividend (Div) index. The model can be represented as:[6]

$$R_{it} = \beta_{it} + \beta_{2i}R_{mt} + \beta_{3i}\bar{\lambda}_{it} + \beta_{4i}L_{it} + \beta_{5i}\,(Div)_{it} + u_{it} \tag{5.8}$$

$$t = 1,2,....n$$

$$i = 1,2,....k$$

where u_{it}'s account for the variable(s) omitted from the model (specification error). If one or more of the omitted variables are common to firms in the same industry, they may be reflected in the disturbance terms. If such is the case, the residuals will be correlated cross-sectionally between firms in the same industries (i.e., all oil stocks tend to move together).

A regression method that appropriately takes note of this fact is that of "Seemingly Unrelated Regressions" (SUR). This procedure, credited to Zellner (1962), yields GLS estimators that are asymptotically more efficient than the OLS estimators obtained from single equation systems. Again, as in the previous subsection, GLS estimators are derived, but a different set of assumptions will be made about the correlations of the error terms.

To illustrate the approach of SUR, let us consider only two firms in the industry, each with n observations. Let us also consider a simpler model (we'll come back to the longer version shortly), such as $R_{it} = \beta_{1i} + \beta_{2i}R_{mt} + \beta_{3i}(Div)_{it} + u_{it}$ for expository convenience, without any loss of generality to the SUR approach. The expanded version of the simplified model as applied to the two firms and n observations can be written as:

[6]In equation (5.8), we are betting that the regression coefficient is only firm-dependent, not time dependent as in the previous subsection.

$$
\begin{bmatrix} R_{11} \\ R_{21} \\ R_{12} \\ R_{22} \\ \vdots \\ R_{1t} \\ R_{2t} \\ \vdots \\ R_{1n} \\ R_{2n} \end{bmatrix}
=
\begin{bmatrix}
1 & R_{m1} & (Div)_{11} & 0 & 0 & 0 \\
0 & 0 & 0 & 1 & R_{m1} & (Div)_{21} \\
1 & R_{m2} & (Div)_{12} & 0 & 0 & 0 \\
0 & 0 & 0 & 1 & R_{m2} & (Div)_{22} \\
\vdots & \vdots & \vdots & \vdots & \vdots & \vdots \\
1 & R_{mt} & (Div)_{1t} & 0 & 0 & 0 \\
0 & 0 & 0 & 1 & R_{mt} & (Div)_{2t} \\
\vdots & \vdots & \vdots & \vdots & \vdots & \vdots \\
1 & R_{mn} & (Div)_{1n} & 0 & 0 & 0 \\
0 & 0 & 0 & 1 & R_{mn} & (Div)_{2n}
\end{bmatrix}
\begin{bmatrix} \beta_{11} \\ \beta_{22} \\ \beta_{31} \\ \beta_{12} \\ \beta_{22} \\ \beta_{32} \end{bmatrix}
+
\begin{bmatrix} u_{11} \\ \updownarrow \\ u_{21} \\ u_{12} \\ \updownarrow \\ u_{22} \\ \vdots \\ u_{1t} \\ \updownarrow \\ u_{2t} \\ \vdots \\ u_{1n} \\ \updownarrow \\ u_{2n} \end{bmatrix}
$$

or

$$R = XB + \Omega$$

What is done essentially is to pool the data on different firms, and to define a Ω matrix that adequately reflects the interaction of disturbance terms (shown by $\leftrightarrow$ in the disturbance vector). In SUR models, the disturbance terms are assumed to be correlated cross-sectionally (contemporaneous covariance) and not otherwise. Hence the assumptions are $E(u_{jt}) = 0$; $E(u^2_{jt}) = \sigma_i^2$ and

$$E(u_{it}, u_{qp}) = \begin{cases} \sigma_{iq}, & t=p \\ 0, & t \neq p \end{cases}$$

The variance-covariance matrix for the disturbance terms for any period t can be written as:

$$\Sigma = \begin{bmatrix} \sigma_1^2 & \sigma_{12} \\ \sigma_{21} & \sigma_2^2 \end{bmatrix}$$

If we have three firms the Σ matrix will be

$$\Sigma = \begin{bmatrix} \sigma_1^2 & \sigma_{12} & \sigma_{13} \\ \sigma_{21} & \sigma_2^2 & \sigma_{23} \\ \sigma_{31} & \sigma_{32} & \sigma_3^2 \end{bmatrix}_{3x3} \tag{5.10a}$$

and so on for k firms. The off-diagonal elements in the Σ matrix are the contemporaneous covariances and $\sigma_{iq} = \sigma_{qi}$. By assumption, the Σ matrix is also independent of time dimensions. The full-blown covariance matrix for all the (kn) observations is the Ω matrix, which can be represented as

$$\Omega = \begin{bmatrix} \Sigma & 0 & 0 \; \dots \; 0 \\ 0 & \Sigma & 0 \; \dots \; 0 \\ \vdots & \vdots & \Sigma \; \dots \; 0 \\ \vdots & \vdots & \ddots \quad \vdots \\ 0 & 0 & 0 \quad\quad \Sigma \end{bmatrix} \tag{5.10b}$$

(n diagonal Σ submatrices)

The above form of the Ω matrix is known as the <u>block-diagonal</u> form. The off-diagonal submatrices are all null matrices because of our assumption that the disturbance terms are temporally independent.

Now, the problem of estimating the Ω matrix is simplified to that of estimating the Σ matrix. Once the Σ matrix is estimated, we can use the GLS procedure to obtain the regression coefficients using equation (5.2),

$$\hat{\beta}=(X'\Omega^{-1}X)^{-1}(X'\Omega^{-1}y)$$

Incidentally, Ω^{-1} is a block diagonal matrix with Σ^{-1} occupying the diagonal blocks.

To estimate Σ^{-1}, we proceed as follows. We run OLS regressions on the time-series data for each one of the firms and obtain the residuals. For example, the residuals for firm 1 are $\{e_{11}, e_{12}, \dots e_{1n}\}$, and so on for other firms. Having obtained these residuals , we can construct the estimator of Σ for the two-firm case, as

$$\hat{\Sigma} = S = \frac{1}{n-m}\begin{bmatrix} \sum_{t=1}^{n} e_{1t} & \sum_{t=1}^{n} e_{1t}e_{2t} \\ \sum_{t=1}^{n} e_{1t}e_{2t} & \sum_{t=1}^{n} e_{2t} \end{bmatrix}$$

where m is the number of estimated parameters.
The estimation of Σ when there are more than two firms can be done by extending the above matrix in accordance with equation (5.10a) (for three firms) and so forth.

The submatrix $\hat{\Sigma}$ enables us to estimate Ω which in turn can be used to estimate the regression coefficients (equation 5.2) and the variance-covariance matrix (equation 5.3).[7] The estimates of SUR coefficients obtained with the aid of $\hat{\Sigma}$ are often called the joint GLS estimates.

Now, let us re-consider the model represented by equation (5.8):[8]

$$R_{it} = \beta_{1i} + \beta_{2i}R_{mt} + \beta_{3i}\pi_{it} + \beta_{4i}L_{it} + \beta_{5i}(Div)_{it} + u_{it}$$

Cheng Lee and Joseph Vinso (1978), investigated the advantage of estimating the above model using SUR over other least-squares estimation techniques. They used seven firms in the oil industry for the period 1945 to 1973. To detect any correlations between the disturbances, OLS regressions were performed independently on data from each firm[9] and a residual correlation matrix was obtained (Table 5.3). As indicated by the asterisks, there were several statistically significant cases of correlation between residuals, thereby warranting a SUR approach. Consequently, the SUR estimation technique was employed.

Results comparing the OLS and SUR estimates are shown in Table 5.4. SUR provides more efficient estimators than OLS as evidenced by higher t-statistic values (note the terms with double asterisks in Table 5.4). As Lee and Vinso used annual data, their SUR results would probably be stronger with quarterly data.

[7]Strictly speaking, asymptotic variance-covariance matrix.
[8]See, for another example, Theil (1971).
[9]The computation of these residuals can be used in the estimation of Σ.

Table 5.3
RESIDUAL CORRELATION MATRIX AFTER OLS

	R_1	R_2	R_3	R_4	R_5	R_6	R_7
R_1	1.0000	.1725	.1687	.4422*	.0571	.1129	.1450
R_2		1.0000	.2062	.2312	.7487*	.4420*	-.0770
R_3			1.0000	.1634	.3542*	.5748*	.2183
R_4				1.0000	.1789	.3645*	.3329*
R_5					1.0000	.6697*	.6234*
R_6						1.0000	.3154*
R_7							1.0000

*Denotes significantly different from zero at .05 level of significance.

Source: see Table 5.4

Before we conclude this section, we want to mention that the SUR estimation reduces to OLS estimation (i) if contemporaneous covariances are absent, and, (ii) if the data matrices of the explanatory variables used in each one of the k equations (i.e., k equations for k firms) are identical (Theil, 1971).

Table 5.4
Lee and Vinso's SUR versus OLS Results*

		α_j	β_j	b_{j1}	b_{j2}	b_{j3}	$\bar{R}^2$
R_1	OLS	-.4479	.7602	6.043	.4582	-2.0840	.2202
		(1.6480)	(2.4770)**	(1.7270)	(.2932)	(-.1749)	
	SUR	-.2861	.7663	4.2020	.8655	-6.9720	
		(1.1890)	(2.5560)**	(1.3600)	(.6268)	(-.6648)	
R_2	OLS	-.8203	.5413	1.0680	-1.2170	5.2960	.0248
		(-.2680)	(1.3140)	(.2359)	(-1.2180)	(.2725)	
	SUR	-.1600	.5822	2.4550	-.8193	-8.509	
		(-.8001)	(1.4340)	(.8517)	(-1.2710)	(.6768)	
R_3	OLS	-.2251	1.1200	2.0550	2.5110	-.5165	.4540
		(-1.7230)	(3.9800)**	(1.4220)	(2.1510)**	(-.0677)	
	SUR	-.3003	1.0880	2.9140	2.665	-2.532	
		(2.633)**	(3.8870)**	(2.393)**	(2.812)**	(-.4126)	
R_4	OLS	-.1550	.7283	2.1070	-.2395	25.2900	.3040
		(-.8648)	(3.0540)**	(.7852)	(-.2707)	(1.8170)*	
	SUR	-.0538	.6458	-.9832	.4262	26.3500	
		(-.3519)	(2.7530)**	(-.4340)	(.5884)	(2.337)**	
R_5	OLS	-.0029	1.1280	-.7520	1.8370	15.600	.0558
		(-.0111)	(2.0820)**	(-.2295)	(1.3410)	(.8942)	
	SUR	-.0047	1.1640	-.8607	1.8860	.9103	
		(-.0271)	(2.3090)**	(-.4143)	(2.4970)**	(.9555)	
R_6	OLS	-.1472	.7098	.6888	.9155	62.2000	.2755
		(1.4350)	(3.0960)**	(.5501)	(1.3050)	(1.7140)	
	SUR	-.1509	.7070	.8508	.9016	54.1100	
		(1.9960)*	(3.1751)**	(1.0101)	(2.0230)**	(2.4020)**	
R_7	OLS	-.1140	1.0141	1.347	.6427	4.5300	.4693
		(-.9173)	(4.7590)**	(.7899)	(1.2400)	(.7579)	
	SUR	-.0661	1.0190	.6500	.9632	3.9660	
		(-.5823)	(4.6800)**	(.4206)	(2.0890)**	(.7431)	

† - t-values appear in parentheses beneath the corresponding coefficients.

*denotes significant at .10 level of significance or better for two-tailed test.

**denotes significant at .05 level of significance or better for two-tailed test.

*Source: Cheng Lee and Joseph Vinso, "The Single versus Simultaneous Equation Model in Capital Asset Pricing: A Synthesis," forthcoming Journal of Business Research.

2. SIMULTANEOUS EQUATION SYSTEMS

In contrast to the above techniques which stressed only correlations within the residual error terms, simultaneous equation problems are concerned with the two-way causal influence among both dependent and independent variables, i.e., $y \leftrightarrows x$ versus the usual $y \leftarrow x$. Ignoring such simultaneous effects causes the presence of correlation between the independent variables and the error terms, thereby resulting in inconsistent and biased OLS estimators. In such a simultaneous situation, the "trick" is to find out if there are enough independent relationships (variables) to allow the parameters of an equation to be estimated ("the problem of identification").

THE IDENTIFICATION PROBLEM

The identification problem asks, "If I have two or more functions, say $D_t = f(P_t)$ and $S_t = g(P_t)$, can I identify the difference between these functions?" For example, assume that the demand (D_t) for a company's stock at time t is a function of the stock's price (P_t); also, that the supply (S_t) of its stock is a function of the corresponding price (P_t); and finally that demand must equal supply to clear the market:

Demand Function $$D_t = \beta_{10} + \beta_{11}P_t + u_t \tag{5.11a}$$

Supply Function $$S_t = \beta_{20} + \beta_{21}P_t + v_t \tag{5.11b}$$

Equilibrium Condition $$D_t = S_t \tag{5.11c}$$

In such a case, identification is impossible. Since $D_t = S_t$ by equation (5.11c), $D_t = \beta_0 + \beta_1 P_t + v_t$ -- which is the supply function! Graphically, Figure 5.2a illustrates the fact that completely different functions could all exist for the same price, and that there is no way to disentangle the effects, unless some new independent relationship is added (such as that "the demand function shifts independently of the supply function," as in (5.2b).

While there are numerous treatises on how to determine if an equation can be identified, a simple trick provides both the necessary and sufficient conditions. To illustrate how this works, let us use the above example, except assume that the demand (D_t) is influenced by both the

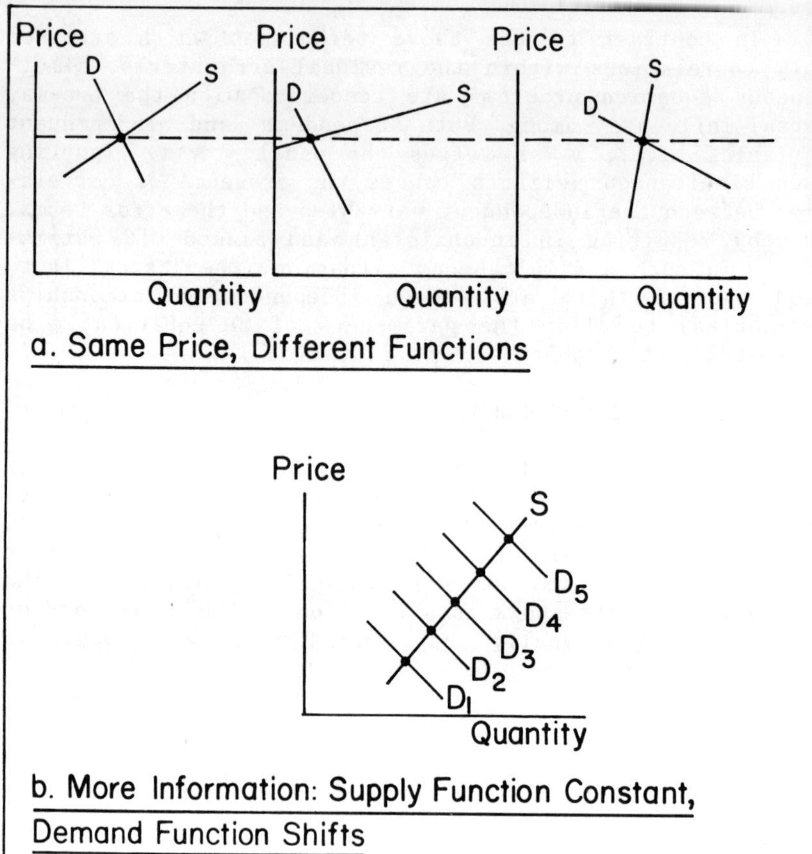

FIGURE 5.2 The Identification Problem

stock's price (P_t) and its earnings (E_t). Thus, our three equations can be written as

$$D_t - \beta_{10} - \beta_{11}P_t - \beta_{12}E_t = u_t$$
$$S - \beta_{20} - \beta_{21}P_t = v_t$$
$$D_t - S_t = 0$$

or by detaching the variable coefficients and putting them into a table

	I	D_t	S_t	P_t	E_t
Eqn. #1	$-\beta_{10}$	1	0	$-\beta_{11}$	$-\beta_{12}$
Eqn. #2	$-\beta_{20}$	0	1	$-\beta_{21}$	0
Eqn. #3	0	1	-1	0	0

Now, for each equation, check the determinant (see Appendix L) of the column coefficients on the variables with zeros in the relevant equation, ignoring the zero coefficient in the row of this equation. For example, for equation #2, the variables D_t and E_t have been excluded, and the determinant of their remaining column coefficients in the other equations is

$$\begin{vmatrix} 1 & -\beta_{12} \\ 1 & 0 \end{vmatrix} = \beta_{12}$$

Because this is nonzero, it has a rank of two (i.e., there are two independent relationships); and because its rank is equal to the number of equations minus one, equation #2 is identified. Since equation #1 has only one zero coefficient, its coefficients cannot be identified even though it has more variables than equation #2 (this is equivalent to the situation in Figure 5.2b where the supply function can be identified after it is specified that the demand function shifts independently of price and supply). Such an equation is said to be underidentified. Also, although the coefficients of the third equation do not need to be estimated because it is an identity and therefore they are combinations of ones, it would be overidentified since there are several determinants of rank two that can be constructed from the column coefficients of its excluded coefficients.[10] Table 5.5 summarizes these results for a four-equation/four left-hand-side ("endogenous") variable system.

[10]The above foregoing explanation of the rank condition provides both the necessary and sufficient conditions for identification. Many current econometrics texts spend a considerable portion of time discussing the order

Table 5.5

THE IDENTIFICATION TRICK

a. The Rank Condition:

In a system with M equations, an equation is identified if and only if at least one determinant of rank (M-1) can be constructed from the column coefficients of the variables excluded from the particular equation being analyzed.

b. A Hypothetical Set of Equations:

Y_{it} = a left hand side (endogenous) variable
X_{it} = a right hand side (exogenous or predetermined) variable

$$
\begin{aligned}
Y_{1t} - \beta_{10} \phantom{- \beta_{21}Y_{1t}} - \beta_{12}Y_{2t} - \beta_{13}Y_{3t} - \beta_{14}Y_{4t} - \gamma_{11}X_{1t} - \gamma_{12}X_{2t} &= u_{1t} \\
Y_{2t} - \beta_{20} - \beta_{21}Y_{1t} - \beta_{23}Y_{3t} - \beta_{24}Y_{4t} - \gamma_{22}X_{2t} &= u_{2t} \\
Y_{3t} - \beta_{30} - \beta_{31}Y_{1t} &= u_{3t} \\
Y_{4t} - \beta_{40} - \beta_{42}Y_{2t} - \beta_{43}Y_{3t} - \gamma_{41}X_{1t} &= u_{4t}
\end{aligned}
$$

c. Filling In the Table

Equation	1	Y_1	Y_2	Y_3	Y_4	X_1	X_2
#1	1	1	$-\beta_{12}$	$-\beta_{13}$	$-\beta_{14}$	$-\gamma_{11}$	$-\gamma_{12}$
#2	1	$-\beta_{21}$	1	$-\beta_{23}$	$-\beta_{24}$		$-\gamma_{22}$
#3	1	$-\beta_{31}$		1			
#4	1		$-\beta_{42}$	$-\beta_{43}$	1	$-\gamma_{41}$	

d. Trying the Condition-Example

Equations #1, #2, and #4 all exclude less than (M-1) = 3 variables, and therefore the excluded variable coefficients cannot possibly form a determinant of rank 3. Thus, they must be underidentified.

The excluded variable coefficients from equation 3 are

$$
\begin{matrix}
-\beta_{12} & -\beta_{14} & -\gamma_{11} & -\gamma_{12} \\
1 & -\beta_{24} & 0 & -\gamma_{22} \\
-\beta_{42} & 1 & -\gamma_{41} & 0
\end{matrix}
$$

which can be shown to contain two different determinants of rank = 3. Therefore, equation #3 is overidentified.

THE TERMINOLOGY OF SIMULTANEOUS EQUATION SYSTEMS

Having covered identification, it is desirable now to broaden our background in other terminology related to simultaneous equations concepts. For illustrative purposes, let us begin by discussing a study about the impact of inflation on stock prices, and in the next section we will show how the two-stage least squares (TSLS) technique was used to estimate the model's parameters.

In this study, Bruno Oudet (1973) set out to prove that common stocks performed poorly during the inflationary periods in the 50's and 60's contrary to the general belief that common stocks provide a partial, if not a complete, hedge against inflation in the long run. To establish his contention, he specified the following simultaneous relationships between both bond yields (R_{Bt}) and common stock returns (R_{St}):

$$R_{Bt} = \alpha_1 + \alpha_2 R_{St} + \alpha_3 R_{Bt-1} + \alpha_4 L_t + \alpha_5 Y_t + \alpha_6 NIS_t + \alpha_7 I_t + u_{1t} \quad (5.12a)$$

$$R_{St} = \beta_1 + \beta_2 R_{Bt} + \beta_3 R_{Bt-1} + \beta_4 L_t + \beta_5 Y_t + \beta_6 NIS_t + \beta_7 E_t + u_{2t} \quad (5.12b)$$

where L ≡ real per capita monetary base (a liquidity variable), Y ≡ real per capita income, I ≡ the expected rate of inflation, S ≡ personal savings as reported in the national income accounts, NIS ≡ a new issue variable (total gross proceeds from all issues scaled by division by GNP), and E was the expected end-of-period stock returns (for which

---

(cont. [10]).
conditions, which are necessary conditions. These conditions merely state that if the zero coefficients in an equation are less than the number of equations, the equation is underidentified; if the numbers are equal, it is exactly identified; if greater, it is overidentified. The order conditions can be checked with less calculations than the rank conditions, but ultimately the rank should be checked.

Finally, this introduction has not included how restrictions other than excluded variables can be used to allow identification. For examples of the use of covariance and linear homogeneity restrictions, see Maddala (1977).

lagged stock price ratios were used as proxies).[11] Oudet chose the explanatory variables based on the following rationale: "The use of Y_t and L_t reflects the liquidity preference approach. The variable I is justified by the theory of Fisher, and S_t and NIS_t introduce flow elements into the estimating equation. The variable R_{Bt-1} allows for the bond market's adjustment to be slow.... ...Since the stock-return series is very volatile, this variation can only be explained... by the constant expected end-of-period prices (Oudet, 1973, pp. 252-253)."

As discussed earlier, the set of equations (5.12a) and (5.12b) is a simultaneous equation model because the variables such as R_S and R_B mutually interact: $R_S \rightleftarrows R_B$. Using OLS to estimate such equations will lead to inconsistent and biased estimators because R_{St} will be correlated with small u_{1t} and R_{Bt} will vary with u_{2t}, as shown later in this section; this condition violates the basic assumption of OLS that the explanatory variables are independent of the error terms. Continuing with the econometric parlance, equations (5.12a) and (5.12b) are called structural equations, because they help in describing the structure of bond and stock markets.[12] Variables R_B and R_S are known as the endogeneous variables because they are determined by the simultaneous interactions of relations making up the system (or model). Other variables L, I, Y, NIS and E are called the exogenous variables since they are determined outside the system. R_{Bt} is called a current endogenous variable. R_{Bt-1} is called a lagged endogenous variable; L_t, I_t, etc., are called current exogenous variables. Current endogenous variables are otherwise known as jointly dependent variables, and all the other variables are called predetermined variables.

To illustrate the remaining concepts, let us consider two simple structural equations that could make up a hypothetical simultaneous system:

$$R_{Bt} = \gamma_1 + \gamma_2 R_{St} + \gamma_3 I_t + u_{1t} \qquad (5.13a)$$

$$R_{St} = \delta_1 + \delta_2 R_{Bt} + \delta_3 E_t + u_{2t} \qquad (5.13b)$$

[11]For measurement of the variables in equations (5.11a) and (5.11b), see Oudet's (1973) article. We see that one of the 'explanatory' variables is the lagged yield on bond R_{Bt-1}. The use of such variables poses several estimation problems because lagged dependent variables can cause small sample biases in LS estimators. See Johnston (1972, pp. 303-320) for methods to get around these problems.

[12]Equations of the type, Earnings = Retained Earnings + Dividends, are called identities and have no error terms.

We can solve equations (5.13a) and (5.13b) simultaneously (see Appendix M-19) to get,

$$R_{Bt} = \frac{\gamma_1 + \gamma_2\delta_1}{(1 - \gamma_2\delta_2)} + \frac{\gamma_2\delta_3}{(1 - \gamma_2\delta_2)} E_t + \frac{\gamma_3}{(1 - \gamma_2\delta_2)} I_t$$

$$+ \frac{(u_{1t} + \gamma_2\delta_{2t})}{(1 - \gamma_2\delta_2)} \qquad (5.14a)$$

$$= \phi_1 + \phi_2 E_t + \phi_3 I_t + v_t$$

and,

$$R_{St} = \frac{(\delta_1 + \delta_2\gamma_1)}{(1 - \gamma_2\delta_2)} + \frac{(\gamma_3\delta_2)}{(1 - \gamma_2\delta_2)} I_t + \frac{\delta_3}{(1 - \gamma_2\delta_2)} E_t$$

$$+ \frac{u_{2t} + \delta_2 u_{1t}}{(1 - \gamma_2\delta_2)} \qquad (5.14b)$$

$$= \theta_1 + \theta_2 I_t + \theta_3 E_t + \omega_t$$

Equations (5.14a) and (5.14b) are called the <u>reduced-form equations</u> of the model. These equations expressly show how the endogenous variables (R_B, R_S,) are jointly dependent on the exogenous variables (I, E) and the (u_{1t}, u_{2t}) of the system. At this juncture, we want to draw the attention of the readers to an earlier statement about correlation between R_{Bt} and u_{2t} on the one hand and between R_{St} and u_{1t} on the other. Equations (5.14a) and (5.14b) explicitly show that such correlations do exist, resulting in <u>simultaneity bias</u>.

As shown in Appendix M-20, we can obtain <u>unique</u> estimates of the original coefficients (exact identification) of the structural equations, (5.13a) and (5.13b), once estimates of ϕ_1, ϕ_2, ϕ_3, θ_1, θ_2, and θ_3 are obtained by performing OLS of R_{Bt} and R_{St} independently against E_t and I_t. The above process of estimating the original coefficients from the reduced-form equations is called the Indirect-Least-Squares Method (ILS), and simple OLS estimators are used to estimate the reduced form's coefficients.

It is not always possible, however, to obtain unique estimates for the system of simultaneous equations. Such a situation occurs when an equation is not exactly identified. We get multiple estimates of the original coefficients if it is overidentified, and the original coefficients cannot be estimated at all if it is underidentified. For example, if our system of structural equations had been

$$R_{Bt} = \gamma_1 + \gamma_2 R_{St} + \gamma_3 I_t + \gamma_4 L_t + v_t \quad (5.15a)$$

$$R_{St} = \delta_1 + \delta_2 R_{Bt} + \varepsilon_t \quad (5.15b)$$

then by our rank condition of the previous section, we know that equation (5.15a) is underidentified whereas equation (5.15b) is overidentified (Appendix M-20). Equation 5.15a has no missing variables, whereas (5.15b) has two missing variables.

TWO-STAGE LEAST-SQUARES METHOD (TSLS)[13]

Let us consider the following equations to explain the TSLS procedure.

$$R_{Bt} = \gamma_1 + \gamma_2 R_{St} + \gamma_3 I_t + \gamma_4 L_t + v_t \quad (5.16a)$$

$$R_{St} = \delta_1 + \delta_2 R_{Bt} + \delta_3 E_t + \delta_4 Y_t + \varepsilon_t \quad (5.16b)$$

[13]As will be indicated again later, only TSLS is discussed here. This choice was made for three reasons: (1) it is the most frequently used method in estimating equations in simultaneous systems; (2) it can be used for both exactly identified and overidentified equations; and (3) it performs reasonably well in many simulation studies [see Johnston (1972) and Intriligator (1978)]. One reason for its frequent use is that it works on each equation separately, as versus a full system's solution method such as Full Information Maximum Likelihood (FIML) which is computationally more consuming. For a discussion of such other techniques, the reader can go to any of the more advanced texts.

Both equations are overidentified, and hence TSLS is appropriate. The steps to be followed are:

Stage 1:

(i) Formulate the reduced-form version of (5.16a) and (5.16b) for the endogenous variables R_{Bt} and R_{St}; i.e., make both R_B and R_S functions of I, L, E and Y.

(ii) Use OLS to estimate the reduced-form coefficients for both R_B and R_S.

Stage 2:

(iii) Substitute the above-estimated $\hat{R}_B$ and $\hat{R}_S$ in equation (5.16a) and (5.16b) and run OLS regressions of $\hat{R}_B$ on $\hat{R}_S$, I and L, and $\hat{R}_S$ on $\hat{R}_B$, E and Y. Thus, $\hat{\gamma}_1$ through $\hat{\gamma}_4$, and $\hat{\delta}_1$ through $\hat{\delta}_4$ can be obtained.

The standard error of the estimated coefficients obtained during the second stage of the TSLS method cannot directly be used in significance tests because $R_{St} = \hat{R}_{St} + \hat{\varepsilon}_t$ when the reduced form estimates are used; substituting R_{St} in equation (5.16a) we see that

$$R_{Bt} = \gamma_1 + \gamma_2 \hat{R}_{St} + \gamma_3 I_t + \gamma_4 L_t + (v_t + \gamma_2 \hat{\varepsilon}_t).$$

The error term of the above equation is no longer the same as the error term in equation (5.16a). Also $\sigma^2(v + \gamma_2\hat{\varepsilon}) > \sigma_v^2$, thus contributing to errors in estimating the standard errors from the familiar OLS variance-covariance matrix of the coefficients $V(\hat{B}) = \sigma^2(X'X)^{-1}$. There are standard procedures (see Maddala, 1977, p. 239, for example) to obtain corrected standard errors, and we will not dwell on them here.

Oudet estimated equation (5.12b) using TSLS as,

$$\begin{aligned} R_{St} = {} & \underset{(2.07)}{6.47} - \underset{(-2.87)}{1.32}(R_B)_t - \underset{(-2.93)}{.02}(NIS) + \underset{(0.54)}{3.30}S_t + \underset{(2.75)}{1.34}R_{Bt-1} \\ & + \underset{(2.36)}{1.26}L_t - \underset{(-.50)}{.01}Y_t + \underset{(.09)}{.06}E_t + \text{error term} \end{aligned}$$

where the t statistics are quoted in parentheses. Since the coefficients of R_{Bt} and R_{Bt-1} are almost equal in magnitude, the above equation can be written as,

$$R_{St} \simeq -1.32\,[R_{Bt} - R_{Bt-1}] + \text{other terms}$$

Since $(R_B)_t$ - $(R_B)_{t-1}$ is equal to the change in the bond yield, we would interpret the results to suggest that the change in bond yield had an opposite effect on the stock returns. Oudet derived a further conclusion, however, by using the reduced-form equations for the stock returns. The reduced form for R_S can be written as

$$R_S = f(NIS, R_{Bt-1}, L, Y, I, E) + \text{error term}$$

and he interpreted the resulting negative coefficients on inflation as being consistent with the results of the structural equation if higher inflation leads to positive changes in bond yields as Irving Fisher has theorized.

What should be learned from the above study? First, that for examining some structural relationships the simple OLS assumptons may be invalid, and thus the methods of this chapter allow a fuller analysis. Second, that care must be exercised in both the use and interpretation of the results (notice how Oudet used the reduced-form results to interpret the structural relationships). This latter point about "care" can be seen in the sometimes conflicting results of the studies discussed below.

Michael Simkowitz and Dennis Logue (1973) estimated a model aimed at examining the possibility of interdependence in returns of securities of firms in the drug and oil industries for the quarters from January 1954 through December 1970. The simultaneous system that was used was:

$$\begin{aligned}
\text{Security 1:}\quad R_{1t} &= \alpha_1 + r_{12}R_{2t} + r_{13}R_{3t} + \ldots + r_{17}R_{7t} + b_{11}X_{11t} \\
&\quad + b_{12}X_{12t} + b_{13}X_{13t} + b_{1m}R_{mt} + \varepsilon_{1t} \\
&\quad \vdots \\
\text{Security 7:}\quad R_{7t} &= \alpha_7 + r_{71}R_{1t} + r_{72}R_{2t} + \ldots + r_{76}R_{6t} + b_{71}X_{71t} \\
&\quad + b_{72}X_{72t} + b_{73}X_{73t} + {}_{7m}R_{mt} + \varepsilon_{7t}
\end{aligned} \tag{5.17}$$

where R_1 through R_7 are each set of returns, X_1 ≡ a profitability index, X_2 ≡ a leverage index, X_3 ≡ a dividend index and R_m ≡ return on the market portfolio. Their results on the oil industry are reproduced in Table 5.6. Comparing the market model with the simultaneous model, they concluded that the significance of R_m is substantially reduced in the simultaneous systems, and that "...the Sharpe model and its variants must be broadened to accomodate variables that affect the returns for a given security and some recognition be given to the fact that some variables are more predictable than the market return."

TABLE 5.6

2SLS STRUCTURAL ESTIMATES FOR OIL INDUSTRY: R_m INCLUDED
(t-values appear in parentheses beneath coefficients)*

Dependent Variable (R_i)	R_1	R_2	R_3	R_4	R_5	R_6	R_7
Endogenous Variables							
R_1	1.0	-.1337 (-.383)	.1508 (.699)	.5723 (1.151)	-.4526 (-.922)	.4127 (1.311)	-.0036 (-.0120)
R_2	-.1629 (.385)	1.0	.6079* (2.932)	.6243 (1.106)	-.7572* (-1.845)	.3569 (.810)	-.3920 (-1.177)
R_3	.0698 (.159)	.5673* (1.698)	1.0	-.1766 (-.275)	.8532 (1.305)	.1472 (.322)	.6227* (1.784)
R_4	.0907 (.458)	.2441 (1.327)	-.0831 (-.711)	1.0	.2072 (.981)	.0929 (.414)	.3155* (1.772)
R_5	-.1923 (-.662)	-.6740* (-1.821)	.4170* (2.478)	.6430* (1.850)	1.0	-.0562 (-.182)	-.0906 (-.378)
R_6	.4304 (1.269)	.2794 (1.030)	.1781 (.726)	-.0039 (-.010)	.2317 (.617)	1.0	-.0503 (-.196)
R_7	.0633 (.245)	.0375 (.148)	.2271 (1.643)	.4294 (1.213)	.0911 (.312)	.1118 (.458)	1.0
Exogenous Variables†							
Constant	-.0238 (-.192)	.1455 (1.467)	-.0549 (-1.050)	-.1189 (1.488)	-.0821 (-.789)	.0168 (.365)	.0573 (.989)
XP_i	.1077 (.250)	-.4987 (-1.297)	.2135 (1.379)	.3667 (1.224)	.4187 (.953)	-.0879 (-.586)	-.2894 (-1.059)
XF_i	.0037 (.566)	-.0017 (-.810)	-.0070* (-2.234)	.0002 (.066)	.0034 (1.110)	-.0001 (-.002)	.0007 (.327)
XD_i	-.0507 (.481)	.0673 (.797)	-.0725 (-.611)	.2264 (1.543)	-.1371 (-.517)	.2605* (2.106)	.3513* (2.667)
R_m	.6460* (1.785)	.5563 (1.655)	-.4563 (-1.632)	-.7972 (-1.734)	.7700* (-.781)	-.3346 (-.781)	.733* (2.070)
Durbin-Watson Statistic††	2.32	2.47	2.54	2.02	2.42	2.64	2.22
R^2†	.385	.181	.615	.350	.263	.343	.584
SEE††	.091	.095	.063	.142	.122	.103	.091

† subscript i, i = 1, . . . , 7, denotes variables in second stage of relevant equation.
†† second-stage estimates for the single equation.
* denotes significance at .10 level of significance or better for a two-tailed test.

Source: Michael A. Simkowitz and Dennis E. Logue, "The Interdependent Structure of Security Returns," Journal of Financial and Quantitative Analysis, March 1973, Table 2c.

Yet, before you run out and dump the Sharpe model, again care must be exercised. For example, in a later study with annual data for 1945-1973 on the same oil companies, Cheng Lee (1976) showed that if the market return (R_m) had been excluded from the first-stage regressions, then it was of significant importance in the second-stage regressions. Basically, he argued that in cases of severe multicollinearity between the variables, such exclusion was appropriate. Thus, one is left to the realization that, while OLS assumptions may not be valid, extreme care must be placed in the use of the more sophisticated simultaneous-equation estimation technqiues.[14] This is further shown by the study discussed below.

RECURSIVE SYSTEMS

Let us reconsider the system of equations in (5.17). Suppose we have evidence to show that R_1 is not influenced by other stock returns (R_2 through R_7), and that R_2 is influenced by R_1 but not by any other returns (R_3 through R_7), and so on. Then, we can rewrite the system of equations ignoring firm-related variables (as was done by Lee and Lloyd, 1976) as,

$$
\begin{aligned}
R_{it} &= b_{11}R_{mt} + a_1 + \varepsilon_{1t} \\
\gamma_{21}R_{it} + R_2 &= b_{21}R_{mt} + a_2 + \varepsilon_{2t} \\
&\vdots \\
\gamma_{71}R_{1t} + \gamma_{72}R_2 + \ldots\ldots R_{77} &= b_{71}R_{mt} + a_7 + \varepsilon_{2t}
\end{aligned}
$$

and if ε_{1t} through ε_{7t} are independent of each other, then each equation is unrelated to the preceding equations so far as the disturbance terms are concerned.

---

[14]Another problem occurs when the R^2 of the first stage regressions is very low. In such a situation, the second stage regressions will be of little value because of the "estimation" error in the variable estimated at the first stage.

For interesting insights into both the small sample sensitivity and impact of multicollinearity on these techniques, one should review the simulation studies comparing each technique (e.g., see Johnston, 1972).

The first equation is the familar single equation, single-variable market model. Since the second equation is 'independent' of the first one, R_{it} can be treated as a predetermined (exogeneous) variable in the second equation, and this reasoning can be extended to all the seven equations.

Now the question is which security is to be designated as '1', which as '2', and so on? Lee and Lloyd 'ordered' the securities by estimating the degree of correlation of each security with the rest of the securities. The multiple coefficient of determination (R^2) obtained by regressing each set of security returns against the rest was used in ordering the securities, with the security having the lowest R^2 being designated security '1,' and the one with the highest R^2 as '7.'

Table 5.7 shows the results obtained via the recursive model. As the significant t statistics indicate, significant intra-industry relationships exist between these stocks. Thus, again, other variables in addition to the market return are of importance in understanding the return-generating process.

3. SUMMARY

This chapter has presented approaches to dealing with problems due to heteroscedasticity and estimation in simultaneous equation systems. For many financial studies, the most useful methods will be those using either LSDV or GLS. This usefulness is because these studies can use a full database on many different companies over different time periods, and GLS adjustments are appropriate for such pooled cross-sectional analyses. The study of Litzenberger and Ramaswamy, discussed in Chapter 1, is an example of this approach.

Methods for estimating in simultaneous equation systems will be used less frequently. Such methods are designed to provide estimates for each of the structural equations in a system of equations based upon a theoretical model (for example, see the general econometric model of the capital markets by Fair, 1979). These structural equations are useful for testing theoretical relationships, but they are not necessary for accurate prediction of a dependent variable; such prediction can be accomplished by a reduced form equation. While Oudet did address the relationships in his structural model, the other studies were emphasizing the statistical significance (and therefore improved predictability) by adding more explanatory variables.

Should more explanatory variables be added to the diagonal model of stock returns? The answer may be yes, and Rosenberg (1974), Ross (1977) and Sharpe (1977) all show why such a result is theoretically appealing, with

Table 5.7
RECURSIVE SYSTEM ESTIMATES FOR THE OIL INDUSTRY

(t-values appear in parentheses beneath the coefficients)

(Linear Form)

	Dependent Variables						
	STANDARD OF INDIANA	SHELL OIL	PHILLIPS PETROLEUM	UNION OIL	STANDARD OF OHIO	SUN OIL	IMPERIAL OIL
STANDARD OF INDIANA							
SHELL OIL	.2100* (2.859)						
PHILLIPS PETROLEUM	.2293* (2.176)	.0791 (1.065)					
UNION OIL	.1754* (2.472)	.2171* (3.177)	.2225* (2.337)				
STANDARD OF OHIO	-.0794 (-1.294)	.0147 (.235)	.4248* (5.501)	.1468* (1.735)			
SUN OIL	.1249 (1.343)	.1710* (1.843)	.0472 (.355)	.1339 (.908)	.0499 (.271)		
IMPERIAL OIL	-.1077 (-1.412)	.0526 (.6804)	.0354 (.319)	.1580 (1.290)	-.2541* (-1.691)	.0828 (.971)	
CONSTANT	.0868 (.681)	-.0384 (1.296)	-.0127 (-.068)	-.2034 (.986)	.3009 (1.204)	.2013 (1.399)	.3710* (2.161)
MARKET INDEX	.3681* (2.165)	.4997* (3.039)	.2884 (1.232)	.7609* (3.069)	.9089* (3.094)	.7161* (4.783)	.6432* (3.774)
R^2	.5020	.4658	.4106	.2532	.0985	.2404	.1247
DURBIN WATSON	2.1083	2.4714	2.2306	2.3468	2.2181	2.3109	1.9592

*Denotes significance at .10 level or better for two-tailed test
Source: Cheng F. Lee and W. P. Lloyd, "The Capital Asset Pricing Model Expressed as a Recursive System: An Empirical Investigation," Journal of Financial and Quantitative Analysis, June 1976, pp. 237-249, Table 3b.

Sharpe providing the conditions under which such a multi-beta model would be consistent with the capital-asset-pricing model. The final decision could depend on the empirical usefulness of an extended version--afterall, numerous studies have shown adequate predictability between returns and portfolio betas when the time period is at least five years (in contrast to the short bear market cycle used in Table 1.1 to compare two mutual funds with the market). Statistical problems of multicollinearity and nonstationarity pose serious estimation problems in addition to the theoretical problems of defining variables other than the market return. Thus, it is difficult to provide a definitive prescription yet.

Questions such as whether to modify the diagonal model illustrate the importance of a solid background in both financial theory and econometrics. The foregoing parts of this text provide the basic tools for empirical analysis. Application of these tools, combined with capital market theory, will provide the answers to such questions through the evolutionary process of hypothesis formulation and testing, a process in which practitioners and academicians are increasingly involved.

appendixes

APPENDIX A:

RULES GOVERNING EXPECTATIONS OPERATOR

"Statisticians are mean lovers"
-- C. Bonini

While the above quote is somewhat facetious, there is an element of truth in it. More often than than not, an analysis of statistical data starts with the calculation of means or averages of the data. The reason for this is that the mean, on most occasions, is an excellent measure of central tendency for a sample distribution, i.e., it succinctly summarises the 'location' of the distribution. Computation of means is almost always followed by the computation of variances, which are measures of dispersion.

Business situations abound with decision making under uncertainty. Hence, one has to be equipped with the basic tools of probability to meet with such situations, and thus the following example presents some of these basic tools.

Table A.1 shows the 'joint probability distribution' of the expected returns of two stocks i and j. The returns on the stocks R_i and R_j are subject to speculation. Such uncertain variables [which have probabilities, $p(\tilde{R}_i)$, associated with them] are called random variables, and will be capped with a tilde (~). If the variables are expected to take on only a few specific values, they are called discrete variables; if the variables can assume all possible values over a range, they are known as continuous variables. Accordingly, we can describe the probability of occurrence of the random events by a probability distribution. The probability distributions of discrete variables are termed 'mass functions' as against 'density functions' in case of continuous variables. Figure 1 shows the mass function for stock i corresesonding to the data shown in Table A.1. In order to derive meaningful conclusions from such a probability distribution, the first and foremost step is to calculate the mean or the expected value of the distribution. This step is followed by several other statistical calculations on the data. The purpose of this appendix is to clearly explain such rudimentary calculations using the expectations operator, which is a compact notation used to summarize the calculation of 'expected values.'

1. EXPECTED VALUE

Let $\tilde{Z}$ be a discrete random variable with a probability mass function $p(\tilde{Z})$. Then the expected value of $\tilde{Z}$ can be obtained from

$$E(\tilde{Z}) = \sum_{\text{all } Z} \tilde{Z} \cdot p(\tilde{Z}) \tag{A-1}$$

which is the mean of $\tilde{Z}$ itself.

$$E(\tilde{Z}) = \mu \tag{A-2}$$

Thus, for a discrete random $\tilde{Z}$ variable, the expectation operator [denote as $E(\cdot)$] is merely a formal statement of weighting each random event by its corresponding probability, thereby calculating the mean.

If $\tilde{Z}$ were a continuous random variable with a probability density function $f(\tilde{Z})$, then

TABLE A.1

JOINT PROBABILITY DISTRIBUTION OF $\tilde{R}_i$ AND $\tilde{R}_j$

		Return on stock j, $\tilde{R}_j$			
		15%	8%	2%	$P(\tilde{R}_i)$
Return on stock i, $\tilde{R}_i$	12%	.05	.15	.07	.27
	6%	.20	.18	.18	.56
	-1%	.06	.07	.04	.17
	$P(\tilde{R}_j)$	.31	.40	.29	1.00

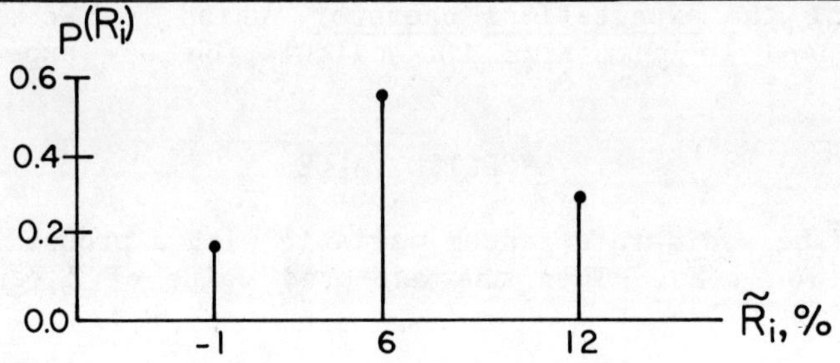

Figure A.1

Probability Mass function for Returns on stock i, $(\tilde{R}_i)$

$$E(\tilde{Z}) = \int_a^b Z \cdot f(Z)\, dZ = \mu \qquad \text{(A-3)}$$

where a and b are the lower and upper limits of the probability density function. We state below certain rules governing the algebra of expectations.

(i) The expected value of a constant, say c, is that constant itself.

$$E(c) = c \qquad \text{(A-4)}$$

(ii) If $\tilde{Z}$ is a random variable with expectation $E(\tilde{Z})$, then

$$E(c\tilde{Z}) = cE(\tilde{Z}) \qquad \text{(A-5)}$$

(iii) The expected value of a sum of random variables $\tilde{X}$ and $\tilde{Z}$ with expectations of $E(\tilde{X})$ and $E(\tilde{Z})$ respectively, is equal to the sum of individual expectations

$$E(\tilde{X}+\tilde{Z}) = E(\tilde{X}) + E(\tilde{Z}) \qquad \text{(A-6)}$$

Based on these rules it follows that

$$E(\tilde{Z}+c) = E(\tilde{Z}) + c \qquad \text{(A-7)}$$

and

$$E(c\tilde{Z}+d\tilde{X}) = E(c\tilde{Z}) + E(d\tilde{X}) = cE(\tilde{Z}) + dE(\tilde{X})$$

2. VARIANCE

Variance, as mentioned earlier, is a measure of dispersion of a random variable, say $\tilde{Z}$, about its mean. It is defined as

$$V(\tilde{Z}) = \sigma^2 = E(Z-\mu)^2 \quad \text{(A-9)}$$

$$V(\tilde{Z}) = \Sigma(\tilde{Z}-\mu)^2 \cdot p(Z)$$
[discrete case] (A-10)

$$V(\tilde{Z}) = \int_{-\infty}^{+\infty} (\tilde{Z}-\mu)^2 \cdot f(Z)\, dZ$$
[continuous case] (A-11)

An alternative way of expressing variance is often found useful:

$$V(\tilde{Z}) = E(\tilde{Z}^2) - [E(\tilde{Z})]^2 \quad \text{(A-12a)}$$

$$= E(\tilde{Z}^2) - \mu^2 \quad \text{(A-12b)}$$

The rules concerning the variances follow directly from the algebra of expectations. Stated simply, if c is a constant, then

(i) $V(c) = 0$ (A-13)

(ii) $V(c\tilde{Z}) = c^2V(\tilde{Z})$ (A-14)

(iii) $V(c\tilde{Z}+d) = c^2V(\tilde{Z})$ (A-15)

It is interesting to note from comparing (ii) and (iii) that the addition of a constant to a random distribution does not change the variance of the distribution.

The square root of the variance is called the standard deviation (σ).

3. COVARIANCE

Covariance is a measure indicating the direction of relationship between two 'jointly distributed' [i.e., statistically dependent] random variables; it also enables us to predict the behavior of one variable from that of another.

$$\mathrm{Cov}(\tilde{X},\tilde{Z}) = \sigma_{XZ} = E\,[(\tilde{X}-\mu_X)(\tilde{Z}-\mu_Z)] \quad \text{(A-16a)}$$

$$= E\,(\tilde{X}\tilde{Z}) - \mu_X\mu_Z \quad \text{(A-16b)}$$

$\mathrm{Cov}(\tilde{X},\tilde{Z}) = 0$ if $\tilde{X}$ and $\tilde{Z}$ are statistically independent, i.e., they do not possess any statistically predictable relationships.

To enumerate some of the rules associated with covariance:

$$\text{(i)} \quad \mathrm{Cov}\,(c,\tilde{Z}) = 0 \quad \text{(A-17)}$$

$$\text{(ii)} \quad \mathrm{Cov}\,(c\tilde{Z},\, d\tilde{X}) = cd\,\mathrm{Cov}\,(\tilde{Z},\tilde{X}) \quad \text{(A-18)}$$

$$\text{(iii)} \quad \mathrm{Cov}\,[(\tilde{X}+\tilde{Z}),\tilde{Y}] = \mathrm{Cov}\,(\tilde{X},\tilde{Y}) + \mathrm{Cov}\,(\tilde{Z},\tilde{Y}) \quad \text{(A-19)}$$

where c and d are constants and $\tilde{X}$, $\tilde{Y}$, $\tilde{Z}$ are random variables. From the earlier discussion on the expected values, one can easily derive the following:

If $\tilde{Z} = \tilde{X}+\tilde{Y}$, then

$$V\,(\tilde{Z}) = V\,(\tilde{X}) + V\,(\tilde{Y}) + 2\,\mathrm{Cov}\,(\tilde{X},\tilde{Y}) \quad \text{(A-20)}$$

<u>Derivation:</u>

$$V(\tilde{Z}) = V\,(\tilde{X}+\tilde{Y}) = E\,[(\tilde{X}+\tilde{Y}) - E\,(\tilde{X}+\tilde{Y})]^2 \quad \text{using (A-9)}$$

$$= E\,[(\tilde{X}+\tilde{Y}) - E(\tilde{X})-E(\tilde{Y})]^2 \quad \text{using (A-6)}$$

$$= E\,[(\tilde{X}+\tilde{Y}) - \mu_X-\mu_Y]^2 \quad \text{using (A-2)}$$

$$= E\,[(\tilde{X}-\mu_X) + (\tilde{Y}-\mu_Y)]^2$$

using the algebraic identity $(a+b)^2 = a^2+2ab+b^2$ we have,

$$V\,(\tilde{X}+\tilde{Y}) = E\,[(\tilde{X}-\mu_X)^2 + 2(\tilde{X}-\mu_X)(\tilde{Y}-\mu_Y) + (\tilde{Y}-\mu_Y)^2]$$

$$= V(\tilde{X}) + 2\,\mathrm{Cov}\,(\tilde{X},\tilde{Y}) + V(\tilde{Y}) \quad \text{using (A-7), (A-9) and (A-16)}$$

4. COEFFICIENT OF CORRELATION

The magnitude of the covariance is very much influenced by the units in which the variables are represented. In order to circumvent this possibility, we 'scale down' the covariance to a <u>dimensionless number</u> that can adequately reflect the strength of relationship between two variables, without tampering with the direction of relationship predicted by the covariance. This is achieved by dividing the covariance by the product of the standard deviations of the two variables in question. The correlation coefficient between random variables $\tilde{X}$ and $\tilde{Z}$ can be represented as

$$r_{XZ} = \frac{\text{Cov}\ (\tilde{X},\tilde{Z})}{\sigma_X \sigma_Z} \qquad \text{(A-21)}$$

5. APPLYING THE RULES--AN EXAMPLE

We now proceed systematically to apply the basic concepts to the data in Table A-1. Since the stock returns R_i are random, we have,

$$E(\tilde{R}_i) = \Sigma \tilde{R}_i \cdot p(\tilde{R}_i) \qquad \text{using (A-1)}$$

$$= (12 \times 0.27) + (6 \times 0.56) + (-1 \times 0.17)$$

$$= 3.24 + 3.36 - 0.17$$

$$= 6.43 = \mu_i$$

$$E(\tilde{R}_i^2) = \Sigma(\tilde{R}^2 \cdot p(R))$$

$$= (144 \times 0.27) + (36 \times 0.56) + (1 \times 0.17)$$

$$= 38.88 + 20.16 + 0.17$$

$$= 59.21$$

$$V(\tilde{R}_i) = E\ (\tilde{R}_i^{\,2}) - \mu_i^{\,2} \qquad \text{using (A-12b)}$$

$$= 59.21 - 41.35$$

$$= 17.86$$

Hence, the standard deviation of stock i's returns is

$$\sigma(\tilde{R}_i) = \sqrt{17.86} = 4.23\%$$

Similarly, the mean and the standard deviation for stock j can be calculated as $\mu_j = 8.43\%$ and $\sigma(\tilde{R}_j) = 5.04\%$ respectively.

The covariance between the returns of stocks i and j can be calculated using eqn. (A-16b)

$$\text{Cov}(\tilde{R}_i, \tilde{R}_j) = E(\tilde{R}_i\tilde{R}_j) - \mu_i\mu_j$$

$$E(\tilde{R}_i\tilde{R}_j) = (12 \times 15 \times .05) + (12 \times 8 \times .15) + \ldots \ldots + (-1 \times 8 \times .07) + (-1 \times 2 \times .04)$$

$$= 45.54$$

Hence, $\text{Cov}(\tilde{R}_i \tilde{R}_j) = 45.54 - (6.43 \times 8.43) = -7.57$

It then follows from the equation for correlation coefficient (A-21) that

$$r_{ij} = \frac{\text{Cov}(\tilde{R}_i\tilde{R}_j)}{\sigma(\tilde{R}_i)\ \sigma(\tilde{R}_j)}$$

$$= \frac{-7.57}{4.23 \times 4.74}$$

$$= -0.38$$

To illustrate the use of the various statistics so computed, let us consider a portfolio management problem. Suppose a portfolio is created by combining stocks i and j in the proportions 0.25 and 0.75 respectively

$$\tilde{R}_P = 0.25\ \tilde{R}_i + 0.75\ \tilde{R}_j$$

$$E(\tilde{R}_P) = \mu_P = 0.25\ E(\tilde{R}_i) + 0.75\ E(\tilde{R}_j) \qquad \text{using (A-8)}$$

$$= 0.25\ (6.43) + 0.75\ (8.43)$$

$$= 7.93$$

$$V(\tilde{R}_P) = V(0.25\ \tilde{R}_i + 0.75\ \tilde{R}_j)$$

$$= (0.25)^2\ V(\tilde{R}_i) + (0.75)^2\ V(\tilde{R}_j) + 2(0.25)(0.75)\ \text{Cov}(\tilde{R}_i, \tilde{R}_j)$$

$$= (0.0625)(17.86) + (0.5625)(25.45) + (0.375)(-7.57)$$

$$= 12.60$$

Therefore,

$$\sigma(\tilde{R}_P) = \sqrt{12.60} = 3.55\%$$

If one were to add a risk-free security, yielding a return of $R_f = 4.5\%$, to the existing portfolio in the ratio of

0.4:0.6, a new portfolio, say P*, is created. The means and variances of this new portfolio P* are:

$$E(R_{P*}) = 0.40\ E\ (R_f) + 0.60\ E(\tilde{R}_p)$$

$$= 0.40\ (4.5) + 0.60\ (7.93)$$

$$= 6.56\%$$

Noting that R_f is risk free and hence constant, $V(R_f) = 0$ using (A-12) and therefore $Cov\ (R_f, \tilde{R}_p) = 0$ using (A-17). So

$$V\ (\tilde{R}_{P*}) = 0.16V(R_f) + 0.36V(\tilde{R}_P) + 2(0.4)(0.6)Cov(R_f, \tilde{R}_P)$$

$$= 0 + (0.36)(12.60) + 0$$

$$= 4.54$$

References

1. Robert L. Winkler and William L. Hays, Statistics - Probability, Inference, and Decision, Holt, Rinehart and Winston (New York), 1975, 2nd Edition, Chapter 3.

2. Charles W. Haley and Lawrence D. Schall, The Theory of Financial Decisions, 2nd Edition, McGraw-Hill Book Company (New York), 1979, Chapter 4.

APPENDIX B

CALCULATION OF SAMPLE STATISTICS

Columns 1 and 2 of Table B.1 show quarterly returns (1970-75) on both IBM (R_j) and on the University of Chicago's Center for Research on Security Prices (CRSP) Index (R_m). Since these are occurrences of the past, they are known values. Such historical data are well depicted with the use of a frequency distribution. The diagramatic representation of the frequency of occurrence of each value in the data set is known as the raw distribution. Where the number of observations are numerous, the data are grouped into several intervals for ease of computation. Such grouped distributions, depicted using bar graphs, are called histograms (e.g., see Appendix H).

If x is a variable (e.g., quarterly returns), and x_1, x_2, x_3 ... x_n are n actually observed values of x, then the sample mean and variance of x can be calculated as follows:

I. Sample Mean:

$$\bar{x} = m = \frac{1}{n}(\sum_{j=1}^{n} x_j) \tag{B-1}$$

II. Sample Variance
biased estimate:

$$s^2 = \frac{1}{n}\sum_{j=1}^{n}(x_j - m)^2 \tag{B-2a}$$

$$= \frac{n\Sigma x_j^2 - (\Sigma x_j)^2}{n^2} \tag{B-2b}$$

unbiased estimate (see Appendix E):

$$\hat{s}^2 = s^2\ (n/n\text{-}1) \tag{B-2c}$$

The square root of sample variance is known as the standard deviation,

$$\hat{s} = \sqrt{\hat{s}^2} \tag{B-3}$$

III. Covariance:

Let us suppose we have n pairs of observations, (x_1, y_1) (x_2, y_2)....... (x_n, y_n). We can calculate the degree of association between the variables x and y using the following formula:

$$\sigma_{xy} = \text{cov}(x,y) = \frac{1}{n}\sum_{j=1}^{n}(x_j - m_x)\,(y_j - m_y) \qquad \text{(B-4)}$$

IV. Coefficient of Correlation:

$$r = \frac{\text{cov}(x,y)}{s_x s_y} \qquad \text{(B-5)}$$

Table B.2 shows the application of equations (B-1) through (B-5) to the data in Table (B.1).

TABLE B.1

Historical Quarterly Returns on IBM (R_j) and the CRSP Index (R_m) (1970-1975)

R_{jt}	R_{mt}	$(R_{jt}-\bar{R}_j)$	$(R_{mt}-\bar{R}_m)$	$(R_{jt}-\bar{R}_j)^2$	$(R_{mt}-\bar{R}_m)^2$	$(R_{jt}-\bar{R}_j)(R_{mt}-\bar{R}_m)$	R_{jt}^2	R_{mt}^2
-2.322	-2.400	-2.222	-3.618	4.937	13.092	8.039	5.392	5.760
-9.479	-19.830	-9.379	-21.048	87.957	443.032	197.403	89.846	393.229
5.449	17.600	5.549	16.382	30.796	268.359	90.909	29.695	309.760
3.026	9.760	3.126	8.542	9.773	72.960	26.703	9.157	95.258
4.141	11.200	4.241	9.982	17.986	99.634	42.333	17.147	125.440
-3.801	0.090	-3.701	-1.128	13.699	1.273	4.176	14.451	0.008
-1.273	-0.660	-1.173	-1.878	1.375	3.528	2.203	1.620	0.436
3.618	4.620	3.719	3.402	13.828	11.571	12.650	13.094	21.344
4.468	6.500	4.568	5.282	20.868	27.896	24.127	19.963	42.250
0.957	0.060	1.057	-1.158	1.117	1.342	-1.224	0.916	0.004
1.329	2.850	1.429	1.632	2.043	2.662	2.332	1.767	8.123
-0.256	7.120	-0.156	5.902	0.024	34.830	-0.919	0.065	50.694
2.499	-6.930	2.599	-8.148	6.756	66.395	-21.180	6.245	48.025
-2.686	-7.240	-2.585	-8.458	6.685	71.543	21.869	7.212	52.418
-6.519	7.480	-6.419	6.262	41.198	39.208	-40.191	42.493	55.950
-1.337	-10.600	-1.236	-11.818	1.529	139.673	14.613	1.786	112.360
-1.332	-2.200	-1.232	-3.418	1.518	11.685	4.212	1.775	4.840
-3.170	-9.670	-3.070	-10.888	9.426	118.556	33.429	10.051	93.509
-9.015	-24.450	-8.915	-25.668	79.476	658.863	228.832	81.272	597.802
2.139	9.480	2.239	8.262	5.012	68.255	18.497	4.574	89.870
7.389	23.750	7.490	22.532	56.095	507.676	168.754	54.605	564.063
0.615	16.080	0.715	14.862	0.511	220.869	10.621	0.378	258.566
-3.124	-11.550	-3.024	-12.768	9.143	163.030	38.608	9.759	133.402
6.279	8.180	6.379	6.962	40.692	48.465	44.409	39.425	66.912
-2.404	29.240	-0.000	0.000	462.445	3094.396	931.202	462.686	3130.021

SUMMARY STATISTICS

	STKRET		MKTRET
MEAN	-0.100		1.218
VARIANCE	19.269		128.933
STD.DEV	4.390		11.355
COVARIANCE		38.800	
CORR.COEFT		0.778	

TABLE B 2
Computation of Basic Sample Statistics

Statistic	Stock Returns (R_i)	Market Returns (R_m)
1. Mean	$\bar{R}_j = \frac{\Sigma R_{jt}}{n} = \frac{-2.40}{24} = -0.10$	$\bar{R}_m = \frac{\Sigma Rmt}{n} = \frac{29.24}{24} = 1.22$
2. Sample Variance Biased	$S_i^2 = \frac{1}{n}\Sigma(R_{jt}-\bar{R}_j)^2 = \frac{1}{24}(462.5) = 19.27$	$S_m^2 = \frac{1}{n}\Sigma(R_{mt}-\bar{R}_m)^2 = \frac{1}{24}(3094.4) = 128.93$
Unbiased	$\hat{S}_i^2 = S^2 * n/n-1 = 19.27 * \frac{24}{23} = 20.11$	$\hat{S}_m^2 = S_m^2 * n/n-1 = 128.93 * \frac{24}{23} = 134.54$
3. Standard Deviation	$S_i = \sqrt{S_i^2} = \sqrt{19.27} = 4.39$	$S_m = \sqrt{S_m^2} = \sqrt{128.93} = 11.36$
	$\hat{S}_i = \sqrt{\hat{S}_i^2} = \sqrt{20.11} = 4.48$	$\hat{S}_m = \sqrt{\hat{S}_m^2} = \sqrt{134.54} = 11.60$
4. Covariance	$Cov(R_i,R_m) = \sigma_{im} = \frac{1}{n}\Sigma(R_i - \bar{R}_i)(R_m - \bar{R}_m)$ $= \frac{1}{24}(931.20)$ $= 38.80$	
5. Correlation coefficient	$r_{im} = \frac{\sigma_{im}}{S_i S_m} = \frac{38.80}{(4.39)(11.36)} = 0.78$	

APPENDIX C:

THE NORMAL DISTRIBUTION AND THE STANDARD NORMAL TRANSFORMATION

Figure C.1 shows the raw distribution of the monthly returns of IBM common stock (Refer to Table C.1) during 1956-1975. The returns are not totally symmetrical. The symmetrical bell-shaped distribution (which is drawn in) is called the "Normal" or "Gaussian" distribution. Once the mean and the standard deviation have been estimated using the method outlined in Appendix B, the normal distribution can be inscribed for several values of returns on the horizontal axis. The general normal probability density function is of the form:

$$f(x) = \frac{1}{\sqrt{2\pi\sigma^2}} e^{\frac{-\frac{1}{2}(x-\mu)^2}{\sigma}} \qquad \text{(C-1)}$$

where μ = mean and σ = standard deviation. In short, the variable X assumes values from $-\infty$ to $+\infty$ and is distributed normally with a mean μ and standard deviation σ (this statement is written formally as $X \sim N(\mu,\sigma^2)$). Although the returns in Table C.1 are not symmetrically distributed, the normal distribution provides a convenient benchmark; also, many randomly distributed variables can be described by this distribution. For this and other reasons (to be presented later), the normal distribution is important.

Now, suppose that we wanted to have a generalized ("standarized") normal curve -- i.e., one that could be related to any normally distributed variable regardless of its specific mean and standard deviation. Such a dimensionless distribution can be very useful, as will be shown shortly. To create the variable, define

$$Z = \frac{X-\mu}{\sigma}$$

If the mean of X is μ, then the expected value of Z must be,

$$E(Z) = \frac{E(X-\mu)}{\sigma} = \frac{E(X) - E(\mu)}{\sigma} = 0$$

and likewise, the variance of Z will be

$$V(Z) = \frac{V(X-\mu)}{\sigma} = V(X/\sigma) - V(\mu/\sigma) = \frac{1}{\sigma^2} V(X) = \frac{\sigma^2}{\sigma^2} = 1$$

since the variance of the population parameter μ is zero.

So, we can rewrite eqn. (C-1) in terms of the standardized normal random variable Z as follows:

$$f(Z) = \frac{1}{\sqrt{2\pi}} e^{-z^2/2} \tag{C-2}$$

If the random variable X is continuously distributed, the probability of X taking on a particular value is zero (i.e., probability is the area under the probability density function between two points, and as the area between two points approaches zero to represent a single value, the probability also approaches zero in the limit). So we are interested in cumulative probabilities of random variables denoted by F(X)

Figure C.1

Comparison of Actual and Assumed Distributions of Stock Returns

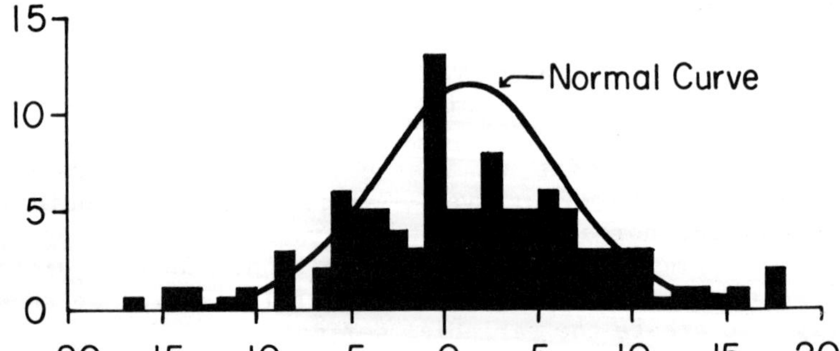

Table C.1
MONTHLY RETURNS ON IBM COMMON STOCK (1956-1975)

PERIOD	STOCK RETURN	PERIOD	STOCK RETURN	PERIOD	STOCK RETURN	PERIOD	STOCK RETURN
1	-3.226	61	7.251	121	-0.601	181	2.439
2	5.128	62	6.250	122	4.133	182	3.779
3	21.027	63	2.963	123	0.194	183	6.241
4	7.071	64	2.734	124	8.043	184	0.070
5	1.533	65	2.752	125	-2.103	185	-8.232
6	13.970	66	-2.661	126	-2.964	186	-3.058
7	5.209	67	2.418	127	-2.782	187	-8.123
8	-5.728	68	6.797	128	-5.620	188	4.824
9	-6.502	69	3.561	129	-0.936	189	-0.082
10	3.090	70	9.201	130	4.567	190	-1.070
11	4.711	71	-1.174	131	13.584	191	2.096
12	10.656	72	-0.172	132	-1.197	192	10.147
13	-4.074	73	-6.390	133	7.537	193	9.361
14	-1.641	74	-0.784	134	7.910	194	0.503
15	2.163	75	-0.791	135	4.884	195	3.731
16	10.106	76	-14.782	136	10.089	196	0.981
17	6.162	77	-13.381	137	-3.523	197	3.394
18	12.394	78	-13.567	138	6.702	198	-1.446
19	1.662	79	14.075	139	2.060	199	2.232
20	-5.914	80	2.584	140	-1.359	200	2.271
21	-4.905	81	-10.789	141	9.705	201	-0.490
22	-0.666	82	-2.122	142	8.254	202	-5.166
23	4.054	83	15.390	143	3.302	203	1.777
24	0.847	84	-2.133	144	2.451	204	2.813
25	5.410	85	8.654	145	-5.183	205	8.333
26	2.379	86	-5.428	146	-2.220	206	-0.597
27	5.327	87	5.316	147	5.603	207	0.000
28	1.445	88	10.154	148	10.612	208	-5.446
29	-0.456	89	3.127	149	5.579	209	-3.226
30	5.806	90	-8.591	150	-0.910	210	0.715
31	0.135	91	-0.401	151	-4.240	211	-0.789
32	0.852	92	2.589	152	-0.915	212	-3.936
33	9.677	93	1.630	153	0.000	213	-14.286
34	6.618	94	9.292	154	-8.164	214	8.624
35	2.908	95	-1.518	155	8.713	215	-5.042
36	22.679	96	4.482	156	-5.618	216	-6.887
37	-6.495	97	6.903	157	-5.952	217	-0.608
38	5.877	98	5.212	158	-0.700	218	-2.485
39	2.646	99	4.438	159	7.030	219	-0.893
40	7.919	100	-4.039	160	4.459	220	-3.605
41	20.435	101	5.491	161	-2.500	221	-5.927
42	-4.681	102	-0.625	162	5.878	222	0.118
43	-4.464	103	-3.145	163	-3.923	223	-5.229
44	-0.701	104	-4.383	164	6.626	224	-4.030
45	-3.062	105	-0.908	165	0.072	225	-17.188
46	-0.607	106	-3.780	166	4.417	226	18.946
47	6.748	107	-1.488	167	-0.694	227	-5.486
48	0.516	108	-0.727	168	2.101	228	-5.219
49	-5.077	109	9.524	169	-8.025	229	12.054
50	0.661	110	1.951	170	1.849	230	15.272
51	5.024	111	-0.329	171	-0.514	231	-4.118
52	3.075	112	6.769	172	-11.964	232	1.573
53	11.547	113	-1.134	173	-6.309	233	3.157
54	3.571	114	-4.184	174	-10.072	234	-2.791
55	0.479	115	4.585	175	1.380	235	-8.971
56	2.336	116	4.488	176	5.550	236	-1.183
57	-3.731	117	2.705	177	9.578	237	1.074
58	-0.969	118	4.000	178	1.182	238	12.749
59	9.149	119	-1.219	179	4.507	239	7.479
60	6.463	120	-4.952	180	3.417	240	-0.939

$$F(X) = P\ (X \leqslant x) = \int_{-\infty}^{X} f(X)dX \qquad \text{(C-3)}$$

Figure C.2 shows the meaning of this expression diagrammatically:

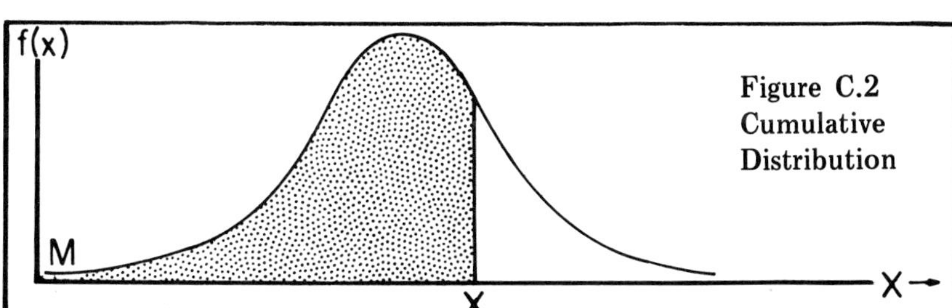

Figure C.2
Cumulative Distribution

The cumulative probability is simply the area under the curve between the two points $(-\infty, x)$. Similarly, we can also evaluate probabilities between intervals a,b as depicted in Figure C.3.

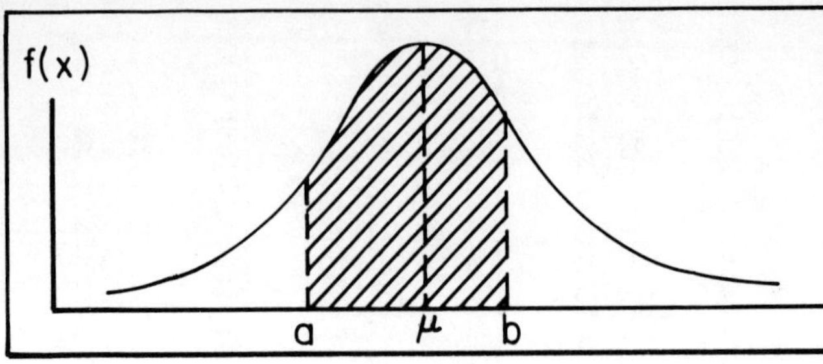

Figure C.3
Probabilities between Intervals

$$P(a<X<b) = F(b) - F(a) \qquad \text{(C-4a)}$$

$$= \int_a^b f(X)dX \qquad \text{(C-4b)}$$

Thus, by knowing the cumulative probabilities, we can calculate the probabilities of intervals. Fortunately, the cumulative probabilities are tabulated, for different values of our previously discussed standardized random variable (Appendix N, Table 1). Thus, the cumulative probability is

$$P(X \leqslant x) = P(Z) \leqslant \frac{(X - \mu)}{\sigma} \qquad \text{(C-5)}$$

and because the normal distribution is symmetrical

$$F(-Z) = 1-F(Z) \qquad \text{(C-6)}$$

as shown in Figure C.4.

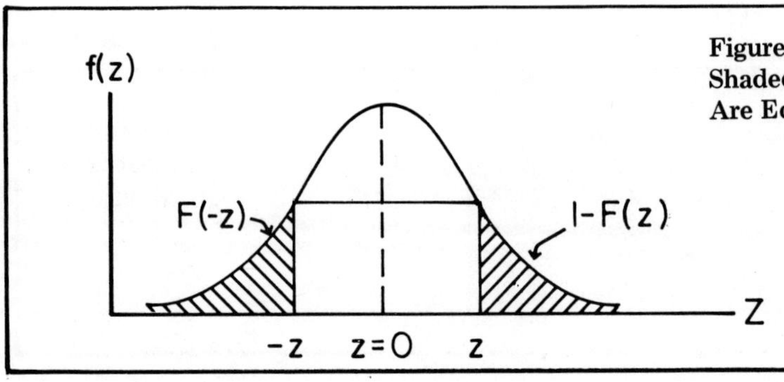

Figure C.4
Shaded Areas Are Equal

Now, let us ask the question: what is the probability that the price of a stock, whose mean $\mu = 25$ and variance $\sigma^2 = 4$, is less than or equal to 29?

Given X = 29, we calculate

$$Z = \frac{X - \mu}{\sigma} = \frac{29 - 25}{2} = 2$$

Referring to Table in Appendix N, thus the probability is

$$F(Z) = F(2) = 0.977$$

As a rule of thumb, about 95% of the cases comprising the population fall within plus or minus two (1.96 to be exact) standard deviations from the mean. This is illustrated in Figure C.5.

Figure C.5

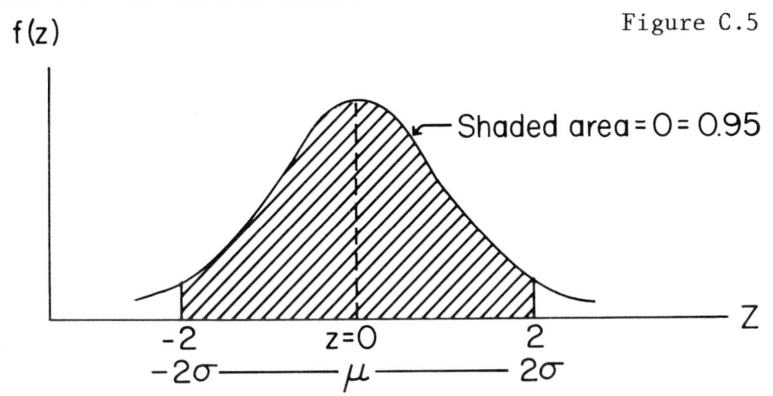

References

1. Robert L. Winkler and William L. Hays, "Statistics - Probability, Inference, and Decision," Holt, Rinehart and Winston (New York), 1975, 2nd Ed., 236-52.

APPENDIX D

THE SAMPLING DISTRIBUTIONS OF POINT ESTIMATORS

Drawing meaningful inferences from a body of data starts with relating the sample to the population of which it forms a subset. Two kinds of estimation, namely, point estimation and interval estimation are used to achieve this purpose. In point estimation, we derive a single estimate (e.g., $\mu = 10$) that serves as a 'proxy' or an adequate substitute for the population parameter. Interval estimation, by contrast deals with the determination of an interval (e.g., $\mu = 10 \pm 1$) that would include the true value of the population parameter, with a given level of "confidence" or probability. Such an interval is termed a "confidence interval." This Appendix deals with point estimation. Interval estimation will be taken up in Appendix F.

SAMPLE STATISTICS

Assume the data in Table C.1 (see Appendix C), where the returns of the stock, R_i, are viewed as a random variable with n observations ($i = 1, \ldots, n$), with unknown population mean μ and population variance σ^2. We can calculate the sample mean, m and the sample variance, σ^2 from a set of n observations as follows (see Appendix B):

$$m = \frac{\sum_{i=1}^{n} x_i}{n}$$

and

$$s^2 = \frac{\sum_{i=1}^{n} (x_i - m)^2}{n} = \frac{\sum_{i=1}^{n} x_i^2}{n} - m^2$$

where x_i is the ith observation. m and s^2 are used to describe the sample distribution, which has actually occurred according to Table C.1. That is, these statistics are calculated ex post from the sample in Table C.1.

APPENDIX E

PROPERTIES OF SAMPLING DISTRIBUTIONS: SMALL AND LARGE SAMPLE ESTIMATORS

When we calculate a sample statistic (such as the mean $\bar{x}$ or β), our goal is to obtain an estimate of the true (population) parameter. We would like such estimators to possess certain desirable properties so that they will serve as a satisfactory estimators; these properties, in turn, may depend on the size of the sample under observation. Some estimators prove satisfactory even if the samples are small, and others tend to be useful only when the samples are large. The former estimators are said to have "finite small sample properties," and the latter, "asymptotic or large sample properties."

SAMPLE PROPERTIES ILLUSTRATED

(a) Unbiasedness:

$\hat{\phi}$ is an unbiased estimator of ϕ if $E(\hat{\phi}) = \phi$; i.e., bias$(\hat{\phi})=E(\hat{\phi})-\phi=0$. In other words the mean, $E(\hat{\phi})$, of the sampling distribution reflects the true value of ϕ.

In the preceding Appendix, it was explicitly proved that the sample mean M is indeed an unbiased estimator of μ, i.e., $E(M) = \mu$. On the other hand, the sample variance s^2 provides a good example of a biased estimator; to prove this,

$$s^2 = \frac{\sum_{i=1}^{n} X_i}{n} - M^2 \text{ and } \sigma_M^2 = \frac{\sigma^2}{n}$$

$$E(s^2) = E\left[\frac{\Sigma E(x_i^2)}{n} - M^2\right] = E\left[\frac{\Sigma(x_i^2)}{n} - \right]E[M^2] = \frac{\Sigma E(x_i^2)}{n} - E[M^2]$$

$$= \frac{n(\sigma^2 + \mu^2)}{n} - \left(\frac{\sigma^2}{n} + \mu^2\right) \text{ since } E(x_i^2) = \sigma^2 + \mu^2$$

$$E(M^2) = \sigma_m^2 + \mu^2$$

$$= \frac{\sigma^2}{n} + \mu^2$$

$$E(\sigma^2) = \frac{n-1}{n}\,\sigma^2 \qquad \text{(E-1)}$$

Thus, $E(s^2) \neq \sigma^2$, for a finite n, making s^2 a biased estimator.

Fortunately, it is easy to obtain an unbiased estimator of σ^2 by simply multiplying the sample variance $\hat{s}^2$ by a factor of $(\frac{n}{n-1})$. Calling the new estimator s^2, we then have,

$$\hat{s}^2 = \frac{n}{n-1}\,s^2 \qquad \text{(E-2)}$$

Taking the expected value,

$$E(\hat{s}^2) = \frac{n}{n-1}E(s^2) = (\frac{n}{n-1}) \cdot (\frac{n}{n-1})\sigma^2 = \sigma^2$$

It should be noted that the square root of $\hat{s}^2$, or $\hat{s}$, is <u>not</u> an unbiased estimator of σ, the standard deviation; however, $\hat{s}$ can still be used as the estimator of σ without making gross errors.

<u>(b) Efficiency</u>:

$\hat{\phi}_1$ is said to be more efficient than $\hat{\phi}_2$ (where $\hat{\phi}_1$ and $\hat{\phi}_2$ are both <u>unbiased</u> estimators of ϕ if $v(\hat{\phi}_1) < v(\hat{\phi}_2)$.

For instance, the mean and the median of a symmetric unimodal distribution (e.g., normal distribution) are both unbiased estimators of the population mean μ; but, the mean is more efficient than the median since it can be shown that $\sigma_M{}^2 < \sigma_{Md}{}^2$.

<u>(c) Sufficiency</u>:

$\hat{\phi}$ is a sufficient estimator if it utilizes all the information that can be gleaned from the sample, as relevant to the parameter at issue. Again, it can be proven the sample mean is a sufficient estimator of μ.

<u>ASYMPTOTIC DISTRIBUTION</u>

Recall from above, that the sample variance s^2 was dubbed as a biased estimator of σ^2 since $E(s^2) \neq \sigma^2$ in a finite sample case. Is it possible to use s^2 as an estimator of σ^2, without bothering to calculate s^2 in a large sample case? To answer this and other related questions, we now turn to the case of asymptotic or limiting distributions.

Broadly speaking, if the sampling distribution of an estimator converges to a certain specific distribution with increasing sample size, then such a specific distribution is called the asymptotic distribution. For example, as suggested by the Central Limit Theorem, the sampling distribution of sample means with $E(M) = \mu$ and $V(M) = \frac{\sigma^2}{n}$ approaches a normal distribution. Under such conditions, the normal distribution is described as the asymptotic distribution of the sample means. As n tends to infinity ($n \to \infty$), V(M) approaches zero[1], implying that the distribution will collapse on the population mean and result in a bias of zero in the estimation of the population mean.[2] Expressed mathematically,

$$\lim_{n\to\infty} V(M) = \lim_{n\to\infty} E[(M-\mu)^2] = \lim_{n\to\infty} \frac{\sigma^2}{n} = 0$$

So, the final form of the distribution as n increases indefinitely is not a continuous distribution, but a mass function concentrated solely at the population mean; such a distribution is called a degenerate distribution. The asymptotic distribution can now be appropriately defined as the form that the sampling distribution takes on before it reaches the final form which may or may not be degenerate.

Asymptotic distributions can be characterized in most instances by the asymptotic mean and asymptotic variance.[3] For an estimator $\hat{\phi}$ with a mean $E(\hat{\phi})$, the asymptotic mean is represented as $\lim_{n\to\infty} E(\hat{\phi}) = E(\hat{\phi})$. Thus, for a distribution

sample means the asymptotic mean is the population mean itself; i.e., $\lim_{n\to\infty} E(M) = \mu$.

But, if we attempt to define asymptotic variance in a similar vein, we run into problems. For example, note that $\lim_{n\to\infty} E(M) = \lim_{n\to\infty} E(\text{Median}) = \mu$, and both $V(M) = \frac{\sigma^2}{n}$ and $V(\text{Median}) = \frac{\pi\sigma^2}{2n}$ go to zero as n goes to infinity, thus making the final form of the sampling distribution of the

---

1. Note that $\lim_{n\to\infty} (\frac{1}{n}) = 0$
2. Obviously, the best sample one can ask for, when estimating the population mean, is indeed the sample encompassing the whole population at issue!
3. Since most sampling distributions can be treated as normal, we need only the variance to characterize them.

mean indistinguishable from that of the median. Thus, to distinguish between the asymptotic distribution of different estimators (for instances, sample mean versus the sample median) purporting to estimate the same parameter (say, the population mean), the asymptotic variance is formulated as follows:

$$\text{Asymptotic Var } (\hat{\phi}) = \frac{1}{n} \lim_{n\to\infty} E[\sqrt{n}[(\hat{\phi}-\varepsilon(\hat{\phi})]]^2 \qquad \text{(E-3)}$$

Such a structure permits us to make large sample comparisons. To illustrate, distributions of sample means (M) and sample medians (Md) can be compared by looking at the limiting distributions of $\sqrt{n}\cdot M$ and $\sqrt{n}\hat{\ }Md$ whose limiting variances are σ^2 and $\pi\sigma^2/2$ respectively if x is normally distributed.

ASYMPTOTIC PROPERTIES

(a) Asymptotic Unbiasedness:

ϕ is an asymptotically unbiased estimator of ϕ if $\varepsilon(\phi) = \lim_{n\to\infty} E(\phi) = \phi$. For the sample mean, it can be easily proved that $\varepsilon(M) = \mu$. For the sample variance,

$$s^2 = \frac{n-1}{n}\sigma^2$$

$$\lim_{n\to\infty} s^2 = \lim_{n\to\infty} \frac{n-1}{n}\sigma^2 = \sigma^2$$

Thus, although s^2 is a biased estimator of σ^2 for small samples, it is an adequate estimator for large samples!

(b) Asymptotic Consistency:

Consider Figure E.1. ϕ is the population parameter that we are after. As the sample size increases from n_1 to n_2, the bias decreases from $(\hat{\phi}_1 - \phi)$ to $(\hat{\phi}_2 - \phi)$, and also the variance of the distribution decreases. A small interval around ϕ (say $\phi \pm \delta$) occupies more density under the n_2 distribution than under the n_1 distribution. Therefore, it is theoretically possible to increase the sample size indefinitely so as to compact the bulk of the distribution within the internal $\phi \pm \delta$. Stated rigorously,

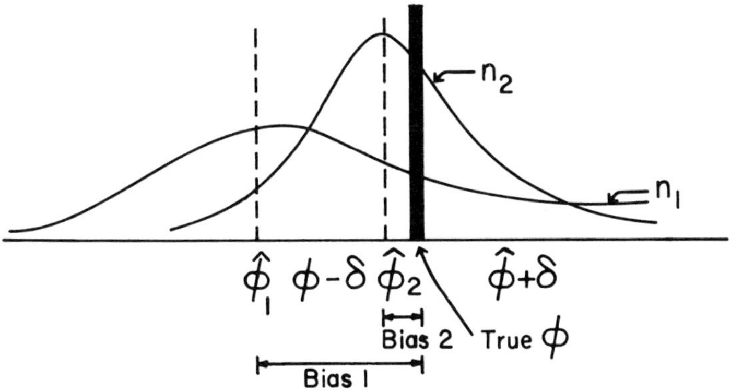

Figure E.1 Asymptotic Bias - Effect of Sample Size

$$\lim_{n\to\infty} \Pr [\hat{\phi}-\phi < \delta] = 1. \qquad \text{(E-4)}$$

Under such conditions, $\hat{\phi}$ is said to be consistent, and ϕ is known as the probability limit (plim) of $\hat{\phi}$, i.e., plim $\hat{\phi}=\phi$. It can also be seen that consistent estimators have degenerate distributions in the limiting case. An interesting corrollary concerning consistency can be mentioned here: $\hat{\phi}$ is a consistent estimator of ϕ if $\lim_{n\to\infty} \text{MSE}(\hat{\phi})=0$.

(c) Asymptotic Efficiency:

For the sake of completeness, let us state that: $\hat{\phi}$ is an asymptotically efficient estimator of ϕ if $\hat{\phi}$: (1) has a limiting distribution with finite mean and finite variance; (ii) is consistent; and (iii) has the least asymptotic variance among the estimators of ϕ.

(d) Some useful results:

$$\text{plim } (\hat{\phi}^2) = [\text{plim } (\hat{\phi})]^2$$

$$\text{plim } (\hat{\phi}^{-1}) = [\text{plim } (\hat{\phi})]^{-1}$$

REFERENCES

1. Robert L. Winkler and William L. Hays, Statistics - Probability, Inference, and Decision, Holt, Rinehart and Winston (New York), 1975, 2nd edition, pp. 334-43.
2. Jan Kmenta, Elements of Econometrics, Macmillan Publishing Co., (N.Y.), 1971, Chapter 6.
3. Arthur S. Goldberger, Econometric Theory, John Wiley and Sons, Inc., (N.Y.), 1964, pp. 115-135.
4. J. Johnson, Econometric Methods, McGraw-Hill Book Co., (N.Y.), 1972, 2nd ed., pp. 267-74.

APPENDIX F

CONFIDENCE INTERVALS AND HYPOTHESIS TESTING

It is quite obvious from Appendix D that a point estimate is seldom equal to the population parameter. However, if you have to quote one and only one number as representative of a population parameter, then that point estimate, which has those desirable properties enumerated in Appendix E, is generally the number to quote. Unfortunately, such a point estimate still does not give us any idea about the accuracy of estimation. Also, as pointed out earlier, the point estimate can be very sample-specific.

In order to account for the sampling error, we calculate an interval that is expected to contain the population parameter with a specified probability. To see a practical example, Table F.1 contains randomly generated[1] percentage daily stock price movements that are "known" to be normally distributed. Let us assume that we know the variance of such price movements (say $\sigma^2 = 2.25$ or $\sigma = 1.5$), but that the true mean μ is unknown! Let us now proceed to construct the confidence interval for the true mean μ.

We learned in Appendix C that

$$P[-1.96 \leq Z \leq 1.96] = p = 0.95 \qquad (F.1)$$

where p (=0.95) is called the confidence coefficient. For sampling distributions of sample means, Z is defined as (Appendix C)

$$Z = \frac{m - \mu}{\sigma/\sqrt{n}} \qquad (F\text{-}2)$$

where n is the number of observations making up the sample and m is the sample mean. So we can rewrite equation (F-1) as

$$P(-1.96 \leq \frac{m - \mu}{\sigma/\sqrt{n}} \leq 1.96) = 0.95$$

or

$$P(-1.96\frac{\sigma}{\sqrt{n}} \leq m - \mu \leq 1.96\frac{\sigma}{\sqrt{n}} = 0.95$$

[1]These numbers were generated using a computer, with μ=0 and σ = 1.5.

or

$$P(-m - 1.96\frac{\sigma}{\sqrt{n}} \leq -\mu \leq -m + 1.96\frac{\sigma}{\sqrt{n}}) = 0.95$$

Therefore,

$$P(m - 1.96\frac{\sigma}{\sqrt{n}} \leq \mu \leq m + 1.96\frac{\sigma}{\sqrt{n}}) = 0.95 \qquad \text{(F-3)}$$

So, for our stock price example, a 95% confidence interval for μ is

$$.09 - \frac{1.96\text{x}1.5}{\sqrt{16}} \leq \mu \leq .09 + \frac{1.96\text{x}1.5}{\sqrt{16}}$$

The classical interpretation of equation (F-3) is that the probability is 0.95 that the interval $m \pm 1.96\sigma/\sqrt{n}$ will include the true mean μ (that is, if such a calculation is made for many samples, 95% of the intervals would contain the true population mean). Similarly, other confidence intervals can be constructed for various levels of significance. In general, as shown in Fig. F.1, if

$$P(-h \leq Z \leq h) = p$$

then, $m \pm h\sigma/\sqrt{n}$ is a p% confidence interval for μ. $\alpha = (1 - p)$ is known as the significance level.

TABLE F.1

Hypothetical Data of Daily Stock Price Movements

Period	Change in Stock Price, (ΔP)%
1	-0.28
2	-1.54
3	.04
4	2.05
5	0.50
6	-0.05
7	0.86
8	-0.46
9	-1.98
10	1.43
11	-0.28
12	-0.35
13	-0.58
14	0.73
15	0.78
16	1.22

Mean $\overline{\Delta P}$ = 0.09
Standard deviation = 1.04

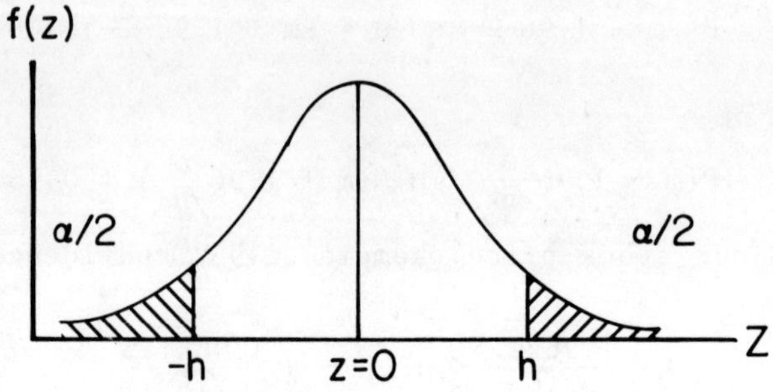

Figure F.1 $P[-h \leq Z \leq h] = p = 1 - \alpha$

HYPOTHESIS TESTING:

Sample data are often gathered to test a belief about the population parameters. For instance, you might hypothesize that "...the population mean of the daily stock price changes is zero." The hypothesis that one sets out to test is called the <u>null</u> hypothesis, denoted by H_0. The competing hypothesis, pitted against the null hypothesis, called the alternative hypothesis (H_1). Typically, there are two kinds of hypotheses:

$\mu = 0$ exact

$\mu \geq 0$ inexact

To test such hypotheses, there are two common types of significance tests, that will be widely used in the text. We will illustrate each below. To provide data for our illustration, we again use the results on daily stock movements from the previous section i.e. $m = .09$, $\sigma = 1.5$ and $n = 16$ to aid in our illustrations.

<u>Two-tail Test</u>:

Let us say that we have

$$H_0 : \mu = 0$$

$$H_1 : \mu \neq 0$$

Does the sample estimate of μ, $m = .09$, support the null hypothesis? Or, is the value of m so grossly different from $\mu = 0$ that we are "confident" that we should reject H_0? For a moment, let us accept the hypothesis that $\mu = 0$. Then we can find a value 'g' such that

$$P\left(\left|\frac{m-\mu}{\sigma/\sqrt{n}}\right| \leq g\right) = 1 - \alpha$$

or equivalently,

$$P\left(-g \leq \frac{m - \mu}{\sigma/\sqrt{n}} \leq g\right) = 1 - \alpha$$

or $$P(\mu - g\sigma/\sqrt{n} \leq m \leq \mu + g\sigma/\sqrt{n}) = 1 - \alpha$$

The above equation suggests that we will accept the null hypothesis if m falls within the interval $(\mu \pm g\sigma/\sqrt{n})$, i.e., the "Acceptance Region" (Figure F.2). Returning to our example (Table F.1), $\mu = 0$, $\sigma = 1.5$, $n = 16$, and using $\alpha = .05$, then the corresponding 95% confidence coefficient would be $g = 1.96$ (Table 1 Appendix N). Hence, the acceptance region is $(0 \pm \frac{1.96 \times 1.5}{16})$ or (-0.735 to + 0.735). Since the sample mean is .09, we accept the null hypothesis with 95% confidence. Similarly, it is common to test whether the estimator is significantly different than the null hypothesis, and this can be done by the test statistic $\frac{m-0}{\sigma/\sqrt{n}}$, and if this is greater than 1.96 then signficant difference is concluded at the 5% significance level.

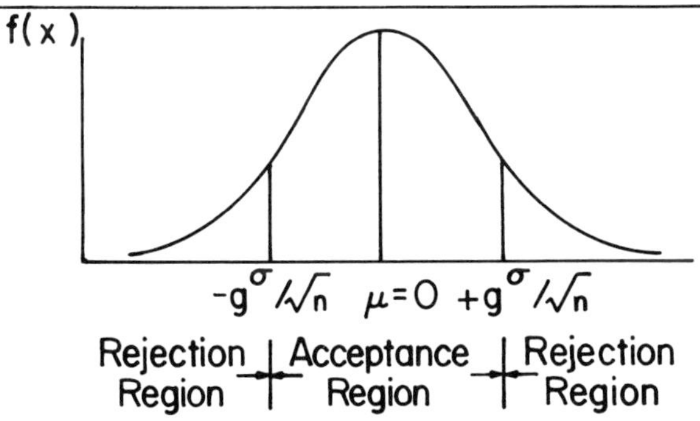

Figure F.2 Two Tail Test

Unfortunately, it is often forgotten that the above only considers the Type I error--viz., rejecting a true hypothesis. That is, the above test insured that the null hypothesis would not be rejected more than 5% of the time if it were correct. What if the true mean were only slightly different than zero--say $\mu_t = 0.001$. In such a case, the probability of accepting the false null hypothesis ($H_0: \mu = 0$) will be almost 95%!!! Thus, <u>for a given sample size</u>, the smaller the Type I error, the larger the

Type II error. While we will generally ignore the Type II error, readers should realize that the null hypothesis should be stated in such a way that its acceptance will insure against later problems in methodology. We find an easy way to remember the odd implications of these errors is to note that, while all "random walk" studies have found "no significant difference" between managed portfolios and randomly selected ones, this result would be expected in about 95% of the studies if the true difference were very small, say ¼%!!

One-tail Test

A one-tail test arises if we have the following sort of hypothesis before us:

$$H_0: \ \mu \geq 0$$

In this case we will be looking for a cutoff point (g) such that (see Figure F.3)

$$P\left(\frac{m - \mu}{\sigma/\sqrt{n}} \leq g\right) = 1 - \alpha$$

In other words, we will accept the hypothesis if

$$P(m \leq g\sigma/\sqrt{n} + \mu) = 1 - \alpha$$

Let us now test the null hypothesis: $\mu = 0$ at a significance level $\alpha = .15$ with $m = 0.09$, $\sigma = 1.5$, $n = \sqrt{16}$. Referring to Table 1, (Appendix N) we observe that $g = 1.04$, so that $\mu + g\sigma/\sqrt{n} = 0 + 1.04 \times \frac{1.5}{\sqrt{16}} = 0.39$; that is, since the sample mean $m = 0.09$, we accept the null hypothesis at $\alpha = 0.15$.

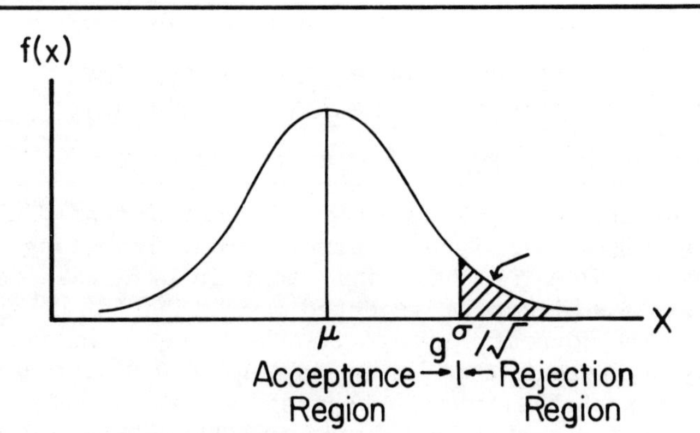

Figure F.3 One Tail Test

THE CHI-SQUARE DISTRIBUTION

The Chi Square distribution is an interesting extension of our previous discussion of the normal distribution. Recall the standardized random variable Z, which was normally distributed with a mean of zero and a standard deviation of 1 (i.e., $Z \sim N(0,1)$). For this variable, calculate the sum of n observations, with each observation squared--e.g.,

$$\chi_n^2 = \sum_{i=1}^{n} Z_i^2 \qquad \text{(G-1)}$$

where each Z_i is the individual observation from the standardized normal distribution. This statistic has certain intriguing properties, as shown both below and in the next Appendix (Appendix H: "Goodness of Fit Tests").

Let us begin by hypothesizing the following example: A financial analyst feels strongly that the price of a particular stock is normally distributed with a mean of \$23.70 and a price variation of within \$8--95% of the time. He takes observations of the price data for 17 days and finds that the variance, $\hat{s}^2 = 4.25$. We ask ourselves, does the estimated variance support or deny the analyst's claim?

Implicitly, our analyst has hypothesized that $\sigma^2 = 4$. Referring to the rule of thumb stated in Appendix C, the range of \$8 (over 95% of the observations) represents a spread of 4σ. Hence $\sigma = \$2$, and $(n-1) = 16$. Thus we want to test whether his hypothesis of $\sigma^2 = 4$ is likely, given the sample result of $\hat{s}^2 = 4.25$. Unfortunately, the tests in Appendix C using the normal distribution do not apply here. Such tests require that we know the population variance. But, for the problem at hand, we assume that the mean is given and testing of the variance happens to be the center of focus. All we have is the sample variance $\hat{s}^2$ to draw inferences from.

As was shown in Appendix E, the adjusted sample variance $\hat{s}^2$ is an unbiased estimator of the population variances σ^2, i.e., $E(\hat{s}^2) = \sigma^2$. In repeated sampling, the variance of the estimator would be:

$$V(\hat{s}^2) = \frac{2\sigma^4}{(n-1)} \qquad \text{(G-2)}$$

Thus, the estimate, $\hat{s}^2$, is itself distributed[1], conditioned on the true population variance σ^2 and the sample size n. This makes it difficult for us to compute the cumulative probabilities for a given s^2.

As was done with the normal distribution, we obtain a standardized variable; instead of the z statistic, here 'Chi-Square' is used. Because χ^2 is defined by the sum of standardized random variables in equation G-1, it can be shown that it can also be defined as

$$\chi^2_{n-1} = \frac{(n-1)\hat{s}^2}{\sigma^2} \qquad \text{(G-3)}$$

The chi-square distribution is skewed to the right, Fig (G.1), for small samples and becomes more symmetric for larger samples. Table 2 (Appendix N) shows the χ^2 values for various significance levels, and degrees of freedom v, (v = n-1).

Now the stage is set to test the analyst's claim of $\sigma = 2$ with v = 16 and $s^2 = 4.25$. The corresponding χ^2 -statistic is

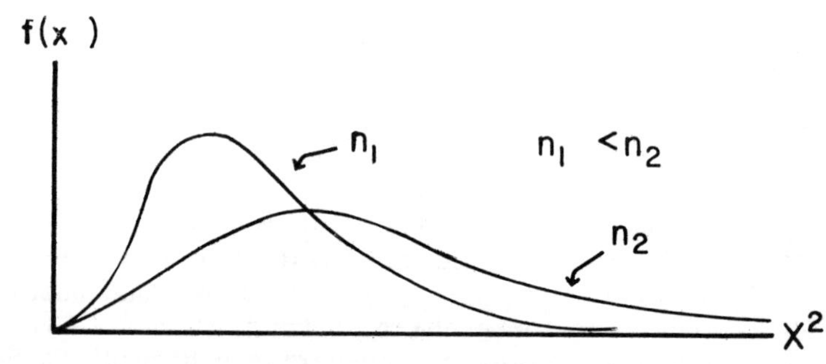

Figure G.1. Chi Square Distribution for n_1 and n_2 Degrees of Freedom

$$\chi^2 = \frac{16*4.25}{4} = 17.0$$

---

[1]This pertains to the sampling distributions of the variance estimator. See Appendix D for an insight into sampling distributions of means.

To evaluate the analyst's claim, let us test the null hypothesis,

$$H_0: \sigma^2 = 4$$

against the alternative

$$H_1: \sigma^2 > 4$$

This would require a one-tailed test, referring to Table 2 we see that for v = 16 and a significance level $\alpha = .05$, $\chi^2 = 26.29$. The computed χ^2 value is 17.0 and is well within the acceptance region of $0 \leq 26.29$, see Figure G.2, thereby supporting the analyst's contention.

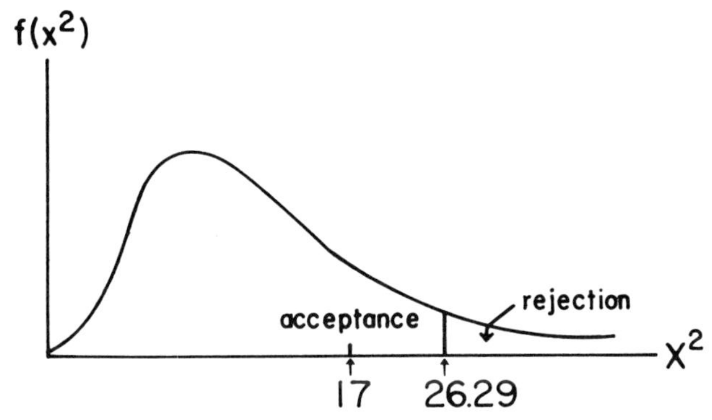

Figure G.2. Graphical Representation of χ^2 Decision

REFERENCES

1. William Mendenhall, Introduction to Probability and Statistics, Duxburg Press (Mass.), 1975, 4th ed., pp. 232-37.

2. Robert L. Winkler and William Hays, Statistics-Probability, Inference and Decision, Holt, Rinehart and Winston (N.Y.), 1975, 2nd ed., pp. 375-80, 453-55.

APPENDIX H

GOODNESS OF FIT TESTS

In Appendix C, we assumed that the distribution of stock returns (Table C.1) could be assumed to come from a normal distribution. But, "Do the data provide enough evidence to justify such an assumption?"

Such a question can be answered by applying 'goodness of fit tests' to the sample data. The general procedure is:

(a) Formulate a null hypothesis about the distribution of the sample data.
(b) Classify the data (n observations in all) into several intervals (i = 1, 2,...k), and calculate the actual observed frequencies (Θ_i) falling under each interval.
(c) Compute estimates of population parameters for the distribution assumed in (a), say ℓ such estimates.
(d) Assuming that the null hypothesis is correct, calculate the expected frequencies e_i for each interval.
(e) Calculate the test statistic

$$\sum_{i=1}^{k} \frac{(\Theta_i - e_i)^2}{e_i}$$

whose distribution, for large samples, approximates the chi-square distribution (Appendix G). Thus, for large samples,

$$\sum_{i=1}^{k} \frac{(\Theta_i - e_i)^2}{e_i} \sim \chi^2_{k-\ell-1}$$

where $(k-\ell-1)$ = degrees of freedom associated with the chi-square distribution of the test statistic.

(f) Specify a decision criterion; accept or reject the null hypothesis following such criterion. It is essential that $k \geq 5$, and $e_i \geq 5$ for the test to prove satisfactory.

To apply the general procedure to a specific problem, let us test whether we can assume that the monthly returns of a particular stock are normally distributed (null hypothesis). Table H.1 contains the monthly return data (R_j,

$j=1, 2,\ldots n$) for $n = 240$ months, classified into intervals (Column #2) with the corresponding observed frequencies (Θ_i) in Column #3. The histogram showing the grouped distribution of stock returns is shown in Figure H.1. We know from Appendix C that the population normal distribution is characterized by two population parameters, the mean and variance. Obviously, the population parameters are not known. So, we estimate them by using the sample data as follows:

$$\text{Sample Mean} = m = \frac{\sum_{j=1}^{n} R_j}{n} = \frac{351.4}{240} = 1.5$$

and

$$\text{Sample Variance} = \hat{s}^2 = \frac{\sum_{j=1}^{n}(R_j - m)^2}{n-1} = \frac{9450}{239} = 39.54$$

and the sample standard deviation is $\hat{s} = 6.3$.

Now to calculate the expected frequencies, we set out in the following manner. Let us take the first interval (-11.99 -10.00). The same interval can be written into terms of standardized values as

$$\frac{-11.99-1.5}{6.3}, \frac{-10.0-1.5}{6.3} = 2.14, -1.83.$$ [1]

Then by using equations (C.4a) and (C.6), the cumulative probability of returns within this interval is

$$P_{i=1}\ (-2.14 \leq -1.83) = F(2.14)-F(1.83)$$

$$= .4838 - .4664 = .0174$$

from the table of Cumulative Standard Normal Probabilities (Table 1). Then, the expected frequency for any interval can be calculated using the formula $e_i = P_i x\ n$, and hence, $e_i = .0174 \times 240 = 4.18$.

Column #4 shows these expected frequencies for each one of the intervals, and Column #5 contains the corresponding $(\Theta_i - e_i)^2/e_i$. By following the above-mentioned

[1]Recall from Appendix C that $Z = X_i - \mu/\sigma$.

TABLE H.1

CHI SQUARE TEST FOR NORMALITY OF STOCK RETURNS

INTERVAL CODE	STOCK RETURNS, INTERVALS	ACTUAL FREQUENCY	EXPECTED FREQUENCY, e_i	$\frac{(\Theta_i - e_i)}{e_i}$
1	-11.99 to -10.00	8	4.18	3.49
2	- 9.99 to - 8.00	6	8.59	0.78
3	- 7.99 to - 6.00	5	11.42	3.61
4	- 5.99 to - 4.00	26	18.05	3.50
5	- 3.99 to - 2.00	21	22.92	0.16
6	- 1.99 to 0.00	40	28.20	4.94
7	0.01 to 2.00	24	30.41	1.35
8	2.01 to 4.00	32	29.64	0.19
9	4.01 to 6.00	27	25.37	0.10
10	6.01 to 8.00	18	20.98	0.42
11	8.01 to 10.00	14	15.12	0.08
12	10.01 to 12.00	7	9.84	0.83
13	12.01 to 14.00	5	5.66	0.08
14	14.01 to 16.00	3	3.17	0.01
15	16.01 to 18.00	4	1.51	4.11
				$\chi^2 = 23.65$

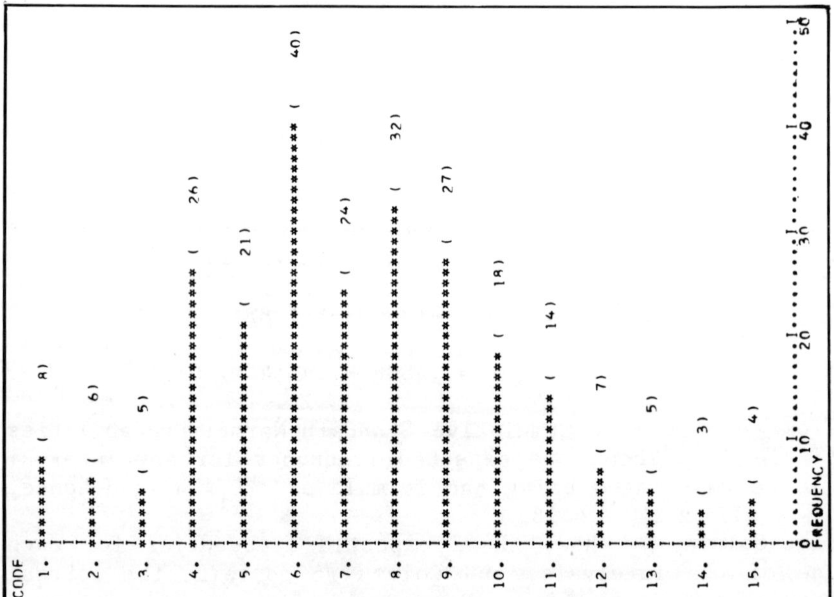

Figure H.1. Histogram of Stock Returns

method, the χ^2 - statistic is seen to be 23.65. Thus, assuming a significance level of 0.01 (decision criteria), χ^2_{12} value from Table 2 is 26.2, and the null hypothesis of no significant difference between the assumed and actual distribution is not rejected at the .01 level of significance since χ^2-calculated $<$ χ^2-theoretical, (i.e., $23.65 < 26.2$).

Obviously, the above procedure can be applied to any probability distribution. As such, goodness-of-fit tests by the χ^2 statistic are a very adaptable procedure.

APPENDIX I

t and F Distributions and Their Relation to the Chi-square distribution

t-DISTRIBUTION

While testing hypotheses concerning means, we have assumed that the variance of the population σ^2 is known--but such an assumption may be questionable. To fully account for such an assumption, let us define a statistic called the 't-statistic' which parallels the Z-statistic of the standard normal distribution (where σ^2 is known):

$$t = \frac{m-\mu}{\hat{\sigma}_m} = \frac{m-\mu}{\hat{s}/\sqrt{n}} \qquad \text{(I-1)}$$

where m is the sample mean of the variable $\tilde{x}$, μ is the population mean, from (Appendix D),

$$\hat{s}^2 = \frac{\Sigma(x_i-m)^2}{(n-1)}$$

and $\hat{s}$ is approximate equal to $\sqrt{\hat{s}^2}$.

How, then, is the t-statistic distributed? Rewriting (I.1) as

$$t = \frac{(m-\mu)\sqrt{n}}{\sqrt{\hat{s}^2}}$$

and rearranging the expression by introducing both the population variance σ^2 and an (n-1) term, without affecting the equality we get,

$$t = \frac{(m-\mu)/(\sigma/\sqrt{n})}{\sqrt{(n-1)\ s^2/(n-1)\sigma^2}}$$
$$= \sqrt{(n-1)}Z/\sqrt{\chi^2_{n-1}} \qquad \text{(I-2)}$$

from equation G-3.

But why should one go through all this mathematical juggling? Just to see that the t-statistic is indeed a ratio of the Z to χ^2-statistics with (n-1) degrees of freedom, and thus to understand the theoretical underpinnings of the distribution for the t-statistic, which goes by the name of 't-distribution'. Similar to the normal distribution, the cumulative probabilities of the t-distribution are also conveniently tabulated (Appendix N, Table 3). With increasing sample size, the t-distribution tends to the normal distribution, as would be expected from examination of the terms in I-2.

To see how this distribution is used, recall that in Appendix F, the sample mean of the randomly generated stock price movements was 0.09 and the sample standard deviation was 1.0. To test whether the population mean is significantly different from zero (H_o: $\mu=0$), we compute the t statistic as:

$$t = \frac{.09-0}{1.0/\sqrt{16}} = 0.36$$

Referring to the Table 3 of t-values for 15 degrees of freedom and a 95% confidence level, we find, for a two-tailed test, t = 2.131, which is far greater than the t value calculated from the sample. Thus, we cannot reject the null hypothesis that the mean μ is equal to zero.

F-Distribution

The foregoing section illustrated that the t statistic could be viewed as a ratio whose numerator contained the standard normalized Z, while the denominator contained χ^2 which adjusted for the difference between the sample versus population variance. This section illustrates that the F statistic is a ratio of two χ^2, thereby measuring the relationship between two sample variances adjusted for their relation to their population variance.

To see how this ratio is used, assume that we have gathered the following data about two stocks, stock P and stock Q.

$n_p = 25 \qquad n_q = 16$

$\hat{s}_p^2 = 15 \qquad \hat{s}_q^2 = 6$

$m_p = m_q = 15\%$

where n_p and n_q are the sample sizes of stock returns. Suppose now that we want to compare the "riskiness" of P versus Q, and that we define riskiness by their respective variances. That is, given that the stocks P and Q have approximately the same historic mean returns, $E(R_p) = E(R_q)$, $(m_p = m_q)$, a risk averse person would be expected to opt for the one with lower variance,[1] thereby reducing his(her) risk. For instance, if the returns of stock P showed significantly higher variance than stock Q, then stock Q would be the natural choice. Thus, we have set the stage to test the hypothesis

$$H_o: \sigma_P^2 = \sigma_Q^2$$

versus

$$H_A: \sigma_p^2 > \sigma_q^2$$

If σ_p^2 were equal to σ_q^2, one will be indifferent to the choice of stocks.

In the absence of information about the population variances of stock returns, we resort to using the sample variances $\hat{s}_p^2$ and $\hat{s}_q^2$ as estimates for σ_p^2 and σ_q^2 respectively. An appropriate test statistic in this case would be the ratio $\hat{s}_p^2/\hat{s}_q^2$. If the null hypothesis were to hold, this ratio would tend to unity as the sample sizes become larger. Before we can make any statements for or against the hypothesis, we have to know the sampling distribution of $\hat{s}_p^2/\hat{s}_q^2$. If the null hypothesis is valid, then $\sigma_p^q/\sigma_q^2 = 1$. Hence dividing the numerator of the test statistic by σ_p^2 and the denominator by σ_q^2 should not really affect the statistic, i.e.,

$$\frac{\hat{s}_p^2}{\hat{s}_q^2} = \frac{(\hat{s}_p^2/\sigma_p^2)}{(\hat{s}_q^2/\sigma_q^2)}$$

Rewriting this to include the sample size (but without changing the values) this expression is

$$\frac{(n_p-1)\hat{s}_p^2/(n_p-1)\sigma_p^2}{(n_q-1)\hat{s}_q^2/(n_q-1)\sigma_q^2}$$

The net result of these manipulations is that the test statistic, $\hat{s}_p^2/\hat{s}_q^2$, under the condition that the null hypothesis is true, is a ratio of two independent chi-square distributions with two parameters (n_p-1) and (n_q-1), which is the F-distribution.

[1]We are ignoring the covariance impact for expository convenience.

We write this as,

$$\frac{\hat{s}_p^2}{\hat{s}_q^2} \sim F_{n_p - 1,\; n_q - 1}$$

Tables 4.a and 4.b give the boundary values for the F-distribution for 5% and 1% level of significance for a one tail test.

Returning to our previous example, let us complete the test statistic

$$F = \frac{\hat{s}_p^2}{\hat{s}_q^2} = \frac{15}{6} = 2.5$$

Referring to the F-Tables (4.a and 4.b), the values for two different levels of significance (i.e., $\alpha = 0.05$ and $\alpha = 0.01$) are

$$F_{.05,24,15} = 2.29$$

$$F_{.01,24,15} = 3.29$$

So, if one were to allow a signifiance level of 5%, the null hypothesis is rejected whereas for a 1% level it is accepted. This example illustrates the fact that depending upon the level of significance that one is willing to assume, the conclusions may vary; obviously, the choice of a significance level should always be based upon the consequences of an erroneous decision.

As can be seen from the above, the F ratio tests the ratio of two variances. As such it is the basis for (ANOVA) tests. Also, as shown in the text, it can be used to test the significance of a sample coefficient of determination (R^2), which itself is a ratio of the variance explained by a regression equation divided by the total variance. In general, it is useful for testing the significance of difference between any two sample variances.

APPENDIX J

MAXIMUM LIKELIHOOD ESTIMATION

One of the questions that may haunt security analysts is, "What is the probability that the price of a stock will go up tomorrow?" One might be tempted to say "0.5" (considering two states, up or down), in the absence of any historical data about the stock. But, if we do have the necessary historical data, is it at all possible for us to come up with a more statistically reliable estimate of the probability that the stock price would rise? Certainly, and this is where the maximum likelihood (ML) estimation procedure comes in very handy.

In general terms, let us say we can postulate the distribution of a random variable (e.g., price changes, stock returns) in terms of a population parameter ϕ, (for example, $\phi = .5$) which is assumed to be an unknown. Let us now draw a sample of n observations, $(Z_1, Z_2, \ldots, Z_n)$ for a given value of ϕ. We can depict the probability density ("likelihood") as $L(Z_1, Z_2, \ldots, Z_n \mid \phi)$, given the sample information $(Z_1, Z_2, \ldots, Z_n)$.

With this much of background information, let us resume with our stock price example. Suppose ΔP is the change in the stock price, and let p be the probability that the stock price goes up. Assuming that the stock price can only go up or down (dichotomous event), we can describe the stock price movements (changes) by the binomial distribution. If, out the n sample observations available, we have m cases where the stock prices actually went up, then we can write the binomial distribution of ΔP as

$$L\ (\Delta P_1, \Delta P_2, \ \ldots, \ \Delta P_n \mid p) = \binom{n}{m} p^m (1-p)^{n-m} \qquad (J.1)$$

for a given value of p^1. To set the perspective of our example in line with the general method of ML we see,

$$Z \leftrightarrow \Delta P$$

$$\phi \leftrightarrow p$$

So then, to obtain the ML estimate of p, we will maximize L $(\Delta P_1, \Delta P_2, \ldots, \Delta P_n \mid p)$ with respect to p. Rewriting (J-1) as,

---

[1] $\binom{n}{m} = \frac{n!}{m!(n-m)!}$, where $n! = n(n-1)(n-2)\ldots.(2)(1)$.

$$L = \binom{n}{m} p^m (1-p)^{n-m}$$

Taking logarithms on both sides $\ln L = \ln \binom{n}{m} + m \ln p + (n-m) \ln (1-p)$. Then, using simple calculus to maximize lnL with respect to p[2]

$$\left.\frac{d \ln L}{dp}\right|_{p=p*} = \frac{m}{p*} - \frac{n-m}{1-p*} = 0$$

where p* will be the value of p which maximizes the likelihood function. Hence, it is easily seen that the ML estimate of p is p* = m/n. In other words, the ML probability that the price would rise is just the proportion of price increases in the sample.

The above result seems incredibly intuitive, and thus one is led to ask, "Why all the fuss about maximum likelihood." The answer is ML estimators can be shown to have the desirable properties of efficiency and consistency, although they are not necessarily unbiased in small samples (as can be shown by the fact that the ML estimate of σ^2 is biased). Additionally, this method has the intuitive appeal of providing an estimator which has the greatest relative chance ("likelihood") of being the population parameter of the process which generated the sample sequence.

An Example For Those Wanting To Go A Little Farther

In contrast to the simple Binomial distribution example above, examples can be easily developed for estimators of the parameters for distributions such as the Normal distribution, i.e., the estimators of μ, σ. Also, as the derivation below shows, if the error terms in a regression are assumed normally distributed, then the ML estimators are the same as the OLS estimators.

To see that the ML and OLS regression estimators are the same when normally distributed error terms are assumed, recall that, in Chapter 2, we assumed that $E(u_t) = 0$, $E(u_t^2)$

---

[2]Irrespective of whether we maximize ln L or L, we will have the same value of p=p*, for which both ln L and L attain their maximum; this is because the logarithmic transformation is a strictly monotonically increasing function of L.

Also note,

$$\frac{d \ln y}{dx} = \frac{1}{y}\frac{dy}{dx}$$

$= \sigma_u^2$ and u_t were independently and normally distributed. Observing that $u_t = R_{jt} - \alpha - \beta R_{mt}$, we can write the likelihood function as

$$L(u_1, u_2, \ldots, u_n | \alpha, \beta, \sigma_u^2) = \frac{1}{(\sigma_u^2 2\Pi)^{n/2}} \exp \left[-\frac{1}{2\sigma_u^2} \Sigma (R_{jt} - \alpha - \beta R_{mt})^2 \right]$$

Taking natural logarithms,

$$\ln L = -\frac{n}{2} \ln 2\pi - \frac{n}{2} \ln \sigma_u^2 - \frac{1}{2\sigma_u^2} \Sigma(R_{jt} - \alpha - \beta R_{mt})^2$$

We can maximize lnL (which is equivalent to maximizing L) by partially differentiating with the parameters α, β and σ_u^2 independently, i.e.,

$$\frac{\partial \ln L}{\partial \alpha} = \frac{1}{\sigma_u^2} \Sigma(R_{jt} - \alpha - \beta R_{mt}) = 0 \text{ [using } \frac{\partial(ay^n)}{\partial X} = any^{n-1} \frac{\partial y}{\partial x}$$

$$\frac{\partial \ln L}{\partial \beta} = \frac{1}{\sigma_u^2} \Sigma (R_{jt} - \alpha - \beta R_{mt}) R_{mt} = 0$$

$$\frac{\partial \ln L}{\partial \sigma_u^2} = \frac{n}{2\sigma_u^2} + \frac{1}{2\sigma_u^4} \Sigma(R_{jt} - \alpha - \beta X_i)^2 = 0 \text{ [using } \frac{\partial(\ln y)}{\partial x} = \frac{1}{y} \frac{\partial y}{\partial x}\text{]}$$

Solving the above three equations simultaneously we get the ML estimates of α, β, and σ_u^2 as

$$a = \frac{\Sigma R_{jt} \; \Sigma R_{mt}^2 - \Sigma R_{mt} \; \Sigma r_{mt} \; R_{jt}}{n \; \Sigma R_{mt}^2 - (\Sigma R_{mt})^2}$$

$$b = \frac{n \; \Sigma R_{mt} \; R_{jt} - \Sigma R_{jt} \; \Sigma R_{mt}}{n \Sigma R_{mt}^2 - (\Sigma R_{mt})^2}$$

$$\hat{\sigma}_u^2 = \frac{1}{n} \Sigma(R_{jt} - a - bR_{mt})^2$$

A Useful Tool--The Likelihood Ratio

The above discussion has been directed at using the likelihood function to derive formulas for parameter estimation. Another use is to construct a ratio of two likelihood functions as a vehicle for hypothesis testing. This principle, developed by Neyman and Pearson (1928), can be shown to be the basis for many other hypothesis tests, and as such is quite general.

Let us present an example that applies to the discussion in the preceding subsection about OLS estimators. Suppose you hypothesized that $0 \leq \alpha \leq 1$, $0 \leq \beta \leq 1$ and $0 < \sigma_u^2 \leq 100$. Then assume that you maximized $L(u_1, u_2, \ldots, u_n | \alpha_H, \beta_H, \sigma^2_u)$ where H_0 indicates that $\hat{\alpha}_H$, $\hat{\beta}_H$, and $\hat{\sigma}_u^2$ are constrained as hypothesized above. The likelihood ratio (LR) would test how "close" the above likelihood function was after its parameters were chosen (via a constrained nonlinear optimization method) compared to an unconstrained likelihood function; that is, the likelihood ratio (λ) is

$$\lambda = \frac{\text{Max } L(\alpha,\beta,\ldots.) \text{ where } (\alpha,\beta,\ldots.) \text{ are specified by } H_0}{\text{Max } L(\alpha,\beta,\ldots.) \text{ where } (\alpha,\beta,\ldots.) \text{ are unconstrained}}$$

Since the denominator can use any values of α, β, and σ_u^2 to enlarge $L(\cdot)$, the numerator must be less than the denominator, i.e., $0 \leq \lambda \leq 1$. Further, it can be proven that the value of $(-2 \cdot \ln\lambda)$ will be distributed, in large samples, according to a χ^2 distribution with the degrees of freedom equal to the number of hypothesized parameters in the numerator's function. Thus, it is possible to test whether value the estimated parameters in the denominator produce a likelihood function which is so much greater than the value for the numerator that one should reject the hypothesis that the sample could have come from a population with the hypothesized parameters.

More generally, likelihood functions are often examined for comparative purposes. For example, suppose that you thought that you had a powerful technique for obtaining accurate estimates of α, β and σ_u^2 when certain types of autocorrelation were present. You might compare the power of your procedure versus ordinary-least-squares estimation by calculating the values of the likelihood functions for the parameters estimated by each procedure. Another example of comparison is illustrated in a study where Rogalski and Vinso (1978) compared likelihood functions based upon a Student t-distribution and a symmetric stable distribution in order to determine which provided a better description of changes in foreign exchange rates.

REFERENCES

1. Richard Rogalski and Joseph D. Vinso, "Empirical Properties of Foreign Exchange Rates," Journal of International Business Studies, Fall 1978, pp. 69-80.

2. Taro Yamane, "Mathematics for Economists: An Elementary Survey," Prentice-Hall, Inc., (N.J.), 1962, pp. 444-49, pp. 475-479.

3. Thomas H. Wonnacott and Ronald J. Wonnacott, "Introductory Statistics for Business and Economics," John Wiley and Sons, Inc. (New York), 1972, Chapter 18.

APPENDIX K:

THE COCHRANE-ORCUTT PROCEDURE FOR AUTOCORRELATION

When autocorrelation is present, estimates of the linear models parameters (α and β) will be unbiased and consistent, but not efficient. Econometric literature abounds with methods that provide efficient estimators in the presence of autocorrelation [see Gujarati (1978) for an excellent introduction, as well as Maddala (1977) for a survey], and we choose to present a classic one proposed by Cochrane and Orcutt (1949). This procedure is known as the quasi-first-difference method.

Consider the model

$$R_{jt} = \alpha + \beta R_{mt} + u_t \qquad \text{(K-1)}$$

where it is assumed that

$$u_t = \rho u_{t-1} + \varepsilon_t \qquad \text{(K-2)}$$

and ε_t is assumed to follow the spherical assumptions, α and β are the usual population parameters to be estimated, but is has been assumed that there is some <u>one-period</u> correlation (ρ) between successive error terms in the original model. Because such one period autocorrelation causes inefficient estimators, we must transform equation (K-1) to permit an independently distributed error term.

To transform (K-1) to an equation without autocorrelation, simply first difference it by the correlation coefficient ρ, as shown below. First, merely write (K-1) for period t-1 as

$$R_{j,t-1} = \alpha + \beta R_{m,t-1} + u_{t-1} \qquad \text{(K-3)}$$

Then, multiplying both sides by ρ, we get

$$\rho R_{j,t-1} = \rho\alpha + \rho\beta R_{m,t-1} + \rho u_{t-1} \qquad \text{(K-4)}$$

And subtracting equation (K-4) from equation (K-1) gives

$$(R_{jt} - \rho R_{j,t-1}) = \alpha(1-\rho) + \beta(R_{mt} - \rho R_{m,t-1}) + (u_t - \rho u_{t-1})$$

This latter equation then contains an uncorrelated error term by equation (K-2)

$$(R_{jt} - \rho R_{j,t-1}) = \alpha(1-\rho) + \beta(R_{mt} - \rho R_{m,t-1}) + \varepsilon_t \qquad \text{(K-5)}$$

Denoting $(R_{jt} - \rho R_{j,t-1}) = R^*_{jt}$, $(R_{mt} - \rho R_{m,t-1}) = R^*_{mt}$, $\alpha(1-\rho) = A$ and $\beta = B$ equation (K-5) can be written as:

$$R^*_{jt} = A + BR^*_{mt} + \varepsilon_t \qquad \text{(K-6)}$$

Assuming that ρ can be estimated R^*_{jt} and R^*_{mt} can be computed. This is followed by regressing R^*_{jt} on R^*_{mt}. The estimates of the intercept and slope of equation (K-6) can now be used to calculate the estimates of α and β in equation (K-1) which is the model we started out with:

$$\hat{\alpha} = \frac{\hat{A}}{1-\hat{\rho}}$$

and

$$\hat{\beta} = \hat{B}$$

Unfortunately, ρ is not known, and must be estimated. Several methods have been proposed for this, including the iterative one by Cochrane and Orcutt. They suggest that ρ be estimated from the OLS residuals such that

$$\hat{\rho} = \frac{\Sigma\, e_t e_{t-1}}{\Sigma\, e^2_{t-1}}$$

This is done repeatedly, the first time from equation (K-1), then later from equation (K-6). The procedure is continued until successive estimates of ρ are not changing substantially. Of course, such an iterative procedure may be computationally costly and sensitive to local optima, and thus other procedures (Durbin, Hildreth-Lu, and so on) have been developed as discussed in the above references.

APPENDIX L:

MATRIX ALGEBRA - WHERE 'SYMBOLISM' IS THE WORD!

Matrix Notations, Operations, and Definitions.

Consider the following linear relation:

$$Y = \beta_1 X_1 + \beta_2 X_2 + \beta_3 X_3 + \ldots \beta_m x_m + u$$

where Y, for example, may be the return on a stock, which is posited to be a function of market and firm related variables X_1 through X_m (e.g., market index, dividend yield, earning variability and so on). Suppose there are n observations for each variable; then, the functional relationship should hold good for each one of the n sets of observations:

$$\begin{aligned}
Y_1 &= \beta_1 X_{11} + \beta_2 X_{21} + \beta_3 X_{31} + \ldots + \beta_m X_{mi} + u_1 \\
Y_2 &= \beta_1 X_{12} + \beta_2 X_{22} + \beta_3 X_{32} + \ldots + \beta_m X_{m2} + u_2 \\
&\vdots \\
Y_j &= \beta_i X_{1j} + \beta_{2j} X_{3j} + \beta_3 X_{3j} + \ldots + \beta_m X_{mj} + u_j \\
&\vdots \\
Y_n &= \beta_1 X_{1n} + \beta_2 X_{2n} + \beta_3 X_{3n} + \ldots + \beta_m X_{mn} + u_n
\end{aligned}$$

Obviously, we need a more compact, yet powerful, way to represent such cumbersome equations.

Matrix notation provides a simplified way to depict the above set of equations as:

$$Y = XB + u$$

A matrix is a rectangular array of elements in rows or columns; e.g.,

Columns

$$X = \begin{bmatrix} X_{11} & X_{21} & X_{31} \cdots & X_{m1} \\ X_{12} & X_{22} & X_{32} \cdots & X_{m2} \\ \vdots & \vdots & \vdots & \vdots \\ X_{1j} & X_{2j} & X_{3j} \cdots & X_{mj} \\ \vdots & \vdots & \vdots & \vdots \\ X_{1n} & X_{2n} & X_{3n} \cdots & X_{mn} \end{bmatrix} \quad \text{rows}$$

$$Y = \begin{bmatrix} Y_1 \\ Y_2 \\ . \\ . \\ . \\ Y_n \end{bmatrix} \qquad u = \begin{bmatrix} u_1 \\ u_2 \\ . \\ . \\ . \\ u_n \end{bmatrix} \qquad B = (B_1 B_2 \ldots B_n)$$

X is said to be a matrix of order n x m, where n is the number of rows and m, the number of columns (generally, the row subscript is written first, but the reverse was done above to keep symmetry with the foregoing set of equations). Matrices such as Y and u which are of order (nx1) are called column vectors, and matrices of order (1xm) such as B are called row vectors.

a. Matrix Addition

Two matrices Q and R can be added if, and only if, they are of the same order. The corresponding elements of Q and R are added to obtain the new matrix S. i.e., S = Q + R => ($s_{ij} + q_{ij} + r_{ij}$ for all i,j).

$$Q = \begin{bmatrix} 7 & -9 \\ 5 & 2 \end{bmatrix} \qquad R = \begin{bmatrix} -1 & 4 \\ 3 & 9 \end{bmatrix}$$

Hence,

$$S = \begin{bmatrix} 7-1 & -9+4 \\ 5+3 & 2+9 \end{bmatrix} = \begin{bmatrix} 6 & -5 \\ 8 & 11 \end{bmatrix}$$

b. Matrix Multiplication

Although matrix addition is much like simple arithmetic, matrix multiplication has its own unique definition. If Q is a matrix of order (nxm) and R is a matrix of order (mxk) then, the matrix that results from the product S=QR is a matrix of n x k. The elements of S are defined by

$$s_{ij} = \sum_{l=1}^{m} q_{il} \times r_{lj} \qquad \begin{array}{l} i = 1,2,\ldots,n \\ j = 1,2,\ldots,k \end{array}$$

The primary condition for matrix multiplication is that number of columns in the first matrix (Q) should be equal to the number of rows in the second matrix (R). S has as many rows as in Q and as many columns as in R.

For example,

$$Q = \begin{bmatrix} 5 & 7 & 0 \\ -4 & 2 & 1 \end{bmatrix} \qquad R = \begin{bmatrix} 8 & 7 & 5 \\ 5 & 1 & -2 \\ -3 & 0 & 2 \end{bmatrix}$$

$$S = QR = \begin{matrix} (5x8 + 7x5 + 0x(-3) & (5x7 + 7x1 + 0x0) \\ (5x5 + 7x(-2) + 0x2) & (-4)x8 + 2x5 + 1(-3) \\ (-4x7 + 2x1 + 1x0) & (-4)x5 + 2x(-2) + 1x2) \end{matrix}$$

$$= \begin{bmatrix} 75 & 42 & 11 \\ -25 & -26 & -22 \end{bmatrix}$$

It can be seen that RQ is not defined since the 'primary condition' for matrix multiplication is not met.

c. Matrix transposition

The transpose of a matrix Q, denoted as either Q^T or Q', is obtained by interchanging rows and columns of Q.

$$Q = \begin{bmatrix} 1 & 2 \\ 4 & -2 \\ 0 & 3 \end{bmatrix} \qquad Q^T = Q' = \begin{bmatrix} 1 & 4 & 0 \\ 2 & -2 & 3 \end{bmatrix}$$

such that the original elements q_{ij} become q'_{ji}.

d. Determinants

All solvable systems of equations have coefficient matrices which possess a nonzero value called a "determinant." A determinant is a scalar quantity associated with a square matrix. Consider, for example, a square matrix X,

$$X = \begin{bmatrix} 4 & 2 \\ 7 & 1 \end{bmatrix}$$

The determinant of X, indicated by the symbol $|X|$, is easily calculated for a 2 x 2 matrix; it is simply the multiplication of the main diagonal elements minus the multiplication of the remaining elements:

$$X = (4 \times 1) - (2 \times 7) = -10$$

For a (nxn) matrix

$$|X| = \begin{vmatrix} x_{11} & x_{12} \cdots\cdots\cdots & x_{1n} \\ x_{21} & x_{22} \cdots\cdots\cdots & x_{2n} \\ \vdots & \vdots & \vdots \\ x_{n1} & x_{n2} \cdots\cdots\cdots & x_{nn} \end{vmatrix}$$

Calculating the determinant for higher-order matrices is slightly more complicated, but it can be obtained from the formula

$$|X| = \sum_{\substack{i \\ \text{or} \\ j}} (-1)^{i+j} x_{ij} |X_{ij}|,$$ for any i or j with the summation

where $|X_{ij}|$ is called the <u>minor</u> of x_{ij} and $(-1)^{i+j}|X_{ij}|$ is called the <u>cofactor</u> of x_{ij}. To see how this formula can be put to use, consider a simple (3X3) determinant.

$$|X| = \begin{vmatrix} 1 & -5 & 8 \\ 7 & -2 & 3 \\ 6 & 0 & 4 \end{vmatrix}$$

Corresponding to the element $x_{11} = 1$, the cofactor is $(-1)^{1+1}\begin{vmatrix} -2 & 3 \\ 0 & 4 \end{vmatrix}$ and so on. The trick is to discard the row and the column which simultaneously contain the element whose minor is being computed.

Hence, $$|X| = (-1)^{1+1}(1)\begin{vmatrix} -2 & 3 \\ 0 & 4 \end{vmatrix} + (-1)^{2+1}(7)\begin{vmatrix} -5 & 8 \\ 0 & 4 \end{vmatrix}$$

$$+ (-1)^{3+1}(6)\begin{vmatrix} -5 & 8 \\ -2 & 3 \end{vmatrix}$$

$$= (1)\ (-2\times4-0\times3)-7\ (-5\times4-8\times0) + 6(-5\times3-8\times-2) = -8 + 140 + 6 = 138$$

Higher-order matrices can be "expanded" down by their elements and cofactors, until a 3x3 is obtained. For larger than a 3x3, such expansion by cofactors is necessary unless one used the standard definition available in any elementary linear algebra textbook.

A matrix whose determinant is zero is called a 'singular matrix'. If a row (or a column) in a matrix can be obtained through a linear combination of the other rows (or columns), the rows (or columns) are said to be linearly dependent. It can be easily proved that the determinant of a matrix consisting of linearly dependent rows (or columns) is zero. To consider a numerical example,

$$|X| = \begin{vmatrix} 10 & 3 & -2 \\ -4 & 8 & 1 \\ 2 & 19 & 0 \end{vmatrix}$$

$$|X| = (-1)^{1+1}(10)(8\times0-19\times1)+(-1)^{2+1}(-4)(3\times0-(-2\times19) + (-1)^{3+1}(2)(3\times1-8\times-2)$$

$$= 10\ (-19) + 4\ (38) + 2\ (19) = -190 + 152 + 38 = 0$$

A closer inspection of X reveals that row 3 = 2x(row 2) + row 1, and hence the rows of the matrix X are linearly dependent, and X = 0.

The concept of determinants will be very useful in finding what is called the inverse of a matrix. Another concept which will aid us in evaluating the inverse of a matrix is that of an identity matrix.

e. Unit, or identity matrix

A diagonal matrix has zeros in all elements for which $i \neq j$, and nonzero elements in the main diagonal. If the diagonal elements of a diagonal matrix are all unity, then we have a unit or identity matrix, represented as I.

$$I = \begin{bmatrix} 1 & 0 & 0 \\ 0 & 1 & 0 \\ 0 & 0 & 1 \end{bmatrix}$$

f. <u>Matrix Inversion</u>

The inverse of a matrix X, represented as X^{-1}, is defined such that $XX^{-1} = I$ = identity matrix. X^{-1} can be obtained using the following matrix manipulation:

$$X^{-1} = \frac{1}{|x|} \begin{bmatrix} X_{11} & X_{21} \ldots X_{i1} & \ldots\ldots X_{ni} \\ \vdots & \vdots & \vdots \\ X_{ij} & X_{ij} & X_{nj} \\ \vdots & \vdots & \vdots \\ X_{1n} & \ldots\ldots\ldots\ldots\ldots\ldots & X_{nn} \end{bmatrix}$$

where X_{ij} is the cofactor of x_{ij} (notice that the subscripts of the matrix of cofactors indicate that the cofactors have been transposed).

As an example of the inverse and its use, consider the system of equations.

$$2x_1 + 3x_2 = 12$$

$$2x_1 + 1x_2 = 8$$

We can represent the above system as

$$Ax = b$$

$$\text{with } A = \begin{bmatrix} 2 & 3 \\ 2 & 1 \end{bmatrix} \quad x = \begin{bmatrix} x_1 \\ x_2 \end{bmatrix} \quad b = \begin{bmatrix} 12 \\ 8 \end{bmatrix}$$

From the definition of an inverse matrix,

$$x = A^{-1} b$$

The system can be solved if $A^{-1}b$ can be obtained. By definition of inverse matrix, $AA^{-1} = I$

$$\text{By if } A^{-1} = \begin{bmatrix} -1/4 & 3/4 \\ 1/2 & -1/2 \end{bmatrix} \text{ then}$$

$$AA^{-1} = \begin{bmatrix} 2 & 3 \\ 2 & 1 \end{bmatrix} \begin{bmatrix} -1/4 & 3/4 \\ 1/2 & -1/2 \end{bmatrix} = \begin{bmatrix} 1 & 0 \\ 0 & 1 \end{bmatrix}$$

and

$$X = \begin{bmatrix} -1/4 & 3/4 \\ 1/2 & -1/2 \end{bmatrix} \begin{bmatrix} 12 \\ 8 \end{bmatrix} = \begin{bmatrix} 3 \\ 2 \end{bmatrix}$$

Clearly X^{-1} is not defined if $|X| = 0$, i.e., if $|X|$ is singular. A useful corollary is that for a matrix X, such that X = 0, then $(X'X)^{-1}$ is not defined. Consider

$$X = \begin{bmatrix} 1 & -2 & 0 \\ -3 & 0 & -6 \\ 2 & 4 & 8 \\ 0 & 1 & 1 \end{bmatrix}$$

$|X| = 0$ because Col. 3 = 2 (Col. 1) + Col. 2

Then,

$$X'X = \begin{bmatrix} 1 & -3 & 2 & 0 \\ -2 & 0 & 4 & 1 \\ 0 & -6 & 8 & 1 \end{bmatrix} \begin{bmatrix} 1 & -2 & 0 \\ -3 & 0 & 6 \\ 2 & 4 & 8 \\ 0 & 1 & 1 \end{bmatrix}$$

$$= \begin{bmatrix} 1+9+4+0 & -2+0+8+0 & 0+18+16+0 \\ -2+0+8+0 & 4+0+16+1 & 0+0+32+1 \\ 0+18+16+0 & 0+0+32+1 & 0+36+64+1 \end{bmatrix}$$

$$= \begin{bmatrix} 14 & 6 & 34 \\ 6 & 21 & 3 \\ 34 & 33 & 101 \end{bmatrix}$$

X'X = 0 because Col. 3 = 2 (Col. 1) + Col. 2). Hence, $(X'X)^{-1}$ does not exist. And this is because, if you have a matrix which is the product of two matrices, then its determinant is the product of the respective determinants.

g. Rank of a matrix:

The rank of a matrix X is defined as the number of linearly independent columns (or rows) in X. If X is a square matrix (see section L-b) of order (nxn) and if $x \neq 0$, then the rank of X is n.

h. Trace of a matrix:

The trace of a matrix X, denoted as Tr X, is the sum of its diagonal elements.

i. Some Basic Results:

We have chosen to merely present a series of important results. To appreciate them and to gain competence and confidence, however, the reader should perform each statement on a set of 3x3 matrices.

(1) $Q + R = R + Q$

(2) $QR \neq RQ$ except in the case of some special square matrices

(3) $(QR)S = Q(RS)$

(4) $Q(R+S) = QR + QS$; $(Q+R)S = QS + RS$

(5) $(QR)' = R'Q'$

(6) $(QR)^{-1} = R^{-1}Q^{-1}$

(7) If q is a column vector such that

$$q = \begin{bmatrix} q_1 \\ q_2 \\ \cdot \\ \cdot \\ \cdot \\ q_n \end{bmatrix}$$

then $q'q = \sum_{i=1}^{n} q_i^2$

(8) If q is a column vector of order (nx1) and R is a symmetric matrix of order nxn, then the product q'Rq can be subjected to partial differentiation with q as either:

$$\frac{\partial(q'Rq)}{\partial q} = 2\,Rq, \text{ where } Rq \text{ is a column vector}$$

or

$$\frac{\partial(q'Rq)}{\partial q} = 2\,q'R, \text{ where } q'R \text{ is a row vector}$$

The choice between the above two equations is situation specific.

(9) With reference to asymptotic properties (Appendix E), consider a column vector B such that

$$\hat{b} = \begin{bmatrix} \hat{\beta}_1 \\ \hat{\beta}_2 \\ \cdot \\ \cdot \\ \cdot \\ \hat{\beta}_n \end{bmatrix}$$

We can write,

$$\text{plim } \hat{B} = B$$

provided that each one of the elements of B is a consistent estimator of the corresponding element in B (B is a column vector containing the population parameters).

Other operations of interest are:

(i) $\text{plim } (Q^{-1}) = (\text{plim } Q)^{-1}$

(ii) $\text{plim } (QR) = (\text{plim } Q)\ (\text{plim } R)$

(iii)

$$\varepsilon(\hat{\beta}) = \lim_{n\to\infty} E(\hat{B}) = \begin{bmatrix} \lim_{n\to\infty} E(\hat{\beta}_1) \\ \lim_{n\to\infty} E(\hat{\beta}_2) \\ \cdot \\ \cdot \\ \cdot \\ \lim_{n\to\infty} E(\hat{\beta}_n) \end{bmatrix}$$

<u>Some Special Matrices</u>

a. <u>Square matrix</u>: A matrix that has equal number of rows and columns is called a square matrix.

$$Q = \begin{bmatrix} q_{11} & q_{12} & q_{13} \\ q_{21} & q_{22} & q_{33} \\ q_{31} & q_{32} & q_{33} \end{bmatrix}$$

is a square matrix of order (3 x 3). Incidentally elements of the type q_{11}, q_{22}, q_{33} are called the <u>'diagonal' elements</u> of matrix.

<u>Triangular Matrix</u>: A matrix whose elements above or below the diagonal elements are zero.

$$Q = \begin{bmatrix} q_{11} & 0 & 0 \\ q_{21} & q_{22} & 0 \\ q_{31} & q_{32} & q_{33} \end{bmatrix}$$

b. <u>Diagonal matrix</u>: One in which all the non-diagonal elements are zero.

$$Q = \begin{bmatrix} q_{11} & 0 & 0 \\ 0 & q_{22} & 0 \\ 0 & 0 & q_{33} \end{bmatrix}$$

c. <u>Scalar Matrix</u>: A diagonal matrix whose diagonal elements are all equal in magnitude.

$$Q = \begin{bmatrix} \lambda & 0 & 0 \\ 0 & \lambda & 0 \\ 0 & 0 & \lambda \end{bmatrix} = \lambda \begin{bmatrix} 1 & 0 & 0 \\ 0 & 1 & 0 \\ 0 & 0 & 1 \end{bmatrix} = \lambda I$$

d. <u>Null matrix</u>: If all the elements of a matrix are zero, the matrix is known as a 'null matrix' [denoted by (Φ)]

$$X = \begin{bmatrix} 0 & 0 \cdots\cdots\cdots 0 \\ & \vdots \\ 0 & 0 \cdots\cdots\cdots \\ \vdots & \vdots & \vdots \\ \cdots\cdots\cdots 0 \cdots\cdots \\ \vdots & \vdots & \vdots & \vdots \\ 0 \cdots\cdots\cdots\cdots 0 \end{bmatrix} = \Phi$$

e. Idempotent Matrix: A square matrix which when multiplied by itself yields itself.

$$X'X = X$$

where X is a square matrix of order (nxn)

f. Orthogonal matrix: If the transpose of a matrix X is equal to its inverse, X is said to be an orthogonal matrix.

$$X' = X^{-1}$$

g. Positive Definite Matrix: Consider a symmetric matrix (where $q_{ij} = q_{ji}$) Q of order (nxn):

$$Q = \begin{bmatrix} q_{11} & q_{12} & \cdots & q_{1n} \\ q_{21} & q_{22} & \cdots & q_{2n} \\ \vdots & \vdots & & \vdots \\ q_{n1} & q_{n2} & & q_{nn} \end{bmatrix}$$

A necessary and sufficient condition to call Q a positive definit matrix is when

$$\begin{vmatrix} q_{11} \end{vmatrix} > 0; \begin{vmatrix} q_{11} & q_{12} \\ q_{21} & q_{22} \end{vmatrix} > 0; \ldots\ldots\ldots\ldots$$

$$\begin{vmatrix} q_{11} & q_{12} & \cdots & q_{1n} \\ q_{21} & q_{22} & \cdots & q_{2n} \\ \vdots & \vdots & & \vdots \\ q_{n1} & q_{n2} & \cdots & q_{nn} \end{vmatrix} > 0$$

It can be shown that a positive definite matrix Q can be written in terms of a nonsingular matrix P such that Q = PP'.

References

1. Howard Anton, "Elementary Linear Algebra," John Wiley and Sons (New York), 1977, 2nd Edition, Chapters 1, 2, 6.

2. Taro Yamane, "Mathematics for Economics: An Elementary Survey," Prentice-Hall, Inc., (N.J.), 1962, Chapters 10, 11, 12.

APPENDIX M:

SOME INTERESTING MATHEMATICAL PROOFS

You will find the following proofs very easy once you realize that each step merely relies on either a former derivation or a simple arithmetic result. To assist you, we have indicated which former derivations are being relied on. Two examples of typical arithmetic results are the ability to subtract a constant from both sides of the equation without changing the equation's validity (e.g., frequently the mean is subtracted in deriving the deviations from the mean) and the fact that a term will become zero if it is the sum of the deviations around the mean (e.g., 2, 3, 4 have the mean of 3 and the deviations of -1, 0, and 1). After examining the first three pages, you will find that your confidence, proficiency and speed will be increased for the latter pages.

APPENDIX M:

SOME INTERESTING MATHEMATICAL PROOFS

1. METHOD OF LEAST SQUARES:

$$R_{jt} = \hat{\alpha} + \hat{\beta} R_{mt} + e_t$$

or $$e_t = R_{jt} - \hat{\alpha} - \hat{\beta} R_{mt}$$

Squaring both sides,

$$e_t^2 = (R_{jt} - \hat{\alpha} - \hat{\beta} R_{mt})^2$$

Summing over n observations (all summations are with respect to t)

$$\Sigma e_t^2 = \Sigma(R_{jt} - \hat{\alpha} - \hat{\beta} R_{mt})^2$$

The method of least-squares is used to choose values of $\hat{\alpha}$ and $\hat{\beta}$ such that Σe_t^2 is a minimum. This is done by taking the partial derivatives of Σe_t^2 with respect to $\hat{\alpha}$ and $\hat{\beta}$, i.e.,

$$\frac{\delta(e_t^2)}{\delta\hat{\alpha}} = -2\ \Sigma(R_{jt} - \hat{\alpha} - \hat{\beta} R_{mt}) = 0$$

$$\frac{\delta(\Sigma e_t^2)}{\delta\hat{\beta}} = -2\ \Sigma\ R_{mt}\ (R_{jt} - \hat{\alpha} - \hat{\beta} R_{mt}) = 0$$

After carrying out some mathematical manipulations we can write the above equations as:

$$\Sigma\ R_{jt} = n\ \hat{\alpha} + \hat{\beta}\ \Sigma\ R_{mt}$$

$$\Sigma\ R_{jt}\ R_{mt} = \hat{\alpha}\ \Sigma\ R_{mt} + \hat{\beta}\ \Sigma\ R^2_{mt}$$

which, incidentally, are called the <u>normal equations</u>. Hence,

$$\hat{\beta} = \frac{n\ \Sigma\ R_{jt}\ R_{mt} - \Sigma\ R_{jt} R_{mt}}{n\ \Sigma\ R_{mt}^2 - (\Sigma R_{mt})^2}$$

which can be proved to be

$$\hat{\beta} = \frac{\Sigma(R_{mt} - \bar{R}_m)(R_{jt} - \bar{R}_j)}{\Sigma(R_{mt} - \bar{R}_m)^2} \qquad \text{(M-1)}$$

similarly,

$$\hat{\alpha} = \frac{\Sigma R_{jt}\Sigma R^2_{mt} - \Sigma R_{jt}\Sigma R_{mt}R_{jt}}{n\Sigma R^2_{mt} - (\Sigma R_{mt})^2}$$

which can also be written in terms of $\hat{\beta}$ as

$$\hat{\alpha} = \bar{R}_j - \hat{\beta}\bar{R}_m$$

2. $$\hat{\beta} = \frac{\Sigma(R_{mt} - \bar{R}_m)(R_{jt} - \bar{R}_j)}{\Sigma(R_{mt} - \bar{R}_m)^2}$$

Dividing both the denominator and the numerator by n

$$\hat{\beta} = \frac{[\Sigma(R_{mt}-\bar{R}_m)(R_{jt}-\bar{R}_j)]/n}{\Sigma(R_{mt}-\bar{R}_m)^2/n}$$

$$= \frac{\text{cov}(R_{jt},R_{mt})}{V(R_{mt})} = \frac{\sigma_{jm}}{\sigma_m^2}$$

by using the definitions of variance and covariance in Appendix B.

3. TO PROVE THAT TOTAL VARIATION = EXPLAINED VARIATION + UNEXPLAINED VARIATION

(a) $\hat{R}_{jt} = \hat{\alpha} + \hat{\beta}\, R_{mt}$

$\bar{R}_j = \hat{\alpha} + \hat{\beta}\, \bar{R}_m$

$\hat{R}_{jt}-\bar{R}_j = \hat{\beta}(R_{mt}-\bar{R}_m)$ (M-2)

(b) $R_{jt} = \hat{R}_{jt} + e_t$

$R_{jt} - \bar{R}_j = \hat{R}_{jt} - \bar{R}_j + e_t$

Hence, $e_t = (R_{jt}-\bar{R}_j) - \hat{\beta}(R_{mt}-\bar{R}_m)$ Using (M-2)

(c) $\Sigma(\hat{R}_{jt}-\bar{R}_j)e_t = \Sigma\hat{\beta}(R_{mt}-\bar{R}_m)[(R_{jt}-\bar{R}_j)-\hat{\beta}(R_{mt}-\bar{R}_m)]$

$= \hat{\beta}[\Sigma(R_{mt}-\bar{R}_m)(R_{jt}-\bar{R}_j)-\hat{\beta}(R_{mt}-\bar{R}_m)^2]$

$= \hat{\beta}[\Sigma(R_{mt}-\bar{R}_m)(R_{jt}-\bar{R}_j)-\hat{\beta}\Sigma(R_{mt}-\bar{R}_m)^2]$

$= 0$ using (M-1)

(d) $(R_{jt}-\bar{R}_j) = (\hat{R}_{jt}-\bar{R}_j) + e_t$

Squaring both sides,

$$(R_{jt}-\bar{R}_j)^2 = [(\hat{R}_{jt}-\bar{R}_j)+e_t]^2$$

$$= (\hat{R}_{jt}-\bar{R}_j)^2 + 2(\hat{R}_{jt}-\bar{R}_j)e_t + e_t^2$$

Summing over all observations,

$$\Sigma(R_{jt}-\bar{R}_j)^2 = \Sigma(\hat{R}_{jt}-\bar{R}_j)^2 + 2\,\Sigma(\hat{R}_{jt}-\bar{R}_j)e_t + \Sigma e_t^2$$

$$= \Sigma(\hat{R}_{jt}-R_j)^2 + \Sigma e_t^2$$

Total Variation = Explained Variation + Unexplained Variation

4. TO SHOW THAT $\hat{\beta}$ AND $\hat{\alpha}$ ARE LINEARLY DEPENDENT ON R_{jt}:

(a) $\Sigma(R_{mt}-\bar{R}_m) = \Sigma R_{mt}-\Sigma\bar{R}_m$

$$= \Sigma R_{mt}-n\bar{R}_m$$

$$= \Sigma R_{mt} - \frac{n\Sigma R_{mt}}{n}$$

$$= 0 \qquad \text{(M-3)}$$

That is, the sum of the deviations from the mean is zero.

(b) $$\hat{\beta} = \frac{\Sigma(R_{mt}-\bar{R}_m)(R_{jt}-\bar{R}_j)}{\Sigma(R_{mt}-\bar{R}_m)^2}$$

$$= \frac{\Sigma(R_{mt}-\bar{R}_m)R_{jt} - \bar{R}_j\Sigma(R_{mt}-\bar{R}_m)}{\Sigma(R_{mt}-\bar{R}_m)^2}$$

$$= \frac{\Sigma(R_{mt}-\bar{R}_m)R_{jt}}{\Sigma(R_{mt}-\bar{R}_m)^2} \text{ using (M-3)}$$

$$= \Sigma f_t R_{jt} \quad \text{where} \quad f_t = \frac{R_{mt}-\bar{R}_m}{\Sigma(R_{mt}-\bar{R}_m)^2}$$

(c) $\hat{\alpha} = \bar{R}_j - \hat{\beta}\,\bar{R}_m$

$$= \frac{\Sigma R_{jt}}{n} - \Sigma f_t\, R_{jt}\, \bar{R}_m$$

$$= \Sigma[\frac{1}{n} - f_t \bar{R}_m]\, R_{jt}$$

5. $\hat{\alpha}$ AND $\hat{\beta}$ ARE UNBIASED LS ESTIMATORS:

(a) $$\Sigma f_t = \Sigma \frac{(R_{mt}-\bar{R}_m)}{\Sigma(R_{mt}-\bar{R}_m)^2}$$

$$= \frac{\Sigma(R_{mt}-\bar{R}_m)}{\Sigma(R_{mt}-\bar{R}_m)^2}$$

$$= 0 \qquad \text{using (M-3)} \qquad \text{(M-4)}$$

(b) $$\Sigma f_t\, R_{mt} = \frac{\Sigma(R_{mt}-\bar{R}_m)R_{mt}}{\Sigma(R_{mt}-\bar{R}_m)^2}$$

$$= \frac{\Sigma(R_{mt}-\bar{R}_m)[(R_{mt}-\bar{R}_m)+\bar{R}_m]}{\Sigma(R_{mt}-\bar{R}_m)^2}$$

$$= \frac{\Sigma(R_{mt}-\bar{R}_m)^2}{\Sigma(R_{mt}-\bar{R}_m)^2} + \bar{R}_m \frac{\Sigma(R_{mt}-\bar{R}_m)}{\Sigma(R_{mt}-\bar{R}_m)^2}$$

$$= 1 \qquad \text{using (M-3)} \qquad \text{(M-5)}$$

(c) $$f_t = \frac{R_{mt}-\bar{R}_m}{\Sigma(R_{mt}-\bar{R}_m)}$$

Since $E(R_{mt}) = \bar{R}_m$, we have

$$E(f_t) = \frac{E(R_{mt}-\bar{R}_m)}{\Sigma(R_{mt}-\bar{R}_m)^2}$$

$$= 0$$

(d) The simple regression model is,

$$R_{jt} = \alpha + \beta\, R_{mt} + u_t$$

Therefore, $\hat{\beta} = \Sigma f_t R_{jt}$

$$= \Sigma f_t(\alpha+\beta R_{mt}+u_t)$$

$$= \alpha\Sigma f_t + \beta\ \Sigma f_t R_{mt} + \Sigma f_t u_t$$

$$= \beta\Sigma f_t R_{mt} + \Sigma f_t u_t \quad \text{by (M-4)}$$

$$= \beta + \Sigma f_t u_t \quad \text{using (M-5)} \qquad \text{(M-6)}$$

$$E(\hat{\beta}) = E(\beta) + \Sigma f_t E(u_t)$$

$$= \beta \text{ [unbiasedness] because } E(u_t) = 0$$

(e) $\hat{\alpha} = \Sigma(\frac{1}{n} - \bar{R}_m f_t)(\alpha + \beta R_{mt} + u_t)$

$$= \alpha - \alpha\bar{R}_m\Sigma f_t + \beta\bar{R}_m - \beta\bar{R}_m\Sigma f_t R_{mt} + \Sigma(\frac{1}{n} - \bar{R}_m f_t)u_t$$

$$= \alpha + \Sigma(\frac{1}{n} - \bar{R}_m f_t)u_t \quad \text{using (M-4), (M-5)} \qquad \text{(M-7)}$$

$$E(\hat{\alpha}) = \alpha + \Sigma(\frac{1}{n} - \bar{R}_m f_t)\ E(u_t)$$

$$= \alpha \quad \text{because } E(u_t) = 0$$

6. DERIVING EXPRESSIONS FOR VARIANCE OF $\hat{\beta}$ AND $\hat{\alpha}$:

(a) $$f_t^{\,2} = \frac{(R_{mt}-\bar{R}_m)^2}{[\Sigma(R_{mt}-\bar{R}_m)^2]^2} \qquad \text{(M-8)}$$

$$\Sigma f_t^{\,2} = \frac{\Sigma(R_{mt}-\bar{R}_m)^2}{[\Sigma(R_{mt}-R_m)^2]^2}$$

$$= \frac{1}{\Sigma(R_{mt}-\bar{R}_m)^2}$$

(b) $$v(u_t) = \sigma_u^{\,2} = E(u_t^2) - [E(u_t)]^2 \text{ using A-12a} \qquad \text{(M-9)}$$

$$= E(u_t^2) \quad \text{since } E(u_t) = 0 \text{ by assumption}$$

Hence,

$$E(u_t^2) = \sigma_u^{\,2} \qquad \text{(M-10)}$$

Also,

$$E(u_t u_{t-j}) = 0 \qquad j \neq 0 \text{ by assumption}$$

(c) $\hat{\beta} = \beta + \Sigma f_t u_t$ from (M-6)

$$\hat{\beta}-\beta = \Sigma f_t u_t$$

$$v(\hat{\beta}) = E(\hat{\beta}-\beta)^2$$

$$= E[\Sigma f_t u_t]^2$$

$$= E[f_1^2 u_1^2 + f_2^2 u_2^2 + \ldots + f_n^2 u_n^2 + 2f_1 f_2 u_1 u_2 + \text{other cross-product terms}]$$

$$= f_1^2\, E(u_1^2) + f_2^2 E(u_2^2) + \ldots\; f_n^2 E(u_n^2) + 2f_1 f_2 E(u_1 u_2) + \ldots\ldots$$

$$= \sigma_u^{\,2} \Sigma f_t^{\,2} \qquad \text{using (M-9)}$$

$$= \frac{\sigma_u^{\,2}}{\Sigma(R_{mt}-\bar{R}_m)^2}, \quad \text{using (M-8)}$$

We can rewrite this expression as,

$$E(\hat{\beta}-\beta)\ \Sigma(R_{mt}-\bar{R}_m)^2 = \sigma_u^2 \qquad \text{(M-11)}$$

(d)

$$\hat{\alpha} = \alpha + \Sigma(\tfrac{1}{n} - \bar{R}_m f_t)u_t \qquad \text{from (M-7)}$$

$$v(\hat{\alpha}) = E(\hat{\alpha} - \alpha)^2$$

$$= E[\Sigma(\tfrac{1}{n} - \bar{R}_m f_t)u_t]^2$$

$$= \Sigma(\tfrac{1}{n} - \bar{R}_m f_t)^2\ E(u_t^2) \qquad \text{since } E(u_t u_{t-j}) = 0 \quad j \neq 0$$

$$= \sigma_u^{\,2}\ \Sigma(\tfrac{1}{n} - \bar{R}_m f_t)^2$$

$$= \sigma_u^{\,2}\ \Sigma(\tfrac{1}{n^2} + \bar{R}_m^2 f_t^2 - \frac{2\bar{R}_m f_t}{n})$$

$$= \sigma_u^{\ 2}\ [\frac{1}{n} + \Sigma\bar{R}_m^2 f_t^2 - \frac{2R_m}{n}\ \Sigma f_t]$$

$$= \sigma_u^{\ 2}\ [\frac{1}{n} + \bar{R}_m^2\ \Sigma f_t^{\ 2} - \frac{2\bar{R}_m}{n}\ \Sigma f_t]$$

$$= \sigma_u^{\ 2}\ [\frac{1}{n} + \frac{\bar{R}_m^2}{\Sigma(R_{mt}-\bar{R}_m)^2}] \qquad \text{using (M-8), (M-4)}$$

$$= \sigma_u^2\ \{\frac{[\Sigma(R_{mt}-\bar{R}_m)^2] + n\ \bar{R}_m^2}{n\ \Sigma(R_{mt}-\bar{R}_m)^2}\}$$

$$= \sigma_u^2\ \{\frac{[\Sigma\ R_{mt}^2 - 2R_{mt}\bar{R}_m + \Sigma\bar{R}_m^2] + n\bar{R}_m^2}{n\ \Sigma(R_{mt}-\bar{R}_m)^2}\}$$

$$= \sigma_u^{\ 2}\ \{\frac{\Sigma R_{mt}^2 - 2\bar{R}_m\ R_{mt} + \bar{R}_m^2 + n\bar{R}_m^2}{n\ \Sigma(R_{mt}-\bar{R}_m)^2}\}$$

$$= \sigma_u^{\ 2}\ \{\frac{\Sigma R_{mt}^2 - 2n\bar{R}_m^2 + n\bar{R}_m^2 + n\bar{R}_m^2}{n\ \Sigma(R_{mt}-\bar{R}_m)^2}\}$$

$$= \ _u^{\ 2}\ [\frac{\Sigma\ R_{mt}^2}{n\ \Sigma(R_{mt}-\bar{R}_m)^2}]$$

7. TO OBTAIN AN UNBIASED ESTIMATOR FOR $\sigma_u^{\ 2}$:

(a) $(u_t-\bar{u}_t)^2 = u_t^2 + \bar{u}_t^2 - 2u_t u_t$

$$\Sigma(u_t-\bar{u}_t)^2 = \Sigma(u_t^2 + \bar{u}_t^2 - 2u_t\bar{u}_t)$$

$$= \Sigma[u_t^2 + (\frac{\Sigma u_t}{n})^2 - 2u_t\frac{\Sigma u_t}{n}] \qquad \text{since } \bar{u}_t = \frac{\Sigma u_t}{n}$$

$$= \Sigma\ u_t^2 + \Sigma(\frac{\Sigma u_t}{n})^2 - 2\Sigma u_t\frac{\Sigma u_t}{n}$$

$$= \Sigma\ u_t^2 + n(\frac{\Sigma u_t}{n})^2 - 2\ \frac{(\Sigma u_t)^2}{n}$$

$$= \Sigma\ u_t^2 - \frac{(\Sigma u_t)^2}{n}$$

$$E\,\Sigma(u_t-\bar{u}_t)^2 = E(\Sigma u_t^2) - E\,\frac{(\Sigma u_t)^2}{n}$$

$$= n\,\sigma_u^2 - \frac{n\sigma_u^2}{n} \qquad \text{because } E(u_t u_{t-j}) = 0 \quad j\neq 0$$

$$= (n-1)\,\sigma_u^2 \qquad \text{(M-12)}$$

(b) $E(\hat{\beta}-\beta)\,\Sigma(u_t-\bar{u}_t)(R_{mt}-\bar{R}_m) = E[\Sigma\, f_t\, u_t\, (\Sigma u_t(R_{mt}-\bar{R}_m) - u_t\Sigma(R_{mt}-\bar{R}_m)]$

$$= E\left\{\frac{\Sigma(R_{mt}-\bar{R}_m)u_t}{\Sigma(R_{mt}-\bar{R}_m)^2}\,[\Sigma u_t(R_{mt}-\bar{R}_m)]\right\}$$

$$= E\,\frac{[\Sigma u_t(R_{mt}-\bar{R}_m)]^2}{\Sigma(R_{mt}-\bar{R}_m)^2}$$

$$= E\,\frac{[u_1^2(R_{m1}-\bar{R}_m)^2 + u_2^2(R_{m2}-\bar{R}_m)^2 + \ldots + \text{cross-product terms}}{[(R_{m1}-\bar{R}_m)^2 + (R_{m2}-\bar{R}_m)^2 + \ldots\,]}$$

$$= \frac{(R_{m1}-\bar{R}_m)^2E(u_1^2)+(R_{m2}-\bar{R}_m)E(u_2^2)+\ldots+E(\text{cross-product terms}]}{[(R_{m1}-\bar{R}_m)^2+(R_{m2}-\bar{R}_m)^2+\ldots]}$$

But $E(u_1^2) = E(u_2^2) = \ldots E(u_n^2) = \sigma_u^2$ by (M-10) and also, E (cross-product terms) equal zero. So then,

$$E(\hat{\beta}-\beta)\,\Sigma(u_t-\bar{u}_t)(R_{mt}-\bar{R}_m) = n\sigma_u^2$$

(c) Considering the sample,

$$R_{jt} = \hat{\alpha} + \hat{\beta}\,R_{mt} + e_t$$

$$\bar{R}_j = \hat{\alpha} + \hat{\beta}\,\bar{R}_m$$

Subtracting $\bar{R}_j$ from R_{jt},

$$R_{jt} - \bar{R}_j = \hat{\beta}(R_{mt}-\bar{R}_m) + e_t$$

Hence,

$$e_t = (R_{jt}-\bar{R}_j) - \hat{\beta}(R_{mt}-\bar{R}_m) \qquad \text{(M-13)}$$

(d) Considering the population,

$$R_{jt} = \alpha + \beta R_{mt} + u_t \qquad \text{eqn. (2.1)}$$

$$\bar{R}_j = \alpha + \beta \bar{R}_m + \bar{u}_t$$

Therefore,

$$R_{jt} - \bar{R}_j = \beta(R_{mt} - \bar{R}_m) + (u_t - \bar{u}_t) \qquad \text{(M-14)}$$

(e) Using both (M-13) and (M-14)

$$e_t = \beta(R_{mt} - \bar{R}_m) + (u_t - \bar{u}_t) - \hat{\beta}(R_{mt} - \bar{R}_m)$$

$$= (R_{mt} - \bar{R}_m)(\beta - \hat{\beta}) + (u_t - \bar{u}_t)$$

Therefore,

$$e_t^2 = (\beta - \hat{\beta})^2 (R_{mt} - \bar{R}_m)^2 + (u_t - \bar{u}_t)^2 + 2(\beta - \hat{\beta})(u_t - \bar{u}_t)(R_{mt} - \bar{R}_m)$$

Summing over all n observations and noting $(\beta - \hat{\beta})^2 = (\hat{\beta} - \beta)^2$

$$\Sigma e_t^2 = (\hat{\beta} - \beta)^2 \, \Sigma(R_{mt} - \bar{R}_m)^2 + \Sigma(u_t - \bar{u}_t)^2 - 2(\hat{\beta} - \beta) \, \Sigma(u_t - \bar{u}_t)(R_{mt} - \bar{R}_m)$$

$$E(\Sigma e_t^2) = E[(\hat{\beta} - \beta)^2 \, \Sigma(R_{mt} - \bar{R}_m)^2] + E\Sigma(u_t - \bar{u}_t)^2 - 2\, E[(\hat{\beta} - \beta) \, \Sigma(u_t - \bar{u}_t)(R_{mt} - \bar{R}_m)]$$

$$= \sigma_u^2 + (n-1)\,\sigma_u^2 - 2\sigma_u^2 \qquad \text{using (M-11) and (M-12)}$$

$$= (n-2)\,\sigma_u^2$$

Hence,

$$E\left(\frac{\Sigma e_t^{\,2}}{n-2}\right) = \sigma_u^{\,2}$$

So, we can conclude that $\frac{\Sigma e_t^{\,2}}{n-2}$ is an unbiased estimator of σ_u^2.

8. Equation (2.12c) can be rewritten (Appendix C) as

$$\frac{\hat{\beta} - \beta}{\sigma_{\hat{\beta}}} \simeq N(0,1) \qquad \text{(1-18)}$$

Also, referring to Appendix G, we can write[1]

$$\frac{\Sigma(R_{jt} - \hat{\alpha} - \hat{\beta} R_{mt})^2}{\sigma_u^{\,2}} = \frac{\Sigma e_t^{\,2}}{\sigma_u^{\,2}} \simeq \chi^2_{n-2}$$

---

[1] Note that $e_t \simeq N(0, \sigma_u^{\,2})$

The Chi-Square distribution in this case has (n-2) degrees of freedom, since 2 degrees are sacrificed while computing $\hat{\alpha}$ and $\hat{\beta}$. To proceed further, using (2.10). we get

$$\frac{\hat{s}^2(n-2)}{\sigma_u^2} \simeq \chi^2_{n-2}$$

or

$$\frac{\hat{s}^2(n-2)/\Sigma\rho^2_{mt}}{\sigma_u^2/\Sigma\rho^2_{mt}} \simeq \chi^2_{n-2}$$

Hence it follows from (M-12) and (2.12c) that,

$$\frac{(n-2)\hat{s}^2_\beta}{\sigma^2_\beta} \simeq \chi^2_{n-2}$$

As was clearly stated in Appendix I,

$$\frac{(\beta-b)/\sigma_\beta}{\sqrt{(n-2)\hat{s}^2_\beta/\sigma_\beta^2(n-2)}} \simeq t_{n-2}$$

9. $R_{jt} = \alpha + \beta r_{mt} + u_t + \beta\delta_t$

$$= \alpha + \beta r_{mt} + \overline{\lambda}_t$$

where $\overline{\lambda}_t = u_t + \beta\delta_t$

$$\begin{aligned} Cov(r_{mt},\overline{\lambda}_t) &= E[r_{mt}-E(r_{mt})]\overline{\lambda}_t \\ &= E\{[R_{mt}-\delta_t-R_{mt}][u_t+\beta\delta_t]\} \\ &= -E(\delta_t u_t+\beta\delta_t^2) \\ &= -E(\delta_i u_t) - \beta\ E(\delta_t^2) \\ &= -\beta\sigma_\delta^2 \neq 0 \end{aligned}$$

10. $\hat{\beta} = \beta + \dfrac{\Sigma(x_t-\bar{x})u_t}{\Sigma(x_t-\bar{x})^2}$

Considering the second term on the RHS,

$$\frac{\Sigma(x_t-\bar{x})u_t}{\Sigma(x_t-\bar{x})^2} = \frac{\Sigma x_t u_t - \bar{x}\Sigma u_t}{\Sigma x_i^2 + \Sigma\bar{x}^2 - 2\bar{x}\Sigma x_i}$$

$$= \frac{\Sigma x_t u_t - \bar{x}\Sigma u_t}{\Sigma x_t^2 + n\bar{x}^2 - 2\bar{x}\Sigma x_t}$$

$$= \frac{\Sigma x_t u_t - \dfrac{\Sigma x_t}{n}\Sigma u_t}{\Sigma x_t^2 + \dfrac{n(\Sigma x_t)^2}{n^2} - \dfrac{2(\Sigma x_t)^2}{n}}$$

$$= \frac{n\Sigma x_t u_t - \Sigma x_t \Sigma u_t}{n\Sigma x_t^2 - (\Sigma x_t)^2}$$

Hence,

$$\hat{\beta} = \beta + \frac{n\Sigma x_t u_t - \Sigma x_t \Sigma u_t}{n\Sigma x_t^2 - (\Sigma x_t)^2}$$

$$\hat{\alpha} = \alpha + \Sigma\left[\frac{1}{n} - \bar{x}\frac{(x_t-\bar{x})}{\Sigma(x_i-\bar{x})^2}\right]u_t$$

Once again, considering the second term on the RHS,

$$\Sigma\left[\frac{1}{n} - \frac{\bar{x}(x_t-\bar{x})}{\Sigma(x_t-\bar{x})^2}\right]u_t = \frac{\Sigma u_t \Sigma(x_i-\bar{x})^2 - n\bar{x}\Sigma(x_t-\bar{x})u_t}{n\Sigma(x_t-\bar{x})^2}$$

$$= \frac{\Sigma u_t\left[\dfrac{n\Sigma x_t^2 - (\Sigma x_t)^2}{n}\right] - n\bar{x}\Sigma x_t u_t + n\bar{x}\Sigma\bar{x}u_t}{n\Sigma x_t^2 - (\Sigma x_t)^2}$$

using the logic presented above

$$= \Sigma u_t \Sigma x_t^2 - \frac{(\Sigma x_t)^2 \Sigma u_t}{n} - n\,\frac{\Sigma x_t}{n}\,\Sigma x_t u_t + \frac{n(\Sigma x_t)^2}{n^2}\,\Sigma u_t$$

$$= \Sigma u_t \Sigma x_t^2 - \Sigma x_t \Sigma x_t u_t$$

Therefore,

$$\hat{\alpha} = \alpha + \frac{\Sigma u_t \Sigma x_t^2 - \Sigma x_t \Sigma x_t u_t}{n\Sigma x_t^2 - (\Sigma x_t)^2}$$

In matrix form (see Appendix L) we can write,

$$\begin{bmatrix} \hat{\alpha} \\ \hat{\beta} \end{bmatrix} = \begin{bmatrix} \alpha \\ \beta \end{bmatrix} + \frac{1}{n\,\Sigma x_t^2 - (\Sigma x_t)^2} \begin{bmatrix} \Sigma u_t \Sigma x_t^2 - \Sigma x_t \Sigma x_t u_t \\ -\Sigma x_t \Sigma u_t + n\,\Sigma x_t u_t \end{bmatrix}$$

$$= \begin{bmatrix} \alpha \\ \beta \end{bmatrix} + \frac{1}{n\,\Sigma x_t^2 - (\Sigma x_t)^2} \begin{bmatrix} \Sigma\, x_t^2 & -\Sigma x_t \\ -\Sigma x_t & n \end{bmatrix} \begin{bmatrix} \Sigma u_t \\ \Sigma x_t u_t \end{bmatrix} \qquad \text{(M-15)}$$

If we were to designate the matrix of sample observations as X, the matrix of residuals as U and the matrix of the coefficients as B, we can write

$$X = \begin{bmatrix} 1 & x_{11} \\ 1 & x_{12} \\ \vdots & \vdots \\ 1 & x_{1n} \end{bmatrix} \qquad U = \begin{bmatrix} u_1 \\ u_2 \\ \vdots \\ u_n \end{bmatrix} \qquad B = \begin{bmatrix} \alpha \\ \beta \end{bmatrix}$$

Equation (M-15) can now be written as,

$$\hat{B} = B + (x'x)^{-1}\,x'u$$

See Chapter 4 for full length discussion on deriving $\hat{B}$ for a multivariate model.

$$(x'x) = \begin{bmatrix} 1 & 1 & 1 & \dots & 1 \\ x_1 & x_2 & x_3 & \dots & x_n \end{bmatrix} \begin{bmatrix} 1 & x_1 \\ 1 & x_2 \\ 1 & x_3 \\ \vdots & \vdots \\ 1 & x_n \end{bmatrix}$$

$$= \begin{bmatrix} \Sigma 1 & \Sigma x_t \\ \Sigma x_t & \Sigma x_t^2 \end{bmatrix} = \begin{bmatrix} n & \Sigma x_t \\ \Sigma x_t & \Sigma x_t^2 \end{bmatrix}$$

$$(x'x)^{-1} = \frac{1}{\begin{vmatrix} n & \Sigma x_t \\ \Sigma x_t & \Sigma x_t^2 \end{vmatrix}} = \begin{bmatrix} \Sigma x_t^2 & -\Sigma x_t \\ -\Sigma x_t & n \end{bmatrix} = \frac{1}{n\Sigma x_t^2 - (\Sigma x_t)^2} \begin{bmatrix} \Sigma x_t^2 & -\Sigma x_t \\ -\Sigma x_t & n \end{bmatrix}$$

$$x'u = \begin{bmatrix} 1 & 1 & 1 \ldots\ldots\ldots & 1 \\ x_1 & x_2 & x_3 \ldots\ldots\ldots & x_n \end{bmatrix} \begin{bmatrix} u_1 \\ u_2 \\ \vdots \\ u_n \end{bmatrix} = \begin{bmatrix} \Sigma u_t \\ \Sigma x_t u_t \end{bmatrix} \qquad \text{(M-16)}$$

Let us look at $(n^{-1}x'x)^{-1}$:

$$n^{-1}x'x = \frac{1}{n} \begin{bmatrix} n & \Sigma x_t \\ \Sigma x_t & \Sigma x_t^2 \end{bmatrix}$$

$$= \begin{bmatrix} 1 & \Sigma x_{t/n} \\ \Sigma x_{t/n} & \Sigma x^2{}_{t/n} \end{bmatrix}$$

$$(n^{-1}x'x)^{-1} = \frac{1}{\begin{vmatrix} 1 & \Sigma x_{t/n} \\ \frac{\Sigma x_t}{n} & \Sigma x_{t/n}^{\ 2} \end{vmatrix}} \begin{bmatrix} \frac{\Sigma x_t^{\ 2}}{n} & \frac{-\Sigma x_t}{n} \\ \frac{-\Sigma x_t}{n} & 1 \end{bmatrix}$$

$$= \frac{1}{\frac{\Sigma x_t^2}{n} - \frac{(\Sigma x_t)^2}{n^2}} \begin{bmatrix} \frac{\Sigma x_t^2}{n} & \frac{-\Sigma x_t}{n} \\ \frac{-\Sigma x_t}{n} & 1 \end{bmatrix}$$

$$= \frac{n^2}{n\Sigma x_t^2 - (\Sigma x_t)^2} \begin{bmatrix} \frac{\Sigma x_t^2}{n} & \frac{-\Sigma x_t}{n} \\ \frac{-\Sigma x_t}{n} & 1 \end{bmatrix}$$

$$= \frac{n}{n\Sigma x_t^2 - (\Sigma x_t)^2} \begin{bmatrix} \Sigma x_t^2 & -\Sigma x_t \\ -\Sigma x_t & n \end{bmatrix}$$

$$= \frac{1}{s^2} \begin{bmatrix} \frac{\Sigma x_t^2}{n} & \frac{-\Sigma x_t}{n} \\ \frac{-\Sigma x_t}{n} & 1 \end{bmatrix} = \frac{1}{s^2} \begin{bmatrix} \bar{x}_t^2 & \bar{x}_t \\ -\bar{x}_t & 1 \end{bmatrix} \qquad \text{(M-17)}$$

Similarly let us look at $n^{-1}x'u$:

$$n^{-1}x'u = \frac{1}{n}\begin{bmatrix} \Sigma u_t \\ \Sigma x_t u_t \end{bmatrix} \text{, from (M-16)} \qquad \text{(M-18)}$$

So, multiplying equation (M-17) with equation (M-18) we see that

$$(n^{-1}x'x)^{-1}(n^{-1}x'u) = (x'x)^{-1}x'u$$

It follows that

$$\hat{B} = B + (x'x)^{-1}x'u$$
$$= B + (n^{-1}x'x)^{-1}\ n^{-1}x'u$$

Taking probability limits on both sides, (see Appendices E and L)

$$\text{plim } \hat{E} = \text{plim } B + \text{plim } (n^{-1}x'x)^{-1}\ n^{-1}x'u$$
$$= B + \text{plim } (n^{-1}x'x)^{-1}\ \text{plim } n^{-1}x'u$$

since B contains constant elements now,

$$\text{plim}(n^{-1}x'x) = E\frac{1}{s^2}\begin{bmatrix} E\bar{x}_t^2 & -E\bar{x}_t \\ -\bar{x}_t & 1 \end{bmatrix}$$

$$= \frac{1}{E s^2}\begin{bmatrix} E\bar{x}_t^2 & -E\bar{x}_t \\ -Ex_t & E1 \end{bmatrix}$$

$$= \frac{1}{V(x_t)} \begin{bmatrix} E(x_t^2) & -E(x_t) \\ -E(x_t) & 1 \end{bmatrix}$$

If x_t is a random variable,

$$\text{plim } (n^{-1}x'x)^{-1} = \frac{1}{V(\tilde{x}_t)} \begin{bmatrix} E(\tilde{x}_t^2) & -E(\tilde{x}_t) \\ -E(\tilde{x}_t) & 1 \end{bmatrix}$$

Similarly,

$$\text{plim } (n^{-1}x'u) = \begin{bmatrix} E\frac{\Sigma\tilde{u}_t}{n} \\ E\frac{\Sigma\tilde{x}_t\tilde{u}_t}{n} \end{bmatrix}$$

Let us relate these results to the market model, Roll (1969) writes equation (3.4a) as

$$R_{jt} = \beta R_{mt} + \tilde{U}_t$$

where

$$\tilde{x}_t \longleftrightarrow \tilde{R}_m$$

$$\tilde{U}_t \longleftrightarrow (1-\beta)\ \tilde{R}_{Ft} + \tilde{U}_t$$

$$\alpha = 0$$

For the fitted regression,

$$R_{jt} = \hat{\alpha} + \hat{\beta}\ R_{mt} + e_t$$

we have

$$\text{plim}(n^{-1}x'x)^{-1} = \frac{1}{V(\tilde{R}_{mt})} \begin{bmatrix} E(R_{mt}^2) & -E(R_{mt}) \\ -E(R_{mt}) & 1 \end{bmatrix}$$

and

$$\text{plim}(n^{-1}x'u) = \begin{bmatrix} \frac{\Sigma(1-\beta)\tilde{R}_{F,t}}{n} + \frac{\Sigma\tilde{U}_t}{n} \\ \frac{\Sigma(1-\beta)\tilde{R}_{Ft}\tilde{R}_{mt}}{n} + \frac{\Sigma\tilde{R}_{mt}\tilde{U}_t}{n} \end{bmatrix}$$

$$= \begin{bmatrix} (1-\beta) \dfrac{\Sigma\tilde{R}_{Ft}}{n} + \dfrac{\Sigma\tilde{u}_t}{n} \\ (1-\beta) \dfrac{\Sigma\tilde{R}_{Ft}\tilde{R}_{mt}}{n} + \dfrac{\Sigma\tilde{R}_{mt}\tilde{U}_t}{n} \end{bmatrix}$$

$$\begin{bmatrix} (1-\beta)\ E(\tilde{R}_{Ft}) \\ (1-\beta)\ E(\tilde{R}_{Ft}\tilde{R}_{mt}) \end{bmatrix} \quad \text{since } \frac{\Sigma\tilde{U}_t}{n} \text{ and } \frac{\Sigma\tilde{R}_{mt}\tilde{U}_t}{n} = 0 \text{ by assumption.}$$

Hence,

$$\text{plim } \hat{B} = \text{plim}\begin{bmatrix}\hat{\alpha} \\ \hat{\beta}\end{bmatrix} = \begin{bmatrix}0 \\ \beta\end{bmatrix} + \frac{1}{V(\tilde{R}_{mt})}\begin{bmatrix} E(\tilde{R}^2_{mt}) & -E(\tilde{R}_m) \\ -E(\tilde{R}_m) & 1 \end{bmatrix}\begin{bmatrix} (1-\beta) & E(\tilde{R}_{Ft}) \\ (1-\beta) & E(\tilde{R}_{Ft}\tilde{R}_{mt}) \end{bmatrix}$$

$$\begin{bmatrix}0 \\ \beta\end{bmatrix} + \begin{bmatrix} E(\tilde{R}_{Ft})\ E(\tilde{R}^2_{mt}) - E(\tilde{R}_m)\ E(\tilde{R}_{Ft}\tilde{R}_{mt}) \\ -E(\tilde{R}_{Ft})\ E(\tilde{R}_m) + E(\tilde{R}_{Ft}\tilde{R}_{mt}) \end{bmatrix} \frac{1-\beta}{V(\tilde{R}_{mt})}$$

$$\begin{bmatrix}0 \\ \beta\end{bmatrix} + \begin{bmatrix} E(\tilde{R}_{Ft})\ \{[E(\tilde{R}_{mt})]^2 + V(\tilde{R}_{mt})\} - E(\tilde{R}_m)\ E(\tilde{R}_{Ft}\tilde{R}_{mt}) \\ -E(\tilde{R}_{Ft})\ E(\tilde{R}_{mt}) + E(\tilde{R}_{Ft}\tilde{R}_{mt}) \end{bmatrix} \frac{1-\beta}{V(\tilde{R}_{mt})}$$

$$\begin{bmatrix}0 \\ \beta\end{bmatrix} + \begin{bmatrix} E(R_{Ft}) + E(R_{mt}) \dfrac{\{E(R_{Ft})\ E(R_{mt}) - E(R_{Ft}R_{mt})\}}{V(\tilde{R}_{mt})} \\ \dfrac{E(R_{Ft}R_{mt}) - E(R_{Ft})\ E(R_{mt})}{V(\tilde{R}_{mt})} \end{bmatrix} (1-\beta)$$

$$\begin{bmatrix}0 \\ \beta\end{bmatrix} + \begin{bmatrix} E(R_{Ft}) - E(R_{mt}) \dfrac{Cov(R_{mt}, R_{Ft}}{V(\tilde{R}_{mt})} \\ \dfrac{Cov(R_{mt}, R_{Ft})}{V(\tilde{R}_{mt})} \end{bmatrix} (1-\beta)$$

Therefore,

$$\text{plim } \hat{\beta} = \beta + (1-\beta)\frac{Cov(\tilde{R}_{mt}, \tilde{R}_{Ft})}{V(\tilde{R}_{mt})}$$

$$\text{plim } \hat{\alpha} = (1-\beta)\left[E(R_{Ft}) - E(R_{mt})\ \frac{Cov(\tilde{R}_{mt},\tilde{R}_{Ft})}{V(\tilde{R}_{mt})}\right]$$

11. $$\hat{R}_F = \frac{\hat{\alpha}}{1-\hat{\beta}}$$

$$\text{plim } R_F = \text{plim}(\frac{\hat{\alpha}}{1-\hat{\beta}})$$

$$= \text{plim}(\frac{\hat{\alpha}}{1-\hat{\beta}})$$

$$= \frac{\text{plim } \hat{\alpha}}{\text{plim } (1-\hat{\beta})}$$

$$= \frac{(1-\beta)[E(\tilde{R}_F)-E(\tilde{R}_m)\ \frac{Cov(\tilde{R}_m,\tilde{R}_F)}{V(\tilde{R}_m)}}{(1-\beta) - (1-\beta)\ \frac{Cov(\tilde{R}_m,\tilde{R}_F)}{V(\tilde{R}_m)}}$$

$$= E(R_F)\left[\frac{1 - \frac{E(R_m)}{E(R_F)}\ \frac{Cov(R_m,R_F)}{V(R_m)}}{1 - \frac{Cov(\tilde{R}_m,\tilde{R}_F)}{V(\tilde{R}_m)}}\right]$$

Consider the case where,

$$E(\tilde{R}_m) > E(\tilde{R}_F)\ ;$$

then $$\frac{E(\tilde{R}_m)}{E(\tilde{R}_F)} > 1$$

In addition, if $Cov(\tilde{R}_m,\tilde{R}_F) > 0$, then plim $\tilde{R}_F < E(\tilde{R}_F)$.

12. $$R_{jt} = (1-\beta)R_{Ft} + \beta R_{mt} + U_t$$

$$= (1-\beta)\ R_{Ft} + \beta\left[\frac{r_{mt} - R_{Ft}(1- \ _m)}{\beta_m} - \frac{E_{mt}}{\beta_m}\right] + u_t$$

$$= (1-\beta)\ R_{Ft} - \beta\ R_{Ft}\ \frac{(1-\beta_m)}{\beta_m} + \frac{\beta r_{mt}}{\beta_m} - \frac{\beta E_{mt}}{\beta_m} - u_t$$

$$= R_{Ft} - \frac{\beta}{\beta_m} R_{Ft} + \frac{\beta}{\beta_m} r_{mt} - \frac{\beta E_{mt}}{\beta_m} - \frac{\beta E_{mt}}{\beta_m} + u_t$$

$$= \alpha_j + \beta_j\ r_{mt} + u_t$$

13. $y = x\beta + u$

$u = y - x\beta$

objective: minimize $Q = SSE = u'u$

$Q = u'u = (y-x\beta)'(y-x\beta)$

using partial differentiation (see Appendix L)

$$\frac{\partial Q}{\partial \beta} = \left.\frac{\partial (u'u)}{\partial \beta}\right|_{\beta=\hat{\beta}} - 2x'y + 2x'x\hat{\beta} = 0$$

or $x'x = x'y$

which implies (using the definition $(x'x)^{-1}(x'x) = I$)

$$\hat{\beta} = (x'x)^{-1}(x'y)$$

14. $\hat{\beta} = (x'x)^{-1}\ x'y$

$= (x'x)^{-1}\ x'(x\beta + u)$

$= (x'x)^{-1}\ (x'x)\ \beta + (x'x)^{-1}\ x'u$

$= \beta + (x'x)^{-1}\ x'u$

$V(\hat{\beta}) = E\ (\hat{\beta}-\beta)(\hat{\beta}-\beta)'$

$= E[(x'x)^{-1}\ x'uu'x\ (x'x)^{-1}$

$= [(x'x)^{-1}\ x'E(uu')\ x(x'x)^{-1}]$

Observing that $E(uu') = \sigma^2 I$

$$V(\hat{\beta}) = \sigma^2\ (x'x)^{-1}\ x'x\ (x'x)^{-1} = \sigma^2(x'x)^{-1}$$

15. $e = y - x\hat{\beta}$

$e'e = (y-x\hat{\beta})'(y-x\hat{\beta})$

$= y'y - 2\hat{\beta}'x'y + \hat{\beta}'x'x\hat{\beta} = y'y - 2\hat{\beta}'x'y + \hat{\beta}'x'y$

Hence $e'e = y'y - \hat{\beta}'x'y$

16. $SSR + SSE = SST$

$R^2 = (SST - SSE)/SST$

hence, $SSE = (1-R^2)\ TSS = e'e$

Consider models with m and (m+q) variables

$$SSR_m = SST_m - SSE_m$$

$$SSR_{m+q} = SST_{m+q} - SSE_{m+q}$$

Therefore,

$$SSR_m - SSR_{m+q} = (SST_m - SST_{m+q}) - (SSE_m - SSE_{m+q})$$

But $SST_m = SST_{m+q}$

which implies

$$SSR_m - SSR_{m+q} = SSE_{m+q} - SSE_m$$

hence

$$\frac{(SSE_{m+q} - SSE_m)/q}{SSE_{m+q}/(n-m-q)} = \frac{(SSR_{m+q} - SSR_{m+q})/q}{SSE_{m+q}/n-m-q}$$

$$\simeq F_{q},(n-m-q)$$

17. $\tilde{R}_D^{\ *} = \tilde{R}_D - a\ \tilde{R}_E$

$$\mathrm{Cov}(R_D^{\ *},\tilde{R}_E) = \mathrm{Cov}[(\tilde{R}_D - a\ \tilde{R}_E),\ \tilde{R}_E]$$

$$= E(\tilde{R}_D - a\ \tilde{R}_E)(\tilde{R}_E) - (\tilde{R}_D - a\ \tilde{R}_E)\ E(\tilde{R}_E)$$

$$= E(\tilde{R}_D\tilde{R}_E) - a[E(\tilde{R}_E)^2] - E(\tilde{R}_D)\ E(\tilde{R}_E) + a[E(\tilde{R}_E)]^2$$

$$= E(\tilde{R}_D\tilde{R}_E) - a[Var(\tilde{R}_E) + [E(\tilde{R}_E)]^2] - E(\tilde{R}_D)\ E(\tilde{R}_E) + a\ E(\tilde{R}_E)^2$$

$$= Cov(\tilde{R}_D,\tilde{R}_E) - a\ Var(\tilde{R}_E) = 0$$

Hence
$$a = \frac{Cov(\tilde{R}_D,\tilde{R}_E)}{Var(\tilde{R}_E)}$$

18. Simple Example

$$V = QQ' \qquad V^{-1} = (QQ')^{-1}$$
$$= Q'^{-1}Q^{-1} = Q^{-1\prime}Q^{-1}$$

$$\hat{B} = (x^{*\prime}x^{*})^{-1}(x^{*\prime}y^{*})$$

where $x^{*} = Q^{-1}x$ and $y^{*} = Q^{-1}y$

Hence,
$$\hat{B} = \{[(Q^{-1}x)'(Q^{-1}x)]^{-1}[(Q^{-1}x)'(Q^{-1}y)]\}$$
$$= \{(x'Q^{-1\prime}Q^{-1}x)(x'Q^{-1\prime}Q^{-1}y)\}$$
$$= (x'v^{-1}x)^{-1}(x'v^{-1}y)$$

Noting that $((\sigma^2)^{-1}) = \sigma^2$, since $Q^{-1\prime}Q^{-1} = V^{-1}$

$$\hat{B} = [x'(\sigma^2 v)^{-1}x]^{-1}[x'(\sigma^2 v)^{-1}y]$$
$$= (x'\Omega^{-1}x)^{-1}(x'\Omega^{-1}y)$$

$$V(\hat{B}) = \sigma^2(x^{*\prime}x^{*})^{-1}$$
$$= \sigma^2(x'v^{-1}x)^{-1}$$
$$= (x'(\sigma^2 v)^{-1}x)^{-1}$$
$$= (x'\Omega^{-1}x)$$

19. $$(R_B)_t = \gamma_1 + \gamma_2\ (R_s)_t + \gamma_3 I_t + u_t \qquad (5\text{-}13a)$$

$$(R_s)_t = \delta_1 + \delta_2\ (R_B)_t + \delta_3 E_t + \mu_t \qquad (5\text{-}13t)$$

Substituting (5-13b) in (5-13a) we get,

$$(R_B)_t = \gamma_1 + \gamma_2\ [\delta_1 + \delta_2\ (R_B)_t + \delta_3 E_t + \mu_t] + r_3 I_t + u_t$$

$$= (\gamma_1 + \gamma_2\delta_1) + \gamma_2\delta_2(R_B)_t + \gamma_2\delta_3\ E_t + \gamma_2\mu_t + \gamma_3 I_t + u_t$$

Collecting terms containing $(R_B)_t$ together,

$$(R_B)_t = \gamma_2\delta_2(R_B)_t = (\gamma_1 + \gamma_2\delta_1) + \gamma_2\delta_3 E_t + \gamma_3 I_t + (u_t + r_2\mu_t)$$

or,

$$(R_B)_t = \frac{\gamma_1 + \gamma_2\delta_1}{1 - \gamma_2\delta_2} + \frac{\gamma_2\delta_3}{1 - \gamma_2\delta_2} E_t + \frac{\gamma_3 I_t}{1 - \gamma_2\delta_2} + \frac{u_t + \gamma_2\mu_t}{1 - \gamma_2\delta_2}$$

$$= \phi_1 + \phi_2 E_t + \phi_3 I_t + \nu_t$$

where $\phi_1 = \frac{\gamma_1 + \gamma_2\delta_1}{1 - \gamma_2\delta_2}$, $\phi_2 = \frac{\gamma_2\delta_3}{1 - \gamma_2\delta_2}$, $\phi_3 = \frac{\gamma_3}{(1 - \gamma_2\delta_2)}$ and $\nu_t = \frac{u_t + \gamma_2\mu_t}{1 - \gamma_2\delta_2}$

Similarly, we can write,

$$(R_s)_t = \theta_1 + \theta_2 I_t + \theta_3 E_t + w_t$$

where $\theta_1 = \frac{\delta_1 + \delta_2\gamma_1}{(1 - \gamma_2\delta_2)}$, $\theta_2 = \frac{\gamma_3\delta_2}{(1 - \gamma_2\delta_2)}$, $\theta_3 = \frac{\delta_3}{(1 - \gamma_2\delta_2)}$ and $w_t = \frac{\mu_t + \delta_2 U_t}{(1 - \gamma_2\delta_2)}$

Now, the ratio $\frac{\phi_2}{\theta_3} = \gamma_2$; $\frac{\theta_2}{\phi_3} = \delta_2$

Having obtained γ_2 and δ_2 we can obtain δ_3 and γ_3 from the following equations:

$$\delta_3 = \theta_3(1-\gamma_2\delta_2) = \phi_2(1-\gamma_2\delta_2)/\gamma_2$$

and $$\gamma_3 = \phi_3(1-\gamma_2\delta_2) = \theta_2(1-\gamma_2\delta_2)/\delta_2$$

Further, γ_1 and δ_1 can be estimated by solving the simultaneous equation:

$$\delta_1 + \delta_2\gamma_1 = \theta_1\ (1-\gamma_2\delta_2)$$

$$\gamma_1 + \delta_1\gamma_2 = \phi_1\ (1-\gamma_2\delta_2)$$

i.e.,

$$\delta_1 = \theta_1 - \delta_2\phi_1$$

and $$\gamma_1 = \phi_1 - \gamma_2\theta_1$$

20. $$(R_B)_t = \gamma_1 + \gamma_2\ (R_s)_t + \gamma_3\ I_t + \gamma_4\ L_t + \nu_t$$

$$= \gamma_1 + \gamma_2\ [\delta_1 + \delta_2\ (R_B)_t + \delta_t] + \gamma_3\ I_t + \gamma_4\ L_t + \nu_t$$

$$= \frac{\gamma_1 + \gamma_2\delta_1}{1 - \gamma_2\delta_2} + \frac{\gamma_3 I_t}{1 - \gamma_2\delta_2} + \frac{\gamma_4 L_t}{1 - \gamma_2\delta_2} = \frac{\nu_t + \gamma_2 t_t}{1 - \gamma_2\delta_2}$$

$$= \phi_1 + \phi_2\ I_2 + \phi_3\ L_t + \nu_t$$

$$(R_s)_t = \delta_1 + \delta_2\ (R_B)_t + t_t$$

$$= \delta_1 + \delta_2\ [\gamma_1 + \gamma_2\ (R_s)_t + \gamma_3\ I_t + \gamma_4\ L_t + \nu_t] + t_t$$

$$= \frac{\delta_1 + \delta_2\gamma_1}{(1 - \gamma_2\delta_2)} + \frac{\delta_2\gamma_3\ I_t}{(1 - \gamma_2\delta_2)} + \frac{\delta_2\gamma_4\ L_t}{(1 - \gamma_2\delta_2)} + \frac{t_t + \delta_2\nu_t}{(1 - \gamma_2\delta_2)}$$

$$= \theta_1 + \theta_2\ I_t + \theta_3\ L_t + \omega_t$$

Note that δ_2 can be estimated as the ratios of $^{\Theta_3}/_{\phi_2}$ which may not necessarily be equal, thus leading to multiple estimates of δ_2. We can also compute multiple estimates for $\delta_1 = \Theta_1 - \phi_1\delta_2$ corresponding to each of the estimates of δ_2.

On the other hand, we are not able to estimate γ_1 through γ_4 from the reduced form equations and the associated ILS regressions.

references

REFERENCES

Aitken, A. C. "On Least Squares and Linear Combination of Observations," Proceedings of the Royal Society of Edinburgh, 55, 1935, pp. 42-48.

Anscombe, F. J. and John W. Tukey. "The Examination and Analysis of Residuals," Technometrics, Vol. 5, No. 2, May 1963, pp. 141-160.

Black, F., M. C. Jenson, and M. Scholes. "The Capital Asset Pricing Model: Some Empirical Tests," Studies in the Theory of Capital Markets, edited by M. C. Jensen (Praeger, New York, 1972).

Black, Fischer and Myron Scholes. "The Effects of Dividend Yield and Dividend Policy on Common Stock Prices and Returns," Journal of Financial Economics, Vol. 1, 1974, pp. 1-22.

Blume, Marshall. "Betas and Their Regression Tendencies," Journal of Finance, Vol. XXX, June 1975, pp. 785-96.

Box, G. E. P. and G. M. Jenkins. Time Series Analysis: Forecasting and Control, Holden-Day, Inc., Publisher, San Francisco, 1970.

Bronfenbrenner, J. "Sources and Size of Least Squares Bias in a Two-Equation Model," in Studies in Econometric Methods, edited by Hood and Koopmans, John Wiley and Sons, Inc. (N.Y.), 1953.

Chance, Don M. "Comment: A Test of Stone's Two-Index Model of Returns," Journal of Financial and Quantitative Analysis, Vol. XIV (September 1979), pp. 641-644.

Chang, H. and C. F. Lee. "Using Pooled Time-Series and Cross-Section Data to Test the Firm and Time Effects in Financial Anslyses," Journal of Financial and Quantitative Analysis, September, 1977, pp. 457-471.

Chow, G. C. "Tests of Equality Between Sets of Coefficients in Two Linear Regressions," Econometrica, Vol. 28, 3, July 1960, pp. 591-605.

Cochrane, D. and G. H. Orcutt. "Application of Least Squares Regression to Relationships Containing the Autocorrelated Error Terms," Journal of the American Statistical Association, 1969, pp. 32-61.

Dowell, C. D. and R. C. Grube. "Common Stock Return Distributions During Homogenous Activity Periods," Journal of Financial and Quantitative Analysis, March 1978, pp. 79-87.

Durbin, J. and G. S. Watson. "Testing for Serial Correlation in Least-Squares Regression," Biometrica, Vol. 37, pp. 409-428, 1950; Vol. 38, pp. 159-178, 1951.

Fabozzi, F. J. and J. C. Francis, "Beta as a Random Coefficient," Journal of Financial and Quantitative Analysis, Volume XIII (March 1978), pp. 101-116.

Fair, Ray C. "An Analysis of a Macro-Econometric Model with Rational Expectations in the Bonds and Stock Markets," The American Economic Review, Sept. 1979, pp. 539-552.

Fama, Eugene F. "The Behavior of Stock-Market Prices," Journal of Business, Vol. 38 (January 1965), pp. 34-105.

Fama, E. F. and J. D. MacBeth. "Risk, Return, and Equilibrium: Empirical Test," Journal of Political Economy, 1973, Vol. 81, pp. 607-636.

Farrell, J. L., Jr. "Analyzing Covariation of Returns to Determine Homogeneous Stock Groupings," Journal of Business, Vol. 47, No. 2 (April 1974), pp. 186-207.

Farrell, J. L., Jr. "Homogeneous Stock Groupings," Financial Analysts Journal, Vol. 31, No. 3, May/June 1975, pp. 50-62.

Fogler, H. Russell. Analyzing the Stock Market: Statistical Evidence and Methodology, (1978), GRID, Inc., Columbus, Ohio.

Fogler, H. Russell, Kose John, and James Tipton, "Three Factors, Interest Rate Differentials, Stock Groups and Nonstationarity," Journal of Finance, forthcoming May 1981.

Friend, I., R. Westerfield and M. Granito. "New Evidence on the Capital Asset Pricing Model," Journal of Finance, vol. XXXIII, No. 3 (June 1978), pp. 903-917.

Gibson, W. E. "Interest Ratio and Inflationary Expectations: New Evidence," American Economic Review, 1972, pp. 854-865.

Glejser, H. "A New Test for Heteroscedasticity," Journal of American Statistical Association, March 1969, pp. 316-323.

Goldfield, S. M. and R. E. Quandt, "Some Tests for Homoscedasticity," Journal of American Statistical Association, Vol. 60, 1965, p. 539-547.

Gordon, J. J. "Dividends, Earnings and Stock Prices," Review of Economics and Statistics, Vol. 41 (1959), pp. 99-105.

Gujarali, Damodar. Basic Econometrics, 1978, McGraw-Hill Book Company, New York.

Gultekin, N. Bulent and Richard J. Rogalski. "Comment: A Test of Stone's Two-Index Model of Returns, Journal of Financial and Quantitative Analysis, Vol. XIV (September 1979), pp. 629-639.

Intriligator, Michael D. Econometric Models, Techniques and Applications, 1978, Prentice-Hall, Inc., New Jersey.

Jensen, Michael C. "Some Anomolous Evidence Regarding Market Efficiency," Journal of Financial Economics, Vol. 6, June/September 1978, pp. 95-102.

Johnson, Craig G. "Dimensional Analysis and Interpretation of Regression Coefficients," Journal of Financial and Quantitative Analysis, Jan. 1972, pp. 1399-1406.

Johnston, J. Econometric Methods, 2nd edition, 1972, McGraw-Hill Book Company, New York.

King, B. "Market and Industry Factors in Stock Price Behavior," Journal of Business, Volume 39 (January 1966), pp. 139-190

Kmenta, Jan. Elements of Econometrics, 1971, McMillan Publishing Co., Inc., New York.

Kon, S. J. and F. C. Jen. "Estimation of Time-Varying Systematic Risk and Performance for Mutual Fund Portfolios: An Application of Switching Regression," Journal of Finance, Vol. XXXIII, No. 2, May 1978, pp. 457-475.

Kraus, Alan and Robert H. Litzenberger. "Skewness Preference and the Valuation of Risk Assets," Journal of Finance, Vol. XXXI (Sept. 1976), pp. 1085-1100.

Lee, Cheng F. "A Note on the Interdependent Structure of Security Returns," Journal of Financial and Quantitative Analysis, March 1976, pp. 73-86.

Lee, Cheng F. and Son N. Chen, "A Random Coefficient Model for Reexamining Risk-Decomposition Method and Risk-Return Relationship Test," Quarterly Review of Economics and Business, Volume XX (Winter 1980), pp. 58-69.

Lee, Cheng F. and Frank C. Jen. "Effects of Measurement Errors on Systematic Risk and Performance Measure of a Portfolio," Journal of Financial and Quantitative Analysis, Vol. XIII, June 1978, pp. 299-312.

Lee, Cheng F. and W. P. Lloyd. "The Capital Asset Pricing Model Expressed as a Recursive System: An Empirical Investigation," Journal of Financial and Quantitative Analysis, June 1976, pp. 237-249.

Lee, Cheng F. and Joseph Vinso. "The Role of Firm-Related Variables in Capital Asset Pricing," forthcoming in Journal of Business Research.

Levy, H. and M. Sarnat. Investment and Portfolio Analysis, 1972, John Wiley & Sons, Inc., Chps. 6, 7, 8.

Lin, C. Y. and W. L. White. "Four Procedures for Testing Linear Hypothesis," IMR, Fall 1978, pp. 18-20.

Litzenberger, Robert H. and Krishna Ramaswamy. "The Effect of Personal Taxes and Dividends on Capital Asset Prces: Theory and Empirical Evidence," Journal of Financial Economics, Vol. 7, June 1979, pp. 163-195.

Lloyd, W. P. and C. F. Lee. "Block Recursive Systems in Asset Pricing Models," Journal of Finance, 31, 1976, pp. 1101-1114.

Lloyd, William P. and Shick, Richard A. "A Test of Stone's Two-Index Model of Returns," Journal of Financial and Quantitative Analysis, September 1977, pp. 363-367.

Maddala, G. S. "The Use of Variance Components Models in Pooling Cross-Section and Time-Series Data," Econometrica, March 1971, pp. 341-358.

Maddala, G. S. Econometrics, 1977, McGraw-Hill Book Company, New York.

Makridakis, S. and S. C. Wheelwright. Interactive Forecasting, 1978, Holden-Day, Inc., San Francisco.

Miller, M. H. and M. Scholes. "Ratio of Return in Relation to Risk: A Re-examination of Some Recent Findings," Studies in the Theory of Capital Markets, edited by M. C. Jensen, 1972, Praeger, New York, pp. 47-78.

Montgomery, D. B. and D. G. Morrison, "A Note on Adjusting R^2," Journal of Finance, Sept. 1973, pp. 1009-1013.

Nelson, C. R. Applied Time Series Analysis for Managerial Forecasting, 1973, Holden-Day, Inc., San Francisco.

Nie, Norman H., Hadlai C. Hull, Jean G. Jenkins, Karin Steinbrenner, and Dale H. Bent. Statistical Package for the Social Sciences, 2nd ed., 1970, McGraw-Hill Book Company.

Oudet, Bruno A. "The Variation of the Return on Stocks in Periods of Inflation," Journal of Financial and Quantitative Analysis, March 1973, pp. 247-258.

Rogalski, R. J. and J. D. Vinso. "Stock Returns, Money Supply and the Direction of Causality," Journal of Finance, September 1977, pp. 1017-1030.

Rogalski, R. J. and J. D. Vinso. "Hetroscedastic Security Returns," The Financial Review, October 1978.

Rogalski, Richard J. and Joseph D. Vinso. "Empirical Properties of Foreign Exchange Rates," Journal of International Business Studies, Fall 1978, pp. 69-79.

Roll, Richard. "Bias in Fitting the Sharpe Model to Time Series Data," Journal of Financial and Quantitative Analysis, IV, Sept. 1969, pp. 271-89.

Roll, Richard. "A Critique of the Asset Pricing Theory's Tests," Journal of Financial Economics, Vol. 4 March 1977, pp. 129-176.

Roll, Richard. "Ambiguity When Performance is Measured by the Securities Market Line," Journal of Finance, September 1978, pp. 1051-1069.

Rosenberg, B. and V. Marathe. "Common Factors in Security Returns: Microeconomic Determinants and Macroeconomic Correlates," Proceedings of the Seminar on the Analysis of Security Prices, University of Chicago, May 1976, pp. 61-115.

Ross, S. A. "The Arbitrage Theory of Capital Asset Pricing," Journal of Economic Theory, 13, 1976, pp. 341-360.

Rudd, Andrew and H. K. Clasing, Jr., Modern Portfolio Theory: The Principles of Investment Management, Dow-Jones Irwin, 1981.

Sharpe, W. F. "The Capital Asset Pricing Model: A 'Multi-Beta' Interpretation," in Financial Decision Making Under Uncertainty, ed. by H. Levy and M. Sarnat, New York: Academic Press, 1977, pp. 127-135.

Simkowitz, Michael A. and Dennis E. Logue. "The Interdependent Structure of Security Returns," Journal of Financial and Quantitative Analysis, March 1973, pp. 259-272.

Simkowitz, Michael A. and William L. Beedles. "Asymmetric Stable Distributed Security Returns," forthcoming in Journal of the American Statistical Association.

Stone, Bernell K. "Systematic Interest-Rate Risk in a Two-Index Model of Returns," Journal of Financial and Quantitative Analysis, November 1974, pp. 709-721.

Sunder, Shyam, "Stationarity of Market Risk: Random Coefficients Tests for Individual Stocks," Journal of Finance, Volume 35 (September 1980), pp. 883-896.

Theil, H. Principles of Econometrics, 1971, John Wiley and Sons, New York.

Wallace, T. D. and A. Hussain. "The Use of Error Components Models in Combining Cross-Section with Time-Series Data," Econometrica, Vol. 37, January 1969, pp. 55-72.

Wippern, D. "Financial Structure and the Value of the Firm," Journal of Finance, December 1966, pp. 615-633.

Yamane, Taro. Mathematics for Economists, 1962, Prentice-Hall, Englewood Cliffs, New Jersey.

Yamane, T. Statistics - An Introductory Analysis, 2nd ed., 1967, Harper and Row, New York.

Zellner, A. "An Efficient Method of Estimating Seemingly Unrelated Regressions and Tests for Aggregation Bias," Journal of the American Statistical Association, 1962, Vol. 57, pp. 348-368.

statistical tables

Table 1
AREAS UNDER THE STANDARDIZED NORMAL DISTRIBUTION

Example

Pr $(0 \leq z \leq 1.96) = 0.4750$

Pr $(z \geq 1.96) = 0.5 - 0.4750 = 0.025$

z	.00	.01	.02	.03	.04	.05	.06	.07	.08	.09
0.0	.0000	.0040	.0080	.0120	.0160	.0199	.0239	.0279	.0319	.0359
0.1	.0398	.0438	.0478	.0517	.0557	.0596	.0636	.0675	.0714	.0753
0.2	.0793	.0832	.0871	.0910	.0948	.0987	.1026	.1064	.1103	.1141
0.3	.1179	.1217	.1255	.1293	.1331	.1368	.1406	.1443	.1480	.1517
0.4	.1554	.1591	.1628	.1664	.1700	.1736	.1772	.1808	.1844	.1879
0.5	.1915	.1950	.1985	.2019	.2054	.2088	.2123	.2157	.2190	.2224
0.6	.2257	.2291	.2324	.2357	.2389	.2422	.2454	.2486	.2517	.2549
0.7	.2580	.2611	.2642	.2673	.2704	.2734	.2764	.2794	.2823	.2852
0.8	.2881	.2910	.2939	.2967	.2995	.3023	.3051	.3078	.3106	.3133
0.9	.3159	.3186	.3212	.3238	.3264	.3289	.3315	.3340	.3365	.3389
1.0	.3413	.3438	.3461	.3485	.3508	.3531	.3554	.3577	.3599	.3621
1.1	.3643	.3665	.3686	.3708	.3729	.3749	.3770	.3790	.3810	.3830
1.2	.3849	.3869	.3888	.3907	.3925	.3944	.3962	.3980	.3997	.4015
1.3	.4032	.4049	.4066	.4082	.4099	.4115	.4131	.4147	.4162	.4177
1.4	.4192	.4207	.4222	.4236	.4251	.4265	.4279	.4292	.4306	.4319
1.5	.4332	.4345	.4357	.4370	.4382	.4394	.4406	.4418	.4429	.4441
1.6	.4452	.4463	.4474	.4484	.4495	.4505	.4515	.4525	.4535	.445
1.7	.4554	.4564	.4573	.4582	.4591	.4599	.4608	.4616	.4625	.4633
1.8	.4641	.4649	.4656	.4664	.4671	.4678	.4686	.4693	.4699	.4706
1.9	.4713	.4719	.4726	.4732	.4738	.4744	.4750	.4756	.4761	.4767
2.0	.4772	.4778	.4783	.4788	.4793	.4798	.4803	.4808	.4812	.4817
2.1	.4821	.4826	.4830	.4834	.4838	.4842	.4846	.4850	.4854	.4857
2.2	.4861	.4864	.4868	.4871	.4875	.4878	.4881	.4884	.4887	.4890
2.3	.4893	.4896	.4898	.4901	.4904	.4906	.4909	.4911	.4913	.4916
2.4	.4918	.4920	.4922	.4925	.4927	.4929	.4931	.4932	.4934	.4936
2.5	.4938	.4940	.4941	.4943	.4945	.4946	.4948	.4949	.4951	.4952
2.6	.4953	.4955	.4956	.4957	.4959	.4960	.4961	.4962	.4963	.4964
2.7	.4965	.4966	.4967	.4968	.4969	.4970	.4971	.4972	.4973	.4974
2.8	.4974	.4975	.4976	.4977	.4977	.4978	.4979	.4979	.4980	.4981
2.9	.4981	.4982	.4982	.4983	.4984	.4984	.4985	.4985	.4986	.4986
3.0	.4987	.4987	.4987	.4988	.4988	.4989	.4989	.4989	.4990	.4990

Table 2
VALUES OF THE CHI-SQUARE DISTRIBUTION

Degrees of Freedom	Critical probability			
	10%	5%	1%	0.1%
1	2.706	3.841	6.635	10.827
2	4.605	5.991	9.210	13.815
3	6.251	7.815	11.345	16.266
4	7.779	9.488	13.277	18.467
5	9.236	11.070	15.086	20.515
6	10.645	12.592	16.812	22.457
7	12.017	14.067	18.475	24.322
8	13.362	15.507	20.090	26.125
9	14.684	16.919	21.666	27.877
10	15.987	18.307	23.209	29.588
11	17.275	19.675	24.725	31.264
12	18.549	21.026	26.217	32.909
13	19.812	22.362	27.688	34.528
14	21.064	23.685	29.141	36.123
15	22.307	24.996	30.578	37.697
16	23.542	26.296	32.000	39.252
17	24.769	27.587	33.409	40.790
18	25.989	28.869	34.805	42.312
19	27.204	30.144	36.191	43.820
20	28.412	31.410	37.566	45.315
21	29.615	32.671	38.932	46.797
22	30.813	33.924	40.289	48.268
23	32.007	35.172	41.638	49.728
24	33.196	36.415	42.980	51.179
25	34.382	37.652	44.314	52.620
26	35.563	38.885	45.642	54.052
27	36.741	40.113	46.963	55.476
28	37.916	41.337	48.278	56.893
29	39.087	42.557	49.588	58.302
30	40.256	43.773	50.892	59.703

For larger values of n, the expression $\sqrt{2\chi^2} - \sqrt{2n - 1}$ may be used as a normal deviate with unit standard error, interpreting the deviate as in a one-tailed test.

Source: This table is taken from Table IV of Fisher and Yates: Statistical Tables for Biological, Agricultural, and Medical Research, published by Longman Group Ltd., London (1974) 6th Edition, (previously published by Oliver and Boyd, Edinburgh), and by permission of the authors and publishers.

Table 3
STUDENT'S t-DISTRIBUTION FOR SMALL SAMPLES

Degrees of Freedom	Critical Probability (Upper row for two-tailed test; lower row for one-tailed test)					
	.20 / .10	.10 / .05	.05 / .025	.02 / .01	.01 / .005	.001 / .0005
1	3.078	6.314	12.706	31.821	63.657	636.619
2	1.886	2.920	4.303	6.965	9.925	31.598
3	1.638	2.353	3.182	4.541	5.841	12.924
4	1.533	2.132	2.776	3.747	4.604	8.610
5	1.476	2.015	2.571	3.365	4.032	6.869
6	1.440	1.943	2.447	3.143	3.707	5.959
7	1.415	1.895	2.365	2.998	3.499	5.408
8	1.397	1.860	2.306	2.896	3.355	5.041
9	1.383	1.833	2.262	2.821	3.250	4.781
10	1.372	1.812	2.228	2.764	3.169	4.587
11	1.363	1.796	2.201	2.718	3.106	4.437
12	1.356	1.782	2.179	2.681	3.055	4.318
13	1.350	1.771	2.160	2.650	3.012	4.221
14	1.345	1.761	2.145	2.624	2.977	4.140
15	1.341	1.753	2.131	2.602	2.947	4.073
16	1.337	1.746	2.120	2.583	2.921	4.015
17	1.333	1.740	2.110	2.567	2.898	3.965
18	1.330	1.734	2.101	2.552	2.878	3.922
19	1.328	1.729	2.093	2.539	2.861	3.883
20	1.325	1.725	2.086	2.528	2.845	3.850
21	1.323	1.721	2.080	2.518	2.831	3.819
22	1.321	1.717	2.074	2.508	2.819	3.792
23	1.319	1.714	2.069	2.500	2.807	3.767
24	1.318	1.711	2.064	2.492	2.797	3.745
25	1.316	1.708	2.060	2.485	2.787	3.725
26	1.315	1.706	2.056	2.479	2.779	3.707
27	1.314	1.703	2.052	2.473	2.771	3.690
28	1.313	1.701	2.048	2.467	2.763	3.674
29	1.311	1.699	2.045	2.462	2.756	3.659
30	1.310	1.697	2.042	2.457	2.750	3.646

Source: This table is taken from Table III of Fisher and Yates: Statistical Tables for Biological, Agricultural, and Medical Research, published by Longman Group Ltd., London (1974) 6th Edition, (previously published by Oliver and Boyd, Edinburgh), and by permission of the authors and publishers.

Table 4
5 PERCENT POINTS OF THE F DISTRIBUTION*

	Degrees of freedom for numerator																		
	1	2	3	4	5	6	7	8	9	10	12	15	20	24	30	40	60	120	∞
1	161.4	199.5	215.7	234.6	230.2	234.0	236.8	238.9	240.5	241.9	243.9	245.9	248.0	249.1	250.1	251.1	252.2	253.3	254.3
2	18.51	19.00	19.16	19.25	19.30	19.33	19.35	19.37	19.38	19.40	19.41	19.43	19.45	19.45	19.46	19.47	19.48	19.49	19.50
3	10.13	9.55	9.38	9.12	9.01	8.94	8.89	8.85	8.81	8.79	8.74	8.70	8.66	8.64	8.62	8.59	8.57	8.55	8.53
4	7.71	6.94	6.59	6.39	6.26	6.16	6.09	6.04	6.00	5.96	5.91	5.86	5.80	5.77	5.75	5.72	5.69	5.66	5.63
5	6.61	5.79	5.41	5.19	5.05	4.95	4.88	4.82	4.77	4.74	4.68	4.62	4.56	4.53	4.50	4.46	4.43	4.40	4.36
6	5.99	5.14	4.76	4.53	4.39	4.28	4.21	4.15	4.10	4.06	4.00	3.94	3.87	3.84	3.81	3.77	3.74	3.70	3.67
7	5.59	4.74	4.35	4.12	3.97	3.87	3.79	3.73	3.68	3.64	3.57	3.51	3.44	3.41	3.38	3.34	3.30	3.27	3.23
8	5.32	4.46	4.07	3.84	3.69	3.58	3.50	3.44	3.39	3.35	3.28	3.22	3.15	3.12	3.08	3.04	3.01	2.97	2.93
9	5.12	4.26	3.86	3.63	3.48	3.37	3.29	3.23	3.18	3.14	3.07	3.01	2.94	2.90	2.86	2.83	2.79	2.75	2.71
10	4.96	4.10	3.71	3.48	3.33	3.22	3.14	3.07	3.02	2.98	2.91	2.85	2.77	2.74	2.70	2.66	2.62	2.58	2.54
11	4.84	3.98	3.59	3.36	3.20	3.09	3.01	2.95	2.90	2.85	2.79	2.72	2.65	2.61	2.57	2.53	2.49	2.45	2.40
12	4.75	3.89	3.49	3.26	3.11	3.00	2.91	2.85	2.80	2.75	2.69	2.62	2.54	2.51	2.47	2.43	2.38	2.34	2.30
13	4.67	3.81	3.41	3.18	3.03	2.92	2.83	2.77	2.71	2.67	2.60	2.53	2.46	2.42	2.38	2.34	2.30	2.25	2.21
14	4.60	3.74	3.34	3.11	2.96	2.85	2.76	2.70	2.65	2.60	2.53	2.46	2.39	2.35	2.31	2.27	2.22	2.18	2.13
15	4.54	3.68	3.29	3.06	2.90	2.79	2.71	2.64	2.59	2.54	2.48	2.40	2.33	2.29	2.25	2.20	2.16	2.11	2.07
16	4.49	3.63	3.24	3.01	2.85	2.74	2.66	2.59	2.54	2.49	2.42	2.35	2.28	2.24	2.19	2.15	2.11	2.06	2.01
17	4.45	3.59	3.20	2.96	2.81	2.70	2.61	2.55	2.49	2.45	2.38	2.31	2.23	2.19	2.15	2.10	2.06	2.01	1.96
18	4.41	3.55	3.16	2.93	2.77	2.66	2.58	2.51	2.46	2.41	2.34	2.27	2.19	2.15	2.11	2.06	2.02	1.97	1.92
19	4.38	3.52	3.13	2.90	2.74	2.63	2.54	2.48	2.42	2.38	2.31	2.23	2.16	2.11	2.07	2.03	1.98	1.93	1.88
20	4.35	3.49	3.10	2.87	2.71	2.60	2.51	2.45	2.39	2.35	2.28	2.20	2.12	2.08	2.04	1.99	1.95	1.90	1.84
21	4.32	3.47	3.07	2.84	2.68	2.57	2.49	2.42	2.37	2.32	2.25	2.18	2.10	2.05	2.01	1.96	1.92	1.87	1.81
22	4.30	3.44	3.05	2.82	2.66	2.55	2.46	2.40	2.34	2.30	2.23	2.15	2.07	2.03	1.98	1.94	1.89	1.84	1.78
23	4.28	3.42	3.03	2.80	2.64	2.53	2.44	2.37	2.32	2.27	2.20	2.13	2.05	2.01	1.96	1.91	1.86	1.81	1.76
24	4.26	3.40	3.01	2.78	2.62	2.51	2.42	2.36	2.30	2.25	2.18	2.11	2.03	1.98	1.94	1.89	1.84	1.79	1.73
25	4.24	3.39	2.99	2.76	2.60	2.49	2.40	2.34	2.28	2.24	2.16	2.09	2.01	1.96	1.92	1.87	1.82	1.77	1.71
26	4.23	3.37	2.98	2.74	2.59	2.47	2.39	2.32	2.27	2.22	2.15	2.07	1.99	1.95	1.90	1.85	1.80	1.75	1.69
27	4.21	3.35	2.96	2.73	2.57	2.46	2.37	2.31	2.25	2.20	2.13	2.06	1.97	1.93	1.88	1.84	1.79	1.73	1.67
28	4.20	3.34	2.95	2.71	2.56	2.45	2.36	2.29	2.24	2.19	2.12	2.04	1.96	1.91	1.87	1.82	1.77	1.71	1.65
29	4.18	3.33	2.93	2.70	2.55	2.43	2.35	2.28	2.22	2.18	2.10	2.03	1.94	1.90	1.85	1.81	1.75	1.70	1.64
30	4.17	3.32	2.92	2.69	2.53	2.42	2.33	2.27	2.21	2.16	2.09	2.01	1.93	1.89	1.84	1.79	1.74	1.68	1.62
40	4.08	3.23	2.84	2.61	2.45	2.34	2.25	2.18	2.12	2.08	2.00	1.92	1.84	1.79	1.74	1.69	1.64	1.58	1.51
60	4.00	3.23	2.84	2.61	2.45	2.34	2.25	2.18	2.12	2.08	2.00	1.92	1.84	1.79	1.74	1.69	1.64	1.58	1.51
120	3.92	3.07	2.68	2.45	2.29	2.17	2.09	2.02	1.96	1.91	1.83	1.75	1.66	1.61	1.55	1.50	1.43	1.35	1.25
∞	3.84	3.00	2.60	2.37	2.21	2.10	2.01	1.94	1.88	1.83	1.75	1.67	1.57	1.52	1.46	1.39	1.32	1.22	1.00

*Example: With m = 5 degrees of freedom for the numerator and n = 20 for the denominator, an F value larger than 2.71 has .05 probability.
Reprinted by permission from STATISTICAL METHODS by George W. Snedecor and William G. Cochran, Seventh Edition (c) 1980 by The Iowa State University Press, Ames, Iowa 50010.

Table 4 (cont.)

1 PERCENT POINTS OF THE F DISTRIBUTION*

	Degrees of freedom for numerator																		
	1	2	3	4	5	6	7	8	9	10	12	15	20	24	30	40	60	120	∞
1	4052	4999.5	5403	5625	5764	5859	5928	5981	6022	6056	6106	6157	6209	6235	6261	6287	6313	6339	6366
2	98.50	99.00	99.17	99.25	99.30	99.33	99.36	99.37	99.39	99.40	99.42	99.43	99.45	99.46	99.47	99.47	99.48	99.49	99.50
3	34.12	30.82	29.46	28.71	28.24	27.91	27.67	27.49	27.35	27.23	27.05	26.87	26.69	26.60	26.50	26.41	26.32	26.22	26.13
4	21.20	18.00	16.69	15.98	15.52	15.21	14.98	14.80	14.66	14.55	14.37	14.20	14.02	13.93	13.84	13.75	13.65	13.56	13.46
5	16.26	13.27	12.06	11.39	10.97	10.67	10.46	10.29	10.16	10.05	9.89	9.72	9.55	9.47	9.38	9.29	9.20	9.11	9.02
6	13.75	10.92	9.78	9.15	8.75	8.47	8.26	8.10	7.98	7.87	7.72	7.56	7.40	7.31	7.23	7.14	2.06	6.97	6.88
7	12.25	9.55	8.45	7.85	7.46	7.19	6.99	6.84	6.72	6.62	6.47	6.31	6.16	6.07	5.99	5.91	5.82	5.74	5.65
8	11.26	8.65	7.59	7.01	6.63	6.37	6.18	6.03	5.91	5.81	5.67	5.52	5.36	5.28	5.20	5.12	5.03	4.95	4.86
9	10.56	8.02	6.99	6.42	6.06	5.80	5.61	5.47	5.35	5.26	5.11	4.96	4.81	4.73	4.65	4.57	4.48	4.40-	4.31
10	10.04	7.56	6.55	5.99	5.64	5.39	5.20	5.06	4.94	4.85	4.71	4.56	4.41	4.33	4.25	4.17	4.08	4.00	3.91
11	9.65	7.21	6.22	5.67	5.32	5.07	4.89	4.74	4.63	4.54	4.40	4.25	4.10	4.02	3.94	3.86	3.78	3.69	3.60
12	9.33	6.93	5.95	5.41	5.06	4.82	4.64	4.50	4.39	4.30	4.16	4.01	3.86	3.78	3.70	3.62	3.54	3.45	3.36
13	9.07	6.70	5.74	5.21	4.86	4.62	4.44	4.30	4.19	4.10	3.96	3.82	3.66	3.59	3.51	3.43	3.34	3.25	3.17
14	8.86	6.51	5.56	5.04	4.69	4.46	4.28	4.14	4.03	3.97	3.80	3.66	3.51	3.43	3.35	3.27	3.18-	3.00	
15	8.68	6.36	5.42	4.89	4.56	4.32	4.14	4.00	3.89	3.80	3.67	3.52	3.37	3.29	3.21	3.13	3.05	2.96	2.87
16	8.53	6.23	5.29	4.77	4.44	4.20	4.03	3.89	3.78	3.69	3.55	3.41	3.26	3.18	3.10	3.02	2.93	2.84	2.75
17	8.40	6.11	5.18	4.67	4.34	4.10	3.93	3.79	3.68	3.59	3.46	3.31	3.16	3.08	3.00	2.92	2.83	2.75	2.65
18	8.29	6.01	5.09	4.58	4.25	4.01	3.84	3.71	3.60	3.51	3.37	3.23	3.08	3.00	2.92	2.84	2.75	2.66	2.57
19	8.18	5.93	5.01	4.50	4.17	3.94	3.77	3.63	3.52	3.43	3.30	3.15	3.00	2.92	2.84	2.76	2.67	2.58	2.49
20	8.10	5.85	4.94	4.43	4.10	3.87	3.70	3.56	3.46	3.37	3.23	3.09	2.94	2.86	2.78	2.69	2.61	2.52	2.42
21	8.02	5.78	4.87	4.37	4.04	3.81	3.64	3.51	3.40	3.31	3.17	3.03	2.88	2.80	2.72	2.64	2.55	2.46	2.36
22	7.95	5.72	4.82	4.31	3.99	3.76	3.59	3.45	3.35	3.26	3.12	2.98	2.83	2.75	2.67	2.58	2.50	2.40	2.31
23	7.88	5.66	4.76	4.26	3.94	3.71	3.54	3.41	3.30	3.21	3.07	2.93	2.78	2.70	2.62	2.54	2.45	2.35	2.26
24	7.82	5.61	4.72	4.22	3.90	3.67	3.50	3.36	3.26	3.17	3.03	2.89	2.74	2.66	2.58	2.49	2.40	2.31	2.21
25	7.77	5.57	4.68	4.18	3.85	3.63	3.46	3.32	3.22	3.13	2.99	2.85	2.70	2.62	2.54	2.45	2.36	2.27	2.17
26	7.72	5.53	4.64	4.14	3.82	3.59	3.42	3.29	3.18	3.09	2.96	2.81	2.66	2.58	2.50	2.42	2.33	2.23	2.13
27	7.68	5.49	4.60	4.11	3.78	3.56	3.39	3.26	3.15	3.06	2.93	2.78	2.63	2.55	2.47	2.38	2.29	2.20	2.10
28	7.64	5.45	4.57	4.07	3.75	3.53	3.36	3.23	3.12	3.03	2.90	2.75	2.60	2.52	2.44	2.35	2.26	2.17	2.06
29	7.60	5.42	4.54	4.04	3.73	3.50	3.33	3.20	3.09	3.00	2.87	2.73	2.57	2.49	2.41	2.33	2.23	2.14	2.03
30	7.56	5.39	4.51	4.02	3.70	3.47	3.30	3.17	3.07	2.98	2.84	2.70	2.55	2.47	2.39	2.30	2.21	2.11	2.01
40	7.31	5.18	4.31	3.83	3.51	3.29	3.12	2.99	2.89	2.80	2.66	2.52	2.37	2.29	2.20	2.11	2.02	1.92	1.80
60	7.08	4.98	4.13	3.65	3.34	3.12	2.95	2.82	2.72	2.63	2.50	2.35	2.20	3.12	2.03	1.94	1.84	1.73	1.60
120	6.85	4.79	3.95	3.48	3.17	2.96	2.79	2.66	2.56	2.47	2.34	2.19	2.03	1.95	1.86	1.76	1.66	1.53	1.38
∞	6.63	4.61	3.78	3.32	3.02	2.80	2.64	2.51	2.41	2.32	2.18	2.04	1.88	1.79	1.70	1.59	1.47	1.32	1.00

*Example: With m = 5 degrees of freedom for the numerator and n = 20 for the denominator, an F value larger than 4.10 has .01 probability.

Table 5
DURBIN-WATSON STATISTIC (d).
SIGNIFICANCE POINTS OF d_L AND d_V: 5%

n	k' = 1		k' = 2		k' = 3		k' = 4		k' = 5	
	d_L	d_V	d_L	d_V	d_L	d_V	d_L	d_V	d_L	d_V
15	1.08	1.36	0.95	1.54	0.82	1.75	0.69	1.97	0.56	2.21
16	1.10	1.37	0.98	1.54	0.86	1.73	0.74	1.93	0.62	2.15
17	1.13	1.38	1.02	1.54	0.90	1.71	0.78	1.90	0.67	2.10
18	1.16	1.39	1.05	1.53	0.93	1.69	0.82	1.87	0.71	2.06
19	1.18	1.40	1.08	1.53	0.97	1.68	0.86	1.85	0.75	2.02
20	1.20	1.41	1.10	1.54	1.00	1.68	0.90	1.83	0.79	1.99
21	1.22	1.42	1.13	1.54	1.03	1.67	0.93	1.81	0.83	1.96
22	1.24	1.43	1.15	1.54	1.05	1.66	0.96	1.80	0.86	1.94
23	1.26	1.44	1.17	1.54	1.08	1.66	0.99	1.79	0.90	1.92
24	1.27	1.45	1.19	1.55	1.10	1.66	1.01	1.78	0.93	1.90
25	1.29	1.45	1.21	1.55	1.12	1.66	1.04	1.77	0.95	1.89
26	1.30	1.46	1.22	1.55	1.14	1.65	1.06	1.76	0.98	1.88
27	1.32	1.47	1.24	1.56	1.16	1.65	1.08	1.76	1.01	1.86
28	1.33	1.48	1.26	1.56	1.18	1.65	1.10	1.75	1.03	1.85
29	1.34	1.48	1.27	1.56	1.20	1.65	1.12	1.74	1.05	1.84
30	1.35	1.49	1.28	1.57	1.21	1.65	1.14	1.74	1.07	1.83
31	1.36	1.50	1.30	1.57	1.23	1.65	1.16	1.74	1.09	1.83
32	1.37	1.50	1.31	1.57	1.24	1.65	1.18	1.73	1.11	1.82
33	1.38	1.51	1.32	1.58	1.26	1.65	1.19	1.73	1.13	1.81
34	1.39	1.51	1.33	1.58	1.27	1.65	1.21	1.73	1.15	1.81
35	1.40	1.52	1.34	1.58	1.28	1.65	1.22	1.73	1.16	1.80
36	1.41	1.52	1.35	1.59	1.29	1.65	1.24	1.73	1.18	1.80
37	1.42	1.53	1.36	1.59	1.31	1.66	1.25	1.72	1.19	1.80
38	1.43	1.54	1.37	1.59	1.32	1.66	1.26	1.72	1.21	1.79
39	1.43	1.54	1.38	1.60	1.33	1.66	1.27	1.72	1.22	1.79
40	1.44	1.54	1.39	1.60	1.34	1.66	1.29	1.72	1.23	1.79
45	1.48	1.57	1.43	1.62	1.38	1.67	1.34	1.72	1.29	1.78
50	1.50	1.59	1.46	1.63	1.42	1.67	1.38	1.72	1.34	1.77
55	1.53	1.60	1.49	1.64	1.45	1.68	1.41	1.72	1.38	1.77
60	1.55	1.62	1.51	1.65	1.48	1.69	1.44	1.73	1.41	1.77
65	1.57	1.63	1.54	1.66	1.50	1.70	1.47	1.73	1.44	1.77
70	1.58	1.64	1.55	1.67	1.52	1.70	1.49	1.74	1.46	1.77
75	1.60	1.65	1.57	1.68	1.54	1.71	1.51	1.74	1.49	1.77
80	1.61	1.66	1.59	1.69	1.56	1.72	1.53	1.74	1.51	1.77
85	1.62	1.67	1.60	1.70	1.57	1.72	1.55	1.75	1.52	1.77
90	1.63	1.68	1.61	1.70	1.59	1.73	1.57	1.75	1.54	1.78
95	1.64	1.69	1.62	1.71	1.60	1.73	1.58	1.75	1.56	1.78
100	1.65	1.69	1.63	1.72	1.61	1.74	1.59	1.76	1.57	1.78

n = number of observations.
k' = number of explanatory variables.

This Table is reproduced from <u>Biometrika</u>, vol. 41, p. 173, 1951, with the permission of the Trustees.

index

TABLE OF LISTINGS

WITHDRAWN
University of Bristol
UNIVERSITY OF BRISTOL
82 00996